Australia Compared

AUSTRALIA COMPARED
People, Policies and Politics

Edited by Francis G. Castles

ALLEN & UNWIN

© Francis G. Castles 1991
This book is copyright under the Berne Convention.
No reproduction without permission.

First published in 1991
Allen & Unwin Pty Ltd
8 Napier Street, North Sydney NSW 2059 Australia

National Library of Australia
Cataloguing-in-Publication entry:

Australia compared: people, policies and politics.

ISBN 0 04 442339 X.
1. Australia—Social conditions. 2. Australia—Politics
and government—1945– . 3. Australia—Economic
conditions. I. Castles, Francis G. (Francis Geoffrey), 1943–

994.06

Set in 10/11 pt Plantin by Asco Trade Typesetting Ltd
Printed in Singapore by Chong Moh Offset Printing

Contents

Figures

Tables

Contributors

DON ANDERSON is Professorial Fellow in Sociology in the Research School of Social Sciences at the Australian National University. His research interests include education, the professions and the interaction of social science and policy. His interest in the interaction of public and private school systems was stimulated when he chaired a government inquiry on the topic.

CLIVE BEAN is a Research Fellow in Sociology in the Research School of Social Sciences at the Australian National University. He is co-editor of *Australian Attitudes* (1988) and *The Greening of Australian Politics* (1990) and author of a variety of articles on political attitudes and behaviour.

FRANCIS G. CASTLES is Professor of Public Policy and Head of the Australian National University's Public Policy Program. He was formerly Professor of Comparative Politics at the Open University in England and is author and editor of numerous books on comparative politics and public policy, including *The Working Class and Welfare* (1985), *Australian Public Policy and Economic Vulnerability* (1988) and *The Comparative History of Public Policy* (1989).

STEVE DOWRICK is a Research Fellow in Economics in the Research School of Social Sciences at the Australian National University. He has published in leading academic journals in the fields of labour economics and comparative economic growth.

JOHN EDDY, S.J., is Senior Fellow in History in the Research School of Social Sciences at the Australian National University. He is a Fellow of the Royal Historical Society. Recent co-authored books include *From*

Colony to Colonizer (1987), *The Rise of Colonial Nationalism* (1988) and *Federalism in Canada and Australia* (1989).

BOB GREGORY is Professor of Economics and Director of the Division of Economics and Politics in the Research School of Social Sciences at the Australian National University. He is a member of the Board of the Reserve Bank and a member of the Australian Science and Technology Council. Professor Gregory publishes on labour economics and economic policy issues generally.

JAMES JUPP is Director of the Centre for Immigration and Multicultural Studies at the Australian National University. He was general editor of the bicentennial project, *The Australian People*, and chaired the Commonwealth Review of Migrant and Multicultural Programs and Services. His recent publications include *Ethnic Politics in Australia* (1984) and *The Challenge of Diversity* (1989).

GEOFFREY McNICOLL is Professorial Fellow in Demography at the Australian National University. He has written widely on Third World economic demography and population policy. His most recent book is *Rival Development and Population: Institutions and Policies* (1990).

TREVOR MATTHEWS is Associate Professor of Government at the University of Sydney. His contribution to this book was written while a Visiting Fellow in Political Science in the Research School of Social Sciences at the Australian National University. His recent publications have dealt with organised business in Australia, Australia's relations with Japan and elite attitudes to Australian foreign policy. He is co-author of *The Japanese Connection* (1988).

DEBORAH MITCHELL has recently been awarded a Ph.D. in the Public Policy Program of the Australian National University, having just completed a major study of income transfer systems in a range of OECD countries. Before her move into academia, she was a public servant for 10 years, working substantially in social policy areas.

ELIM PAPADAKIS is a Visiting Fellow in Political Science in the Research School of Social Sciences at the Australian National University, and Senior Lecturer in Sociology at the University of New England. He is author of *The Green Movement in West Germany* (1984) and co-author of *The Private Provision of Public Welfare* (1987).

DON RAWSON is Associate Director of the Research School of Social Sciences at the Australian National University and Senior Fellow in Political Science in that school. He is the author of works on various aspects of Australian politics but particularly on political aspects of industrial relations. Recent books include *Unions and Unionists in Australia* (2nd edn, 1986) and, as co-author, *Trade Union Law in Australia: The Legal Status of Australian Trade Unions* (1986).

MARIAN SAWER lectures in Politics at the University of Canberra. Among her publications are *Australia and the New Right* (1982), *Towards Equal Opportunity* (1984) and *Sisters in Suits* (1990). She is co-author of *A Woman's Place* (1984).

Preface

This is a book which is, first and foremost, about Australia, but it is, at the same time, about many other countries. It is a book which looks at many varied aspects of the contemporary Australian experience—its people, its policies and its politics—partly because they are interesting in themselves, but also with the aim of showing the value of looking at that experience in a particular way. That way is through comparison with other nations. The book is predicated on the view that looking at both the development and contemporary reality of Australia in light of a knowledge of other comparable nations helps us to understand that experience better.

The idea of providing the first wide ranging survey of Australian society with an explicitly comparative focus came from the newly formed Division of Economics and Political Science in the Research School of Social Sciences of the Australian National University. However, the idea rapidly proliferated to include the interests of virtually all the disciplines represented in the Research School. To understand the broad contours of the contemporary Australian experience requires the collaborative endeavour of historians, demographers, sociologists, economists, public policy analysts and political scientists, and all those disciplines are represented here.

The fact that the book is the product of the Research School means that it is based on the very latest data available on the many topics covered and that the themes treated are those which are of particular concern to contemporary scholarship. Moreover, some of the contributions are actually research products in the sense of looking at questions hitherto undiscussed in the literature or of looking at familiar topics in new ways. On the other hand, the book's research origins do not mean that it is inaccessible to a broad educated public. Just because we consider that compassion brings a new and quite vital dimension to the study of Australian society, we have designed the book so that it may serve as an Australian Studies or Social Studies text suitable for first year undergraduate use. Our belief is that looking at Australia comparatively provides a mirror in which we may see ourselves more clearly if sometimes in a quite different light from that shed by more parochial studies. We want that mirror to be available to all those who seek to understand the character of the Australian experience, whether as part of their studies or as a background to a more informed approach to the practical tasks of living and working in the Australian environment.

The topics covered are extremely varied and provide the basis of an overview of many of the issues and debates that preoccupy commentary on the fundamental character of Australian social, economic and political life in the 1990s. Every chapter is framed in terms of a question, the answer to which tells us something important and novel about what Australia is like and/or the directions in which contemporary Australia is moving. The first chapter sets the scene by exploring the question: why compare Australia? It is designed to demonstrate what a comparative approach can bring to our understanding in terms of more accurate description, better grounded explanation, a greater ability to explore puzzles and paradoxes, and a capacity for more informed evaluation of features of Australian society and politics. This chapter stands not merely as an introduction to what is covered in subsequent chapters but also as an invitation to the reader to employ comparison as a means of illuminating all aspects of Australian life.

The remaining chapters are loosely grouped into sections covering people, policies and politics respectively. Part I on People starts with a chapter on the origins of Australia's national identity, which seeks to tell us something about what it means to be Australian and whether a national identity initially fashioned by British settlement on shores far distant from Europe and nurtured by democratic self-government in a vast island continent leaves us with a set of self-perceptions in some way different from those of other peoples. Settlement was not, of course, merely by those of Anglo-Irish stock and the migratory processes of this century have left us with a substantial ethnic diversity from which Australia has managed in a rather distinctive way to fashion the basis of a multicultural society. That is the topic of chapter 3, which could as appropriately have been covered in the section on Policies, but is included here, because ethnic diversity and the change from mono to multiculturalism which has been a feature of the post-war era are such vital components of contemporary Australia.

Another fundamental aspect of Australian life, and one which is the subject of much popular debate, is the changing character of the Australian family. The supposed decline of the 'traditional' family structure is always in the news, with stories about the impact of divorce, the shift to single parent families and changes in childbearing patterns. Chapter 4, by comparing our family experience with that of other nations, provides us with a basis for assessing such stories and offers us a series of scenarios of the direction in which the Australian family is going. Finally, chapter 5 looks at the nature of Australian attitudes and, in particular, attitudes to government. This chapter is a vital prelude to later sections on Policies and Politics, for our attitudes to such issues as civil liberties, welfare, equality and the appropriateness of economic intervention clearly shape the context in which policy-makers and politicians operate. Australians often assume, and that is, of course, a specific component of their national identity, that their attitudes are distinctive—they favour the underdog and put a fair go for all at the top of their priority list. By comparing Australian attitudes with those in other nations, this chapter tests such assumptions, sometimes with rather surprising results.

We do not pretend that Part II on Policies offers anything like a comprehensive survey of Australian policy areas in comparative perspective. Such a survey would constitute a long volume in its own right. Rather what we have done is to take a number of important, and sometimes contentious, areas of policy as illustrative of the contribution that comparison can make to an understanding of how policy is shaped and of the choices facing policy-makers. We start from issues of economic policy. Chapter 6 contrasts recent Australian economic performance and policy with EEC and American trends and suggests that the influence of the world economy is a more important determinant than either Australia's highly distinctive trade structure or the policy stances adopted by successive Labor and Coalition governments. A rather similar conclusion emerges from chapter 7 on wages policy. Australian wage-setting arrangements of conciliation and arbitration are quite different from those found in other western nations, but, according to the comparative evidence provided here, the trend of Australian wage outcomes is not distinctively different from those of other advanced nations in recent decades.

But, if recent Australian economic trends are close to the norm, a rather different picture emerges in other areas. Chapter 8 on the privatisation of Australian school education is possibly the most controversial in the book, seeking to explain the dynamic of a trend in education, which is very much at odds with developments elsewhere in the advanced nations and which can be seen as the antithesis of Australia's traditional egalitarian pretensions. Chapter 9 on welfare and social policy focuses on an area in which Australia has adopted policy strategies quite different from those of other nations. Australian attitudes to welfare and equality notwithstanding, this chapter shows us what Australia has actually achieved compared with other similar nations in terms of obviating poverty and distributing income fairly.

From Policies, we proceed in Part III to the Politics which shaped them and will shape Australian responses to the policy-issues of the

1990s. Chapter 10 starts with the organisation of economic interests in Australian society and how this compares with other advanced nations. In particular, the chapter is concerned with the interest coalitions that have been instrumental in fostering the Hawke government's Accord strategy, a consideration highly relevant to Australia's prospects of arriving at viable political solutions to contemporary economic problems, such as inflation, overseas debt and creating the basis of an export-led economic recovery. Chapters 11 and 12 constitute an internal dialogue about the viability and prospects of different forms of party politics in Australia in the 1990s and beyond. Chapter 11 suggests that the existing party structure is likely to remain adequate as a means of channeling political demands and, in particular, that the labour movement (the ALP and the trade unions, the latter already extensively discussed in chapter 10) have found ways of successfully adapting to social change, while chapter 12 forecasts that, as in a number of other countries, we are likely to experience a 'new' politics, in which issues such as the environment reshape our political agenda and party structure. Finally chapter 13 looks at one area in which new politics has undoubtedly made considerable advances, at least in Australia. This development has been the rise of the women's movement and its impact on government and bureaucracy. Here, to end on a comparative high note, Australia is both distinctive and ahead of the rest of the world.

Earlier we noted that comparison provides a mirror in which we may see ourselves better. It is also, of course, a means by which others may better become acquainted with us. Australia is, in population terms, the eighth largest of the advanced western nations, but of those nations it is undoubtedly the least known and understood in America, Europe and Japan. It is very much our hope that the broad range of studies contained in this volume will constitute some kind of a bridge for students and scholars overseas to understand the Australian experience better.

1 Why compare Australia?

FRANCIS G. CASTLES

In its most general formulation, the main objective of this book is to provide a broad overview of some of the more important ways in which Australia's people, policies and politics are similar to those of other nations and ways in which they are distinctive. Where possible, we also seek to understand the causes of such similarities and differences. Each chapter is an illustration of comparative analysis in action. They variously demonstrate how comparison can help us describe, classify, account for, explore and evaluate aspects of the Australian experience. This first chapter sets the scene by attempting to show some of the more important ways in which a comparative approach can promote a greater knowledge of our own society.

DESCRIBING AND CLASSIFYING THE AUSTRALIAN EXPERIENCE

Without some kind of comparison it is impossible to characterise the Australian experience at all. Essentially, the manner in which we describe and classify aspects of social reality is by making statements that depend on an assertion of similarity and/or difference. When, for instance, we describe contemporary Australia as a welfare state, we may imply one of two possible meanings: that Australian public policy has become far more concerned than it once was with the needs of the poor and helpless or that Australia is one of a group of countries which put such objectives to the forefront of its policy agenda. The first comparison is cross-temporal and the second cross-national. To locate adequately the nature of any aspect of the Australian experience, we require comparisons of both types. That is so, because the information we gain from the two types of comparison is quite different. We may be much more welfare-oriented than we once were—certainly; Australians have a far more extensive range of social services available than they did even twenty years ago (see Graycar & Jamrozik, 1989: 2) but, at the same time, we have ceased to be a welfare pioneer, as we were between 1900 and 1910. Compared with the majority of advanced democratic states, Australia is now a low spender on most aspects of welfare provision, although as chapter 8 demonstrates, that does not necessarily imply that we come at the bottom of the distribution in terms of welfare outcomes, such as poverty and inequality.

Without in any way denying the importance of cross-temporal comparison, this book concentrates very largely on cross-national comparison, although some chapters, most notably chapter 2 on the origins of Australian national identity, do seek to capture the temporal dimension as well by comparisons of what has happened to various countries over a stipulated period of time. One obvious reason for the emphasis on the experience of other nations is that cross-temporal comparison is the stuff of history and has not been neglected to anything like the same extent as cross-national comparison. No one doubts that one must know something of the Australian past to understand the Australian present, but the notion that one must know something of other countries to understand our own is much less frequently encountered.

Another reason is simply that, although historical analysis has made the idea of cross-temporal comparison rather familiar, it is cross-national comparison which is usually to the forefront in contemporary debate about the character of Australian society. When commentators argue that our economic growth rate is slow or that our manufacturing performance is weak, they are far more likely to mean that growth is slower and manufacturing performance is weaker than in comparable nations than to be offering a comparison with Australia's recent past. *Implicitly*, other nations serve as a benchmark for our own. In light of that benchmark, we locate various aspects or dimensions of our own experience—whether they are higher or lower, bigger or smaller, strong or weak, advanced or underdeveloped—and taking a more evaluative viewpoint, whether they are better or worse. When comparison relates to an objective of policy (see final section on evaluating the Australian experience) there is a strong tendency for such comparative terms to have at least some evaluative connotation.

The word implicitly is deliberately chosen because, only too often, we make comparisons with other nations without much conscious awareness of what we are doing. That is because, instead of using explicitly comparative phraseology (country A is richer than countries B, C and D), we often make the assertion that a given country falls into a given classificatory category, and the derivation of the comparison is unstated. When we say that Australia is rich, we are locating an aspect of its experience in a classificatory system consisting of, at a minimum, two kinds of economy, affluent and poor. In reality, such a classification and the concepts of which it is composed can only be derived from prior cross-national comparison. We can only describe a nation as rich because we have a conception of what it is to be a rich nation, and that, in turn, can only come from examining a number of nations and finding some criterion which distinguishes the more from the less affluent.

So if classification and description in terms of categories is inherently comparative, why do we need a book like this, which only differs from many other volumes on Australian society in being quite explicit in the comparisons it offers? The reason is that implicit comparison is rarely good comparison. Fundamentally, that is because unless we are aware of the scope of the comparison on which a given classification is based, we have no grounds for establishing the validity or otherwise of the conclusions that emerge from our analysis. Is Australia an advanced welfare state in expenditure terms? Most certainly, yes, if the comparison is between the industrialised countries and the vast majority of less developed nations, but, almost as emphatically, no, if the comparison is restricted to advanced capitalist economies. Only too frequently the descriptions offered us by both academic and journalistic commentators lack the comparative referents that are essential for making a reasoned assessment of the case being put forward.

Equally frequently, such descriptions highlight one particularly dramatic comparison at the expense of all others, as when the Australian economy is compared, and found wanting in almost every respect, with its Japanese counterpart. Comparisons of this sort are always deeply suspect, because the choice of a single reference point by a commentator largely determines the character of the assessment. All the chapters in this book are explicit in the comparisons they make and seek to avoid the partiality that stems from an unduly narrow basis of comparison. Most chapters relate the Australian experience to at least three or four other nations, and many of them include more, sometimes as many as twenty. In nearly every case, there is some comparison with other English-speaking countries, that might be assumed on *a priori* grounds to have much in common with Australia, and some wider contrast with other advanced, usually European, nations with fewer obvious cultural and historical affinities to Australia.

There is no suggestion here that this focus of comparison is intrinsically better than any other. The ideal comparative study is one in which all nations potentially relevant to the question are compared and contrasted. But that is an ideal and usually the absence of sufficient space, data and knowledge force us to choose a somewhat more modest focus: in this case, sufficient cases to locate some of the more important aspects of what is distinctive and similar about the Australian experience as contrasted with other advanced democratic nations. What we do contend is that our self-consciously comparative stance is likely to be far less misleading than a description framed in categories the comparative basis of which is unstated or very partial. Description or classification of social, economic and political reality which makes no explicit reference to the comparative benchmarks it is using is like a cartography

which produces maps lacking any scales of distance. Equipped with
such maps, we would be unable to tell whether the distance between
London and Sydney was greater or smaller than the distance between
Sydney and Melbourne. Without an explicitly comparative approach or
with only a very partial one, we are likely to find it just as difficult to
locate those features of the Australian experience that make it distinctive and those that we have in common with other nations.

The cartography metaphor is appropriate in another way. Large-
scale maps are often useless when we wish to find our way around
particular localities. The separate chapters of this book may be seen as
analogous to maps of particular aspects of the Australian experience and
the stories they tell us about Australia's similarity and distinctiveness
are often quite different. At one extreme, the stories about economic
performance and wage outcomes told in chapters 6 and 7 are of Australia's basic similarity to most other western nations in the period of the
1970s and 1980s. At the other extreme, the stories about the trend towards the privatisation of schooling, the organisation of economic interests (chapter 10), the degree of party identification (chapter 11) and
women's success in reshaping the bureaucracy (chapter 13) concern
areas in which the Australian experience is highly distinctive. Other
chapters deal with topics which fall in between, which is to say that
Australia turns out to be like one group of countries and rather unlike
another. The Australian definition of citizenship is similar to that of
other English-speaking nations, but based on a different principle from
that of most European nations (chapter 3). Our divorce rates are rather
similar to those of Canada, the United Kingdom and Sweden, but very
unlike those of Italy or the USA (chapter 4). Australians are like Americans and, to a lesser extent, the British in disapproving of nationwide
strikes against the government, while Germans, Austrians and Italians
manifest majority support for such actions (chapter 5). We are becoming
like European countries, such as West Germany and Sweden, in having
environmental parties represented in parliament (Tasmania), but are
unlike the United States and the United Kingdom in this respect (chapter 12), showing, incidentally, that the Australian experience is not always wholly akin to that of the other English-speaking countries. The
crucial point to focus on here is that in describing the Australian experience, we cannot be satisfied with broad generalisations. Australia is
similar and different from other nations in different ways depending on
the subject we are examining. A detailed comparative analysis of the
area in question is essential.

ACCOUNTING FOR THE AUSTRALIAN EXPERIENCE

Apart from serving as a benchmark of description and classification,
comparison offers us a logic by which we may account for features of

the Australian experience. That logic rests on the fact that diverse nations are rarely either entirely different or entirely similar. Grouping nations that are similar and contrasting those that are different often produce conclusions about the factors influencing the outcomes. What underlies such conclusions is a guiding assumption that like consequences stem from like causes and diverse consequences from diverse causes, so that when we discover two or more nations having some feature in common, we make at least an initial presumption that this similarity derives from some other shared characteristic. Using the comparative method to account for outcomes or events is a matter of locating patterns of similarity and difference across space (cross-national), time (cross-temporal) or both.

There are two possible strategies by which the comparativist may proceed (Przeworski & Teune, 1970). A 'most different' strategy is that which is used when we are seeking to understand patterns of similarity. If we can locate some particular feature which very diverse nations have in common, we are entitled to suggest that it is attributable to one of the few other attributes they share. Thus, if all or most nations which spend 10 per cent or more of their national product on welfare have more than 8 per cent of their population over the age of sixty-five, we may conclude that the age structure of the population is a prime candidate accounting for the development of the welfare state (see Wilensky, 1975), and, the greater their diversity in other respects, the more that conclusion is reinforced. To the extent that the high welfare spenders exhibit major differences in cultural and historical development and economic, social and political structure, age structure becomes a more and more probable explanation. The mark of a study employing a 'most different' strategy is a conscious effort to increase potential diversity in the group of nations under investigation, since each additional country with new characteristics added to the sample rules out further alternative explanations.

A 'most similar' strategy is that which is used when we are seeking to understand patterns of diversity. If we can locate some particular feature in which otherwise very similar nations differ, we are entitled to suggest that it is attributable to one of the few other factors distinguishing them. Thus, if affluent, democratic capitalist states vary quite appreciably in the degree to which schooling is conducted under private auspices and that variation coincides substantially with the extent of those nations' cultural heterogeneity, as suggested in chapter 8, we may argue that cultural heterogeneity is amongst the determinants of the public/private sector divide in education. In this case, our confidence in our conclusion is not a function of the diversity of the cases, but rather their similarity. Studies employing the 'most similar' strategy generally, but by no means invariably, tend to focus on fewer cases than those using a 'most different' one for the obvious reason that for each attribute on which nations are matched—how rich they are or whether they are democratic, for instance—more and more are ruled out. Which attributes are matched is, of course, a matter of the question we are asking. The 'most similar' strategy is not the only one employed here. In some instances, we are locating a number of English-speaking and advanced European countries as being broadly similar to Australia and seeking to account for remaining differences by factors which differentiate their experience in significant ways. Here, the strategy of comparison is the 'most similar' one. In other instances, we start from the assumption that the Australian experience is in some way unique, and look to other English-speaking and European nations to find factors common to all that may account for remaining similarities or to dissolve the apparent dissimilarities between Australia and other nations. Here, our strategy is 'most different', as for instance in chapter 7 on wages policy, which begins from the apparent distinctiveness of wage-setting arrangements in Australia, but discovers that such institutional differences are irrelevant to wage outcomes.

Our decision always to include some English-speaking nations other than Australia stems from a belief that in many respects these countries are still more similar to us even than the economically advanced and democratic countries of Western Europe because they broadly share elements of a common culture, history, legal and political structure. Nevertheless, it is by no means invariably true that the English-speaking countries are better matched than some English-speaking and some non-English speaking nations. That, too, depends on purpose and the question in mind. For instance, if we want to explain the factors conducive to the early emergence of democratic institutions, it may be more relevant to examine the commonalities of small countries with a strong independent rural sector, such as Australia, New Zealand and Denmark and to contrast them with other nations, including the United Kingdom, in which independent peasant proprietorship was weaker (see Therborn, 1977).

All the countries examined here are characterised by certain common characteristics—they are all modern, industrialised, democratic nations. The decision to restrict ourselves to these comparisons and contrasts stems from our objective of making an assessment of the degree to which the Australian experience is novel and distinctive. In terms of that objective, much that emerges from comparisons with a wider range of nations at very diverse economic levels and with very different political systems is of rather limited value. We already know that Australia differs from the majority of the nations of the world in being relatively rich, democratic, literate, industrialised and so on and we already make the causal attribution that these characteristics are to a large degree interrelated. To say that Australia is more like Canada, The Netherlands and Sweden—to take three advanced nations at random—than it is like Colombia, Niger and Syria is simply to state what is already known and, hence, of little real interest. If asked, we would say that there is no point in making comparisons with these latter countries because they are so different.

What is of interest is comparing ourselves to countries that we generally think of as being of the same order as ourselves. We may still start with an assumption of difference, as, for instance, the assumption that Australians are more egalitarian than most other peoples, but that makes it interesting when, as in chapter 5, we find that Australian attitudes to state action designed to foster greater equality are by no means more positive than in other Western nations. Alternatively, when we start from the assumption of basic similarity, nations in the same category serve to present a mirror of our own experience and permit the 'mental experiment' of reflecting that we too could be like that if circumstances were only a little different or our choices had been somewhat other than they were. But which circumstances and what choices? Finding out involves a location of aspects of the Australian experience by the use of a 'most similar' strategy of comparison. Why is Australia's economic growth rate so slow compared to other affluent, Western nations? There are many rival explanations. Can low growth be attributed to the fact that countries that are already very affluent tend to grow more slowly than those which are less so? To find out, we contrast the growth performance of the richer and poorer of these nations and seek to establish whether there is, indeed, a convergent pattern. Can low growth be attributed to the choices made in some of these nations to utilise a large share of economic resources on welfare and egalitarian redistribution? To find out, we contrast the growth rates of the larger and smaller social spenders amongst the advanced nations.

Problems arise from either a lack of sufficient cases or from an inability to match cases well enough. The former difficulty tends to afflict studies based on a 'most different' strategy, for without enough cases it is impossible to rule out some possible sources of the similarity one is seeking to explain. The latter difficulty is an inherent part of the 'most similar' strategy. Ideally, that strategy would resemble the controlled experiment of the natural sciences in which a single difference is introduced into otherwise identical specimens, leading to the inevitable conclusion that subsequent diversity is a consequence of that difference. But no group of nations is ever anything like that similar, so that there are always alternative sources of difference competing as the rival explanations of diversity (see Roberts, 1978: 294), as, in our previous example, prior levels of affluence and the size of welfare spending compete as rival ways of accounting for the diversity of economic growth rates in the advanced democratic nations.

Although these problems can never be wholly overcome, there are a variety of techniques for testing which of a series of differing accounts has the greatest degree of plausibility. Many of these techniques as used in the more sophisticated comparative literature are statistical. They provide an assessment of the probability of empirical regularities occurring by chance and objective criteria for deciding which of several competing accounts is the most likely to be appropriate. Using such techniques, it is possible to adjudicate the rival claims of affluence and the 'overmighty' state as determinants of low economic growth in favour of an account of the growth rate convergence of rich and poor nations (see Castles and Dowrick, 1990). With only a few exceptions, the chapters here attempt to assess competing accounts without complex statistical manipulations. In the few cases where there is statistical analysis, an effort has been made to make the text comprehensible to those who do not possess numerical skills. Irrespective of whether testing is conducted by statistical or other means, each comparison involves a process by which various hypotheses are matched up with evidence from a variety of nations to find that with the best fit.

In concluding this section, it should be pointed out that the term 'explanation' has been used somewhat loosely at one or two points in the discussion of the logic of comparative analysis. An explanation consists of a set of reasons or a theory which makes sense of empirically observed regularities, that is the similarities or differences revealed by comparison. The location of a convergent pattern of economic growth amongst advanced western states would clearly help us account for an important aspect of the Australian experience, but it would hardly be an explanation as such. For that we would need reasons: for instance, that nations find it easier to copy industrial techniques from other countries than to develop them themselves or that preferences for leisure increase more than proportionately as income rises. So what we are arguing in this section is that comparison provides us with a logic by which we may isolate empirical generalisations which require theoretical examination. As the next section makes clear, that order of analysis is sometimes reversed: on occasions, we may start from theory and use it to identify critical cases, the further comparative investigation of which leads in turn to the redefinition of theory.

EXPLORING THE AUSTRALIAN EXPERIENCE

Although less frequently noted than its role in explanation and hypothesis testing, comparison is also a means of locating and exploring a phenomenon as yet insufficiently understood. This mode of analysis is, in effect, an extension of the task of identifying and describing features of national distinctiveness. The difference is that, whereas, earlier, distinctiveness was located along a single dimension—a country is exceptional in possessing this, that or the other feature to a greater or lesser extent than others—here we are talking of a nation being distinguished by its unusual placing in a two dimensional space constituted, on the one hand, by some fairly well established theoretical proposition and, on the other, by an empirical instance which contradicts or seems to contradict it. Distinctiveness here is defined not in terms of the extremity of events, institutions or outcomes, but rather by the failure of a particular case or cases to conform with regularities which account for the behaviour of the vast majority of cases. Such failures create puzzles or paradoxes which positively demand further exploration.

In some ways, it is easier to demonstrate dramatic instances of such puzzles or paradoxes in an Australian context than would be the case in respect of many of the other advanced western nations. Australia has not hitherto been in the mainstream of comparative social science research and generalisations concerning social, economic and political behaviour are frequently formulated without even a backwards glance at the Australian experience. No competent comparativist would offer such generalisations without seeking to demonstrate that they fitted at least the larger nations of the advanced world—the USA, Japan, the UK, Germany and France—and frequently there would also be at least some examination of the experiences of many of the smaller nations of Western Europe. However, few seem concerned, or even seem to realise, that they are leaving out of consideration a country which, unlike such frequently compared nations as, say, Sweden, Switzerland, Austria and The Netherlands, falls in the top half of the distribution of population size of the advanced democratic states. Certainly, prominent among the reasons for producing this book, is a wish to locate important aspects of Australian experience that should be taken account of by anyone seeking to offer theoretical generalisations applicable to that entire 'most similar' grouping of nations.

So, what are some of the ways in which the Australian experience is paradoxical? The examples offered here are merely illustrative and are drawn from recent work on the development of Australian public policy (Castles, 1988 and Castles, 1989, 16–55). You will be able to discern other examples in the chapters that follow, most notably in chapter 10, where the puzzle posed by the unusual assymetry of interest group organisation in Australia leads the author to a reformulation of theories accounting for the organisational unity of business.

1 Australia is a country with a population which, while not small, is in no way comparable to those of the major powers. Economic theory tells us that the smaller a country's population, the more it is likely to trade with the rest of the world, since it must rely on product specialisation and international trade to make up for the disadvantage of a small internal market (Dahl & Tufte, 1973, 113–16). So why, measured in terms of its export share, does Australia have one of the most closed economies in the OECD, following closely after the vastly larger American and Japanese economies?

2 Australia is a country which, by virtue of its highly unusual system of conciliation and arbitration of industrial disputes and compulsory and centralised wage-fixing, may be regarded as possessing a highly institutionalised form of labour market regulation. In Western Europe, such institutionalisation has been argued to be an important component of the success of neo-corporatist nations in weathering the economic crises of the 1970s (Katzenstein, 1985). Yet Australia's economic performance in the 1970s was as bad as any in the OECD, being only one of two OECD nations which in the period 1974–79 were below the average in respect of economic growth, unemployment and inflation simultaneously. (Wages policy is discussed in chapter 7 and a possible explanation of at least one aspect of this seeming paradox is suggested in the finding that wage movements are determined more by the international environment than by domestic wage-setting arrangements.)

3 Australia is a country in which the strength of the labour movement, whether assessed in terms of union membership or electoral support has been traditionally strong. Indeed, we may note, as an aspect of Australian distinctiveness, that, taking the percentage electoral support since the turn of the century as a measure of labour movement strength, it is Australia and not Sweden, the supposed exemplar of democratic socialist hegemony, which has had the world's most successful democratic socialist party. (Some measures of the persistence and strength of the Australian Labor Party are to be found in chapter 11.) Theories suggesting that politics is an arena of institutionalised class conflict imply that left strength should be translated into an impetus to welfare expenditure growth as a means to greater social and economic equality, but in Australia welfare expansion in expenditure terms has not matched that of other nations. In 1986, of twenty OECD nations only Japan, Spain and the United States spent a smaller share of GDP on social expenditure than Australia, and Australia's expenditure on pensions as a percentage of GDP was lower than any other advanced OECD nation (OECD, 1989). (Again, the research in this volume speaks to this issue in so far as chapter 9 shows that particular instruments of social policy adopted in Australia lead to more egalitarian outcomes than would be presumed on the basis of welfare expenditure alone.)

In each of these examples, we have a puzzle or paradox because generalisations drawn from the comparative literature are contradicted by facets of the Australian experience. In each case also the solution is the same: we need to explore further the nature of that experience with a view either to a refinement of the way in which we describe and classify it or to a modification of the generalisations constituting the literature. Such explorations raise fascinating problems for research.

Referring back to our examples, we can ask a variety of questions. Is economic openness something that develops directly as a consequence of population size or is it a chosen policy stance and, if the latter, why should Australia more than other small nations have opted to shut out the influence of world markets? What are the similarities and differences between the institutional form and outcomes of labour market regulation through conciliation and arbitration in Australia and through corporatist intermediation in countries such as Sweden, Germany and The Netherlands, and why was the Australian variant more vulnerable to economic crisis in the 1970s? How are we to visualise the impact of party ideology on welfare state development in light of the failure of the normal indicators of the strength of class conflict in politics to explain the Australian experience? One possibility might be to turn from a theory of class politics theory to one of party control of government (the ALP has not been successful in those terms). Another might lie in an attempt to explore whether the Australian labour movement possessed a different strategy of equality from movements elsewhere (see Castles, 1985 and chapter 9).

The examples offered here and the new avenues of exploration they suggest are only dramatic illustrations of a process at work in all research: each step in the elaboration of theory leads to a need to describe and classify phenomena in greater detail and with greater precision leading in turn to an impetus for still more elaborated theory. All that we would argue here is that cross-national comparison, and for Australians, at least, cross-national comparison focusing on the distinctiveness or otherwise of the Australian experience, provides an extraordinarily fruitful way of promoting that research process in respect of broader questions concerning the social, economic and political characteristics of whole societies or nation-states.

EVALUATING THE AUSTRALIAN EXPERIENCE

We have left what is, probably, the commonest and, in some ways, perhaps, the most important use of cross-national comparison to last, not least because it is simultaneously the area of the greatest misuse of the comparative method. All the time, in the councils of government, amongst their critics and by commentators of all sorts, evidence concerning other countries is proffered as a means of evaluating our own and, where that evaluation finds us wanting, becomes an important stimulus for proposals for reform.

In recent times, this kind of evaluation has become more common in Australia, particularly at the extremes of politics, where the symbols of Japan and Sweden are frequently used by their adherents to sum up all that is good about capitalism and democratic socialism respectively. We are also beginning to encounter the phenomenon of major interests and governmental agencies using serious comparative research as part of a reasoned case for reform. One example was the ACTU's 1987 report, *Australia Reconstructed*, which signalled the union movement's acceptance of a need for economic restructuring and a shift to competitive exporting along the lines of a model supposedly derived from the experience of Europe's small corporatist economies. Another was the Australian Manufacturing Council (AMC) report on the future of Australian manufacturing (1989), which, amongst other things, pointed to the policy solutions of other similar countries, such as Canada, as potential remedies for our own difficulties.

The evaluative usage of comparison is unproblematic in principle but is sometimes dangerous in practice. Cross-national comparison is clearly a valuable means of assessing the extent to which we achieve desired objectives. If we want to be richer than we are, it makes sense to compare ourselves with the more affluent and the poorer. This is so for several reasons. First, the very fact that some nations are richer than we are suggests the potential conclusion that we could be richer. Secondly, the range between the richest and the poorest nations of any comparable group (that is 'most similar'), gives us an indication of the extent of the challenge we face in effecting desired reforms. Thirdly, to the degree that our comparison produces an acceptable account of the nature of the problem—reasons why some countries are richer than others—it provides us with a recipé for reform, that is it suggests what we must do in order to become richer. Thus, there are very good reasons why evaluation and reform efforts should be informed by comparative analysis and why we should applaud when organisations such as the ACTU and AMC undertake serious cross-national research.

As soon as we compare performance against a measuring rod constituted by our objectives, descriptive statements of a more-or-less character are prone to take on a connotation of better or worse, with location of difference denoted in terms overtly indicating approval or disapproval such as leaders and laggards, and winners and losers. Such terms are not dangerous so long as we always remember that they relate to performance in respect of some stipulated objective, which is not necessarily shared by all members of the community about which they are used. Difficulties do sometimes occur when these terms are taken to imply that failure to achieve desired objectives is a question of deficiencies that could be remedied by more intelligent policy-making. That may or may not be the case. Whether it is is a matter of what determines the outcomes of which we complain. If, for instance, the degree of industry spending on Research and Development (R & D) is a function of the strength of the export manufacturing sector, it may make perfect sense to describe Australia as an R & D laggard, but very little to suggest that there is very much that can be done about it in the short-term (Castles,

1989). More serious problems arise when inappropriate choices are made as to the countries which are compared and those choices, in turn, lead to misleading ways of accounting for the differences and similarities between nations. More than in any other respect, evaluation, leading potentially to reform, requires a 'most similar' research design. The closer the match between cases, the less the chance that some unnoticed difference is the real reason for diverse national performance in the area which we are attempting to evaluate. On such a basis, we might well be more inclined to emulate the lessons of Canada than of Sweden, not necessarily because we prefer Canadian to Swedish outcomes, but rather because the far greater cultural and structural similarities between Canada and Australia are some sort of indication that what will work in one may well work in the other.

Close matching of cases inherently reduces the range of nations that may be meaningfully compared, but reducing it too far is just as dangerous as reducing it too little. When we are being invited to compare ourselves with just one or two other nations, those nations have quite often been picked to make a point. If Australia wants to be rich, she is frequently told she should copy the USA and Japan. And what precisely is it about these countries that we should copy? In commentary emanating from the right, of course, the answer is that it is their low levels of public expenditure that give individuals the incentive to work for the private gain and that lead to the maximisation of aggregate national wealth! But that answer presupposes, first, that the only thing Japan and the USA have in common is low public expenditure, secondly, that all rich nations have low public expenditure and, thirdly, that all countries with low public expenditure are rich. None of these things are true, the final presumption being disproved by the very fact that it is Australia, a low public expenditure country, that is being advised that the road to economic redemption lies in copying the similar practices of the USA and Japan.

So, although some considerable attention to matching cases is required when we set out to use comparison for evaluation and reform, it is crucial not to make the comparison too limited to exclude spurious generalisations. What is required in all cross-national comparison, whether it is merely descriptive or seeks to account for, explore or evaluate the experience of our own or other countries is a balance between the similarity that makes the experience of other nations relevant to our own and the differences that serve to weed out unwarranted generalisations. In what follows, it is the hope of all the contributors to this volume that the balance achieved—somewhat different in each chapter because of the diversity of the substantive questions addressed—demonstrates how much is to be gained by viewing the Australian experience in comparative perspective.

ACKNOWLEDGEMENT

The framework of presentation adopted here is loosely derived from an article by Professor Robert Jackson (1990).

REFERENCES

ACTU/TDC (1987) *Australia Reconstructed* Canberra: Australian Government Publishing Service

Australian Manufacturing Council (1989) *What Part Will Manufacturing Play in Australia's Future?* Canberra: Australian Government Publishing Service

Castles, Francis G. (1985) *The Working Class and Welfare* Sydney: Allen & Unwin

————— (1988) *Australian Public Policy and Economic Vulnerability* Sydney: Allen & Unwin

————— (1989) 'Social Protection by Other Means: Australia's Strategy of Coping with External Vulnerability' in Francis G. Castles ed. *The Comparative History of Public Policy* Cambridge: Polity, pp. 16–55

————— (1989) 'An ABC of R & D or Is Australia's Record as Black as It Has Been Painted?', *Australian Quarterly*, 61, 1, pp. 17–32.

Castles, Francis G. & Dowrick, Steve (1990) 'The Impact of Government Spending Levels in Medium Term Economic Growth in the OECD, 1960–85', *Journal of Theoretical Politics*, 2, pp. 173–204

Dahl, R.A. and Tufte, E.R. (1973) *Size and Democracy* Stanford: Stanford University Press

Graycar, A. & Jamrozik, A. (1989) *How Australians Live* Melbourne: Macmillan

Jackson, R. (1991) 'Australian and Canadian Comparative Political Research: Purposes, Research Designs and Issues' in B. Galligan, ed. *Comparative Political Studies: Australia and Canada* Melbourne: Longman Cheshire

Katzenstein, Peter (1985) *Small States in World Markets* Ithaca: Cornell University Press

OECD (1989) 'OECD in Figures', *OECD Observer*, 158

Przeworski, A. & Teune, H. (1970) *The Logic of Comparative Social Enquiry* New York: Wiley

Roberts, G. (1978) 'The Explanation of Politics: Comparison, Strategy and Theory' in P.G. Lewis, D.C. Potter and F.G. Castles eds *The Practice of Comparative Politics* London: Longman

Therborn, Göran (1977) 'The Rule of Capital and the Rise of Democracy', *New Left Review*, 103, pp. 3–41

Wilensky, H. (1975) *The Welfare State and Equality* Berkeley: University of California Press

PART I   PEOPLE

2 What are the origins of Australia's national identity?

JOHN EDDY

NATIONAL IDENTITY: THE NATURE OF THE CONCEPT

The words 'national' and 'identity' have only been commonly combined since about 1960, though terms such as 'nationalism', 'national character', and 'national consciousness' are older. 'The search for identity has become a fashionable phrase', wrote Arthur Koestler in 1969, 'but in Australia it is a real problem, and a haunting one' (quoted in Inglis, 1988: 8). In recent years, it shows signs of becoming an obsession. The concept itself, to have any validity, must be based on objective geographical, historical and other verifiable factors, but its power and fascination are grounded more subtly on perception. This perception in turn has its origins in a sense of 'general agreement' about the distinctiveness of a society (usually a political nation-state) as expressed normally in the media, general and specialist literature or public debate, for example 'the Australian economy', 'Australian cities, families, sport'. Historical evidence suggests that it has also long referred to a series of unquantifiable, uplifting or sometimes meretricious 'myths' which may be 'invented', consciously or unconsciously, to symbolise, 'identify' or energise the national community, for example 'the pioneers', 'mateship', 'the beach', 'the bush', 'the lucky country', ANZAC valour in a slouch hat, 'New Australians' etc. 'A national identity is an invention. There is no point asking whether one version of this essential Australia is truer than another because they are all intellectual constructs, neat, tidy, comprehensible—and necessarily false' (White, 1981: viii).

The modern nation is itself an 'artifact', powerfully evocative of social, cultural and political movements in space and time, leading to a communal sense of independence achieved and developing in relation to, or in contrast with, neighbours and peers on the world stage. 'Identity' establishes the specific in human affairs and relations, but at

17

18 AUSTRALIA COMPARED

the national level it proves ambiguous at best (Seton-Watson, 1977). In contemporary Australia, as elsewhere, and in different decades, other organising concepts, such as class, clan, colour, gender, age, suburb, religion, political affiliation or profession, may prove equally significant in establishing self-perception—as a rich, old, 'Irish', Quaker, Democrat woman doctor from Peppermint Grove could assure a poor, young, 'Vietnamese', Catholic, Labor-voting carpenter from Cabramatta, with both claiming plausibly to be all-Australian.

Each individual in the national group maintains and identifies himself or herself with a complex web and plurality of reference groups. The impact of national identity is undeniably real, and not merely made up of the sum total, lowest common denominator, or 'average' of the inhabitants of the nation. Each generation is continuous with its predecessor, of course, but is complete in itself, with its own integrity and maturity. The common temptation to see organic change in a nation's self-awareness as though it was a procession from infancy through youth to full flower and so on, may contain a grain of truth, but should be resisted if pressed too far.

Australians have long seen their 'Antipodean' experience as distinct from and in contrast to those of their immediate neighbours in Asia, and also somehow sea-changed from the life of the European nations—and especially England, Ireland, Scotland and Wales—from which so many of the white settlers came. But the folk memories of the original peoples came with them as 'baggage' and remain, occasionally oddly frozen and unnurtured but more often with roots refreshed and 'updated' by successive waves of migration from the source. Although historical attitudes have been remarkably stable in essential particulars, the expression of national sentiment has undergone historical development as genuinely distinct periods, consolidating social, economic or political change, emerged in the collective *curriculum vitae* (Dutton, 1985; Miller, 1987).

Those versions of national identity which are constructed deliberately by the media often prove to be caricatures of any recognisable truth. The very vividness and immediacy of the images certainly serve to distinguish the 'Aussie' they depict from the equally sharply etched specific 'portraits' of for instance 'Yanks', 'Poms', 'Japs', but they suffer from exaggeration, and are impossible to 'ground'. They are for the most part founded on popular prejudice, which is relatively unsophisticated, fickle and unreflective, and they tend, like any fashion, propaganda or advertisement, to change rapidly according to the commercial or demotic need (Carroll, 1982).

The Bicentenary of 1988 elicited much of this hype, and it cannot be denied that the genre produces powerful and specific 'national' images. Thus, for Australia, the 'type' can vary according to the context or intention of the commentator. If the purpose is celebratory and the tone congratulatory, the wishful picture given is of beaches and barbecues, of tall, athletic, bronzed, healthy, sincere men (and nowadays women), brave in adversity, sworn to independence and yet capable of great 'mateship', casual and laconic, witty and practical, patron saints of the 'fair go' and support for the 'underdog'. These are the children of heroic pioneers who tamed a fierce continent and built a hopeful 'new' nation under the Southern Cross, gifted and tolerant, the stuff out of which have naturally sprung Don Bradman, Greg Norman, Crocodile Dundee, Olivia Newton John and Elle. On the other hand, if the purpose of the context is jaundiced, and the intention is to exhort or denounce, Australians are portrayed as a colonially cringing race of lazy, chauvinistic procrastinators, satisfied with derivative mediocrity, envious of 'tall poppies' and frequently self-destructive in a stupor of sand, sin and beer-swilling, incapable of original thought or efficient action, capable management or rational planning, a nation of 'Norms', apathetic and uncultured, careless of tomorrow in 'the land of the long weekend' (Conway, 1978; Rickard, 1988).

Beguiling though this pursuit may be, and obviously profitable for those who make their living by touching on the sensitive spots (and hip-pockets) of the 'great Australian public', creating the felt need for ever more sentimentally 'home-grown' swimwear, wide-brimmed hats, cars and clothing, it is at bottom essentially an advertising game, and the glamorous or horrible *dramatis personae* change subtly from season to season and from weekly magazine to coloured supplement. This chapter is aimed rather at pinpointing those temporal frames of reference and those developmental landmarks which went into the making of the historical consciousness or 'national identity' with which Australia and Australians in the post-war era have faced the range of social, economic and political issues discussed in later chapters of this book.

A HISTORICAL AND COMPARATIVE PERSPECTIVE

Historical events, periods, and landmarks obviously contribute to the sense of 'national identity', independent of the frameworks imposed on them by commentators. There is an element of comparison in any selection of those items which seem best to illustrate the uniqueness of the national grouping under consideration. Many 'trends', happenings and consequences obviously affect a number of nations simultaneously. Sometimes social, economic and military events, for example, can best be seen as global, not primarily as having their impact within the boundaries of one nation or community. Yet even with regard to these more widely felt phenomena there is a real and individual concern applied to each national community or group of nations, for instance 'the Depression in Australia', 'Australia's role in the Great War'.

Quite distinctly there exists a wide range of 'national goals', as put forward by thinkers, scholars or minorities of various kinds, against which the 'nation' is judged. Therefore a nation's 'identity' refers not only to the conglomeration of verifiable facts and figures which outline its history, geography, demography, and other characteristics (and which distinguish it from or make it resemble any other national grouping) but also to its real or putative achievement in living up to sometimes quite complex expectations, as interpreted by a wide variety of 'publics' or interest groups. Some of these elites hold contradictory views as to what constitutes 'maturity' or 'independence' in formal structure, constitution or action. Much of the debate aimed at recognising or capturing the communal 'identity' rests on more or less informed comparisons with other nations or times.

Modern 'white' Australia does not have the historical depth and cultural reach of most of the countries from which its colonising settlers were (and are) drawn. But, as a 'derivative' society, it shares to some extent in the histories of all its constituent peoples. It is, as a 'self-governing' political nation, older than some of its near neighbours, such as Indonesia or Papua New Guinea, or, for that matter, some of the 'constructed' nations of the twentieth century, comparable in size of population, Yugoslavia for example in Europe, or Zimbabwe and Tanzania in Africa. Often seen as a 'new' country, Australia is manifestly more stable than even comparable 'older' nations such as Canada (Jupp, 1988).

Particularly in countries such as Australia, a hybrid in which some leading elements of a colony of settlement were, from the beginning of European colonisation in 1788, mingled with elements of a plantation colony, the original dreams and visions were important in delineating the features of the enterprise. As foundation or 'heroic' myths they went into the construction and quasi-permanent perception of local 'identity'. Australia was seen from the first, despite all the conscious modelling of her institutions and habits after those of Great Britain, as distinctive, but puzzling and even unique. Robert Hughes' 'Fatal Shore' soon became 'the Land of Contrarieties' (Hughes, 1987; Clarke, 1977).

With every 'ideal' society or at least every society 'with a purpose' comes opposition to that purpose, and the expression of alternative possibilities for the organisation and development of the polity, and therefore a succession of 'enemies', whose charters and agenda for change and reform must also be taken into account in any assessment of identity. The convict colonies of the Antipodes, growing into relatively 'free' societies, were no exception. Even their fundamental flaws fell under the trenchant criticism of Jeremy Bentham and others. Every society must undergo a continual process of comparison against the benchmarks of both its supporters and its critics, its 'failures' as well as its 'successes' (Hirst, 1983; McLachlan, 1989).

Modern Australian identity, therefore, has to be measured not only against the background of relatively unchanging physical and geographical facts, but as an ever-changing reflection within the community—often in the process of vigorous internal debate about desirable social, economic, and political goals—of its perceived stage of development. This process of national discernment is impossible without drawing necessary comparisons with other societies, both similar and dissimilar, and with the Australian past. There has to be, with regards to national identity, a historical perspective as well as a recognition of the role of models both internal and comparative.

Richard White, author of one of the best books about Australian national identity, *Inventing Australia* (1981) writes of the 'public culture' that sustains and legitimises the nation-state:

Nations feed off collective memories. A nation claims to be something more than a set of social relations existing at a particular time. A nation, rather, is a community that is imagined as stretching back into the past and forward into the future. Nationalist rhetoric is always looking for a glorious past or a manifest destiny yet to be realised (White, 1990: 57).

In creating this sense of 'nation-ness', historical judgment and communal acts of memory are essential, creating the myths that give meaning to the nation, and providing the formal linkage between past and present.

MYTHS AND REALITIES

The Australian colonies were chips off the block of Great Britain but their nineteenth century experience of 'self-government' and their gradual coming together as a federal Commonwealth were seen as distinct moves towards 'cutting the painter' and 'going it alone'. The creation of an Australian democracy truly independent of its 'colonial' origins was and is seen to be an objective of national maturity. When the Australian nation became a formal entity on 1 January 1901, the past of its component parts seemed only ambivalently palatable, partly because of the convict origins or 'stain', and partly because of the continuing and often irksome symbiosis of colonial life with that of 'the Home country' (Mandle, 1977; Meaney, 1989).

Pastoral Australia was in part a 'plantation colony' too. Donald Denoon, in his *Settler Capitalism* (1983), shows interesting similarities and a number of common features in 'the dynamic of development in the southern hemisphere', linking societies as diverse as Argentina, Chile, Uruguay, South Africa, New Zealand and Australia. Economic comparisons continue to be made between Australia and Argentina, just as social contrasts and similarities are drawn with quite different nations such as Sweden in the northern hemisphere (Denoon, 1983).

The rhetoric of federation, as White points out, 'had to stress future greatness' (White, 1990: 57). Although there were possible elements in the colonial past which might have caught the imagination, it was World War I, and specifically the gallantry of Australian troops in the storied arena of Asia Minor and the Hellespont, that would provide a 'collective memory'. These myths, bolstered by authority and the education networks (always in Australia, as elsewhere, a key transmitter of attitudes and values), would fill the gap that in other nations was filled by the memory of struggles for national independence, civil wars, or other dramatic events or heroic leaders. The power of 'public commemoration' and glorification of the 'national character' overrode the sadder memories proper to private grief over the casualties of Gallipoli or the much greater sacrifice of life entailed by Australia's massive later entanglement on the Western Front.

'Myths', once established, resist even the most stubborn revisions. In vain, at least as far as the popular imagination is concerned, have revisionist historians insisted that the Third British Empire was Athenian rather than Roman in style, that the path of the self-governing colonies, especially in the Antipodes, was by and large smoothed and encouraged by generations of statesmen in Westminster, that the eventual historic Federation of the Australian colonies was fostered by the 'imperial' power and embodied in an Imperial Act prepared almost entirely by colonial politicians to their own liking, and that Australia's long connections with Britain were almost unanimously seen (in the 'colonies' if not always by many 'little Englanders' at home) as mutually advantageous during the era of 'colonial nationalism' (Eddy and Schreuder, 1988).

Recently evidence has been marshalled to show that, although the Australians were by no means the 'tail that wagged the dog', the impact of their dependent position within the British Empire from 1901 to World War II has been exaggerated. Re-assessments are needed to offer sounder judgments concerning Australia's alleged subservience and timidity—especially as regards the constraints placed on her defence and foreign policies, based supposedly on her economic dependence and the consequent warping or stunting of her development (Tsokhas, 1986; Meaney, 1976).

Along with the 'separateness' of full nationhood goes the growth of new patterns in which nations willingly or perforce accept new political or economic alignments. Keith Sinclair, for example, emphasises the impact of changing trading patterns for New Zealand, chiefly because of the advent of the European Common Market—from 90 per cent with Great Britain in 1939 to only 9 per cent now. Australia, whose larger and more diversified economy was broadly more able to sustain this metamorphosis, did not fare so badly. Sinclair also notes the advent of 'biculturalism' and a new 'multiculturalism', a phenomenon seen—

with due flexibility and not always with universal clarity or for that matter goodwill—as characteristic of several other of the old 'settler dominions', especially Canada and Australia. But *plus ça change*. Migrant patterns, especially since 1945 have been quite distinct, and apart from the 'two cultures' which come with each wave of migration, the original 'two cultures' of indigenes and colonists were very different. New Zealand Maoris, Australian Aborigines and American Indians have their own histories, even if their place in the community Pantheon is being bettered. 'National identity proves not to be a permanent state of feeling, but one which is continuously evolving' (Sinclair, 1990: 117).

John Power, in an attempt to analyse the impact of 'modernisation' and 'deregulation' of the economy and the effect of the 'managerial revolution' on Australia's distinctiveness in the late 1980s, notes that there may be a generational periodicity in social, economic and political change as well as the emergence, within a continuous framework, of fairly clearly defined 'eras' in such key national institutions as federalism itself. Thus he outlines the generally agreed division of twentieth century Australian experience, into the foundational ten years or so of 'coordinate' federalism, with relatively little power exercised at the centre; then a period of 'cooperative' or interdependent federalism up to about 1940, during which the constituent States bargained for power with the central government; and a succeeding time of 'organic' growth when the power and control of the federal government had been consolidated. While there is evidence that this section of historical development is now coming to an end, in a 'paradigm shift', the last half-century has 'exhibited a unique combination of fiscal centralisation and functional decentralisation in a society which has exhibited fewer regional differences than either the UK or Canada' (Power, 1989).

These 'phases' present the underlying but changing reality on which myths of national self-perception are built. 'Australians have been welcoming the dawn of a new kind of civilisation in their country like a ritual, without being clear what was coming', wrote Bruce Grant in his *Australian Dilemma* (1983: 284). By the 1980s he esteemed Australia to have become an uneasy mix of past and future—40 per cent British, 30 per cent American, 20 per cent European and 10 per cent Asian. Yet he noted that

> the Australian system is, despite the pushing and the pulling, sufficiently
> established to gain agreement on its essentials; a mixed economy,
> predominantly capitalist, an always-shifting balance between protection and
> free trade, a federal system that, despite rushes of blood to the periphery
> from time to time, is capable of national direction and stimulation

in face of the extended challenges, stemming from shifts in the world economy and balance of power, which must certainly be imminent.

EARLY BEGINNINGS TO FEDERATION

Australia from the first seemed unique to its European settlers. Even before colonisation there had been many versions of a 'Great South Land' as a balance to known northern land masses in the literature and writings of various adventuring European nations. The first contacts of 'the white man' resulted in rumours of a very peculiar country, inhabited by extremely strange people, odder, in William Dampier's phrase, than the 'Hodmadods of Monomatapa' (Clark, 1962: 39). But it would be unfair not to note that there existed, and still persist, alternative interpretations of the 'essence' of Australia, as experienced by the original inhabitants (Reynolds, 1987; Attwood, 1989).

The economic historian, Noel Butlin, has pointed out that the Aborigines had by 1788 many centuries of experience of the land and its ways. Their version of Australia has been ignored, neglected and sometimes positively uprooted, until comparatively recently. The 'dreaming' of the Aborigines has been overlayed almost totally by the 'myths', aspirations and imaginings of the immigrant settlers, the 'conquerors' (Bolton, 1981; Macintyre, 1985). Nevertheless their close and valuable connection with the 'national psyche' or at least 'spirit of the place' has come to be increasingly recognised, and—in the shape of 'public policy towards indigenous people'—currently forms one of the most thorny and complex specific challenges facing the Australian community. In this, Australia resembles Canada, or even the much larger USA, where the Inuit and Indian indigenes were similarly linked—imaginatively, historically and culturally—to the extended national consciousness, and comes close to the experience, *mutatis mutandis*, of the New Zealand people with their larger Maori population, and to some extent to the Boer and British settlers in South Africa relative to the Bantu and Zulu (Butlin, 1987).

Some of these 'First Nations', however, were comparatively more numerous than the Aborigines and in the course of settlement by the 'invaders' managed so to assert their identity that, in contrast, they maintained or increased their majority status (Africa), or won for their contemporary heirs the sometimes dubious but negotiable advantages of treaty rights accorded by the conquerors (New Zealand and North America). Even in the period of the most insensitive and traditional 'White Australia' the conquered culture never really perished, and provided a surprising and unique set of symbols, names and approaches to landscape and environment. Popular lists of Aborigine place names alone serve to delineate Australian-ness, just as Indian titles specify Canadian-ness (Hodgins, Eddy, et al., 1989; Sinclair, 1986).

The first phase of British settlement, the convict era, was sufficiently distinct and historically so bizarre as to distinguish the 'Antipodean' colonies from every other earthly habitat. Such a process of colonisation was never attempted on such a large and methodical a scale by any other nation, although the French were attracted in the first half of the nineteenth century. The gradual swelling of numbers of men and women transported to over 160 000 and their scattering throughout the continent over the years of formal despatch, 1788–1868, ensured that the aura, or 'stain', of convictism would be firmly registered on the consciousness of both Australians and other observers. The experience of the system is often invoked to explain what is seen as a darker side of the 'national character', its insecurity and wariness of authoritarian structures, and its style of pessimistic irony. The phrase 'Botany Bay' soon became an international byword for a depraved and criminal society (Hirst, 1983).

'Convictism' and its stigma were invoked by the free and 'respectable settlers' to distinguish South Australia and Victoria from the 'original' convict colonies. This segregation, based on geographical divisions formally constituted by the Colonial Office in London according to administrative and constitutional boundaries, and still defining the Australian States—to the periodic chagrin of continental nationalists—went far to explain the political fragmentation of the continent until the lengthy process of federation brought new unity of mind and purpose at the beginning of the twentieth century. Despite the admitted sameness of modern Australian suburbia, the State capitals, 'cosmopolitan Sydney', 'marvellous Melbourne', 'Adelaide, city of churches', 'parochial Perth' and so on, have always created real sub-identities for their inhabitants (Goldberg and Smith, 1988; Statham, 1989).

The substantially similar backgrounds of Australians in almost every particular and the relatively smooth path of the colonies through self-government to nationhood should not obscure the still powerful influence of the original 'purpose' of each colony's foundation in each State's self-awareness. It enters still into any explanation of that feature of Australian life, summed up under the heading of 'States' Rights', which contrasts Australian national attitudes from the national, local and parochial loyalties common to other federal democracies such as the United States or Canada, and distinguishes the style and complexity of Australian nationalism even from the strong regional patriotisms of such unitary countries as New Zealand and the United Kingdom (Sinclair, 1988).

The course of Australian colonisation ensured that the English, Irish, Scots and Welsh migrants who made up the overwhelming bulk of the new population would bring with them the attitudes and 'cultural baggage' of their places of origin, along with their institutions and social and political aspirations. That baggage included not only government forms, but laughter, cooking, and music—all that went to make up the 'multitude of little worlds' which distinguish Australian 'total' history and made it like countries where similar things happened (Shaw, 1983).

They realised that they were creating new communities, but saw substantial advantages in participating in the 'imperial adventure' at a privileged level. They valued political, defence, economic and cultural linkages with the 'mother country' very highly. In this they resembled the Canadians, the New Zealanders, and the British South Africans. But, although they may have been what Sir Keith Hancock, in his *Australia* (1928) called 'independent Australian Britons', the majority would soon be and remain native-born. By 1861, 37 per cent were born in Australia; by 1881, 63 per cent; by 1891, 68 per cent; by 1901, 77 per cent; by 1981, 79 per cent; by 1987, still 78 per cent (Jupp, 1988).

Australians at the turn of the twentieth century saw themselves as British first, then as Victorians, South Australians and so on and only gradually became accustomed to being 'Australians'. They did not in a time of 'colonial nationalism' see this as a divided, but rather as a rational and integrated reflection of a complex but 'independent' identity, in which appropriate recognition was accorded to the mutually supportive communities to which they belonged (Eddy and Schreuder, 1988; Meaney, 1989). Much of the Australian experience paralleled that of Canada and New Zealand, rather than that of the USA 'melting-pot'. In a sense, these years were a rehearsal for later chapters in community integration and self-awareness called for by the much more complex patterns of immigration after 1945, as described in other sections of this book.

Federation was one of the major landmarks of Australian history. It was the beginning of a national story rather than the culmination of a popular movement and campaign. It would prove to be the central factor in the constitution and solidity of an independent national identity. Deeply affecting all aspects of Australian life, Federation was the effective and technically impressive achievement of a generation of professional politicians motivated by a need to confront the changing economic realities experienced by middle-class 'anglophiles' who were prepared to accept only a limited form of 'national' government. If economic interest and a balance of local and national gain or loss were the deciding factors, none of the founding fathers could have known how the federal union would eventually affect the role of the individual component States, though they had before them the examples of Canada and the United States, from whose constitutions they freely drew, and the experience of several other federations such as Switzerland to contemplate (La Nauze, 1972; Mathews, 1982).

A 'spirit of nationalism' upon which the colonial politicians were able to build certainly existed, in an atmosphere very different from that encountered by the founders of the United States after the Revolution or those who had to reconstruct the federation after the Civil War, and different again from the rhythm of Canadian Confederation in the 1860s. The 'nationalism' of the 1880s and 1890s had witnessed an impressive output of Australian art and literature and fostered the conditions out of which a new Commonwealth could emerge. But 'the new nation' had to be promoted, to catch the popular imagination and be confirmed in public opinion by a series of referenda as an expression of democratic will in the 1890s. Everyone admitted that there existed an intense local patriotism (Serle, 1973).

Centralisation, or the lack of it, is not only a key factor in government, but also reflects in various ways a sense of 'centre' which must hold if any community is to relate to itself and the world as a coherent whole. In Australia, the federal system was grafted onto a set of Westminster-style state constitutions. The original components of government, despite frequent criticism of 'structural ossification', have remained firm for ninety years. Though State loyalties and identification remain strong, it was perceived in the mid-twentieth century that Australian political parties embodied the social forces of resistance and initiative, rather than representing and identifying specific regions. As a result, Australians have tended to attach greater significance to the role of status and class in creating a certain degree of homogeneity in partisan loyalties at all levels of government. By comparison, many Canadians have identified more closely with region (Hodgins, Wright, 1978; Hodgins, Eddy, 1989). No matter what explanations are presented for the level and pace of centralisation, and its relative success or failure, and what emphasis is placed on regional vis-a-vis economic or party-political factors, certain instructive patterns have emerged in the evolving character of systems such as the Canadian and Australian federations which throw light on how each nation perceives itself and is perceived by others. These are mostly patterns of similarity, despite some dramatic contrasts which serve to differentiate the style or 'icons' of otherwise comparable societies. In the case of Canada, for example, the role of Quebec with its French Canadian majority is always unique, as is the part played in the South African experience by the Boers. Patrick O'Farrell has perhaps come closest to lay the foundation for any analogies by his arguments for attributing to the Irish component in Australian life and history the most colourful and rebellious features of the national character (O'Farrell, 1986).

THE DYNAMIC OF CENTRALISATION IN WAR AND PEACE

The main historical factor, and the surest benchmark in the formation and development of an Australian national identity, has clearly been the increasing centralism of its polity. A comparison with Canada is instructive. The British North America Act of 1867 provided for a more centralised form of federalism than the Commonwealth of Australia

Constitution Act passed in 1900. Yet over time, despite the expectations of the founding fathers, Canada has tended to move erratically
towards a much more decentralist operation of government, while Australia has shifted in the reverse direction. Although there have been
significant similarities in the adaptive procedures forged in both countries, there have also been important differences derived from the inherent geopolitical, social, and economic variants of their 'separate
worlds'.

External crises such as wars and world-wide depression have been
powerful centralising forces, perhaps even more so than social democratic or 'left-of-centre' governments. Decentralising pressures, on the
other hand, would appear to stem from a variety of circumstances;
dynamic Provincial/State populist leadership, economic disparity, or
even a misfit or outdated constitution. In the Canadian experience, particularly, resistance to central authority has most often been rooted in a
bicultural heritage and/or intense regionalism. In turn, this alienation
has encouraged the overall decentralising trend which began immediately after Confederation. In Australia, where there was no distinct
European bicultural tradition, class differences rather than geographical isolation tended to create political and social divisiveness.

As Australia moved towards a more centralised form of national federation than anticipated by the founding fathers, Canada followed the
reverse trend. Both patterns were well-established before the outbreak
of the Great War. By 1914 the Canadian drift towards a more coordinate federalism was set and suffered only a temporary reversal owing to
the highly centralising consequences of the War. In contrast, Australia
appeared to be moving towards a more centralised system than that
intended by its creators. Even if the original Constitution Act was
framed to support ideological nineteenth century liberalism, the structures were not compatible with the social welfare objectives of the
Labor Party in the early 1900s. The pace of immigration, the existence
of a mechanism of consulting the popular will by referenda, and legal
and economic debates with diverse results, tended to separate the
national experiences. Australia's Commonwealth–State conferences
eventually led to State cooperation with the centre, whereas Canada's
less frequent interprovincial and later Dominion–Provincial conferences tended to encourage federal accommodation with the demands of
the periphery.

As far as national perceptions were concerned, Australia, Canada,
and New Zealand had much in common. All three had managed to
submerge the 'problem' of the indigenous peoples, as South Africa of
course could not. Although the latter two had suffered in the nineteenth
century the traumas of insurrection if not outright Civil War, for example the French Canadian revolt of 1837 and the Maori Wars of the
1860s, the Australians could call only on the ambiguous Eureka Stock-

ade incident of 1854 at the goldfields at Ballarat for dramatic incident. Indeed the very tranquility of Australian life, its relative slowness of pace, its 'suburban' character, its 'mediterranean' climate, its high standard of material living, and the lack of stress originating from population pressure or perceived extremes of racial tension, were all noted as prominent among the distinguishing features of the 'Lucky Country'. Australia shared these characteristics with New Zealand, which did not, however, have to bear with less attractive features such as periodic floods, drought, heat-waves and flies.

All three 'old dominions' as they came to be called in the first half of the twentieth century were officially eager participants in the more chauvinistic manifestations of Britain's imperial apogee. It should be pointed out that by no means all the British were enthusiastic expansionists. Nor were all the imperial gestures of the 'colonials'—whether on the occasion of the Sudan incidents, the Boer War or later the global conflicts of 1914–18 and 1939–45—entirely altruistic or untinged with self-seeking and the hope of local aggrandisement. Even if her defence policies have tended to be based on insecurity rather than aggression, Australia came to recognise a military strand in her make-up right from the first days of the Commonwealth.

The war in South Africa (1898–1902) had, despite all the gallant rhetoric, proved a scarifying experience to the now 'weary Titan', as Joseph Chamberlain called Britain. But the despatch of military contingents by the 'white colonies' and the consequent attempts to construct a modern imperial scheme of defence, the formation of civilian militia forces, professional navies and so on, deeply affected Australia, Canada, and New Zealand. They aimed, not only to bolster Britain against the 'German menace', but to give themselves greater and more specific say in imperial networking against those powers (and especially Japan) which they perceived as threats to their own specific way of life. Their priorities 'at the periphery' were often not shared by the imperial power 'at the centre'. Some later myths about colonial sycophancy towards the British would have been ridiculed by such key leaders as Alfred Deakin of Australia, Wilfrid Laurier of Canada, or even Richard Seddon of New Zealand. Later in the twentieth century, Australian Prime Ministers such as Hughes, Scullin, Lyons and Bruce—along with Mackenzie King of Canada and Nash and Savage of New Zealand—would also have been surprised and distressed to find their form of economic and political nationalism characterised as 'collaborationist' or subservient (Eddy and Schreuder, 1988; Meaney, 1976).

World War I was certainly, for Australia as well as most other combatant countries, a great watershed. The experience of overseas conflict was both painful and uplifting, as the legends of Gallipoli and Flanders prove. In time of war the central governments, not only of all the great powers, but of Australia, Canada and New Zealand, were strengthened to ensure the efficient and unified action necessary to defeat a global foe. The War Precautions Act in Australia and the War Measures Act in Canada gave the federal cabinets extraordinary powers overriding those of the States or Provinces on such matters as taxation, price and wage controls, and the regulation of production and distribution. At the same time, patriotic rhetoric reinforced national identities and purpose, and gave impetus to new cultural expressions of nationalism as authors, song writers, and artists increasingly focused on the unique features of their country's landscape and their respective historical roots. As the twentieth century progressed, however, debates on the issue of conscription would show that national loyalty in 'the English-speaking countries' was not wholly synonymous with military power (Alomes, 1988; Sinclair, 1988).

The interwar years witnessed substantial industrial growth and uneven prosperity in Australia, as in Canada, New Zealand, the USA and to a certain extent Great Britain. All were doomed to suffer an unexpected economic disaster, the Depression of the 1920s and 1930s. The unifying impact of the war declined and was tempered by an increasing sense of regionalism. Australian politics became fragmented, with Labor divided and the cobbling together of coalitions necessary to attain or retain power. A narrowing of focus and confidence, in the aftermath of the generous and dramatic language and sentiment of sacrifice demanded in the crucible of war, saw immigration coming under attack as a threat to the standard of living and to the 'White Australia' policy as established earlier in the century. Any fresh delegation of authority to the centre was widely opposed.

Although the national capital, Canberra, was now developing—a potential symbol of a more mature nation or at least of a more centralised federation—it was perceived rather as 'everyone's enemy' and a reinforcement of 'government in isolation' rather than as a unifying factor. If a 'National Capital' is any symbol of identity achieved, Australia's experience has been very different from that of New Zealand, or Canada; although the later case of Brazilia offered parallels. Canberra had to wait until the 1980s, and the location of such national entities as the High Court, the National Gallery, the Institute of Sport, and finally the new Parliament House, to gain acceptance in the popular mind.

As the Depression lengthened, the economic crisis created regional disparities and gave rise to new spheres of national anxiety and dissent. This experience was paralleled in many similar democracies. Whereas local government authorities seemed in a time of distress to be of relatively human dimension, and thus approachable, national governments often seemed impersonal and remote. With the failure of central governments to deal with the hardships of the Depression, new agenda were forged and supported. Some of these were radical, paler contemporaries or parochial versions of international Fascism and Communism, looking towards considerable reconstructions of the existing national consensus and polity. Powerful though some of these proved elsewhere, they did not take deep root in Australia. World War II not only ended an era of disillusionment and decentralisation, but it provided a temporary solution to the longstanding economic distress.

Emergency war measures again provided opportunities to shift powers to the centre and this time greatly augmented the public service to meet the demands of coordinating industrial and transportation sectors which had increased in importance owing to technological advances. In addition, fears of attack by Japan brought about closer military dependence on the United States, and inversely weakened the ties with Great Britain. Some commentators date modern Australian history and national self-consciousness to Pearl Harbour and John Curtin's appeal to the United States. Others see this as merely the beginning of a new phase of national 'dependency' or perhaps only a new landmark in gradual maturation. Curtin and his successor Chifley became national 'heroes', especially to that half of the Australian people who had come to vote Labor, and who regularly continue to do so, just as the 'little Digger' Billy Hughes had been as leader of the nation during World War I (Harper, 1987).

Most of these, or very similar, developments were shared by Canada, and New Zealand, who participated with Australia and other powers of the 'second' rank in the formation of the United Nations. The Australian Dr Evatt became President of the General Assembly in 1948. The bush, with a vengeance, was being tethered to a wider world. Henceforward, although the relatively tranquil and unhurried Australian community would still bask in the slightly ambiguous reputation of 'the Lucky Country', and engage in its routine pursuits without too much dramatisation—disturbed periodically by its characteristic natural disasters—the survival and very substance and style of the nation was perhaps, as never before, at stake. Always a fanatical sporting community, the Australians now began to treat their politics, and much else besides, as a spectator sport. For active participants, arguably engaged in giving new meanings to Australian democracy in a more stormy global environment, the striving to shape or reshape the social agenda and the national psyche became a serious business (Horne, 1964).

Wartime experience, the threat of Japanese invasion and the renewed sense of isolation as a 'European' society at the heel of an Asia in turmoil, and the shift in world power as the United States took the place of Britain as the necessary 'powerful ally', consolidated changes in Australian self-perceptions. The central government gained significant authority through the taxation power in addition to the inevitable national planning entailed by wartime and post-war management. Yet the people resisted the extension of *carte blanche* to the Commonwealth by their reluctance at the referendum of 1944 to prolong the federal government's emergency powers beyond the time of hostilities. Canada experienced a parallel strengthening of the central government but with a determination to redress the balance in favour of the Provinces as soon as possible. By 1945 Australia's place in the world was more forward and her self confidence high (Bolton, 1990).

POST-WAR AND THE REDEFINITION OF AUSTRALIA'S STRATEGIC IDENTITY

At mid-century the main outlines of a distinct Australian identity had been formed, and the patterns shaped which would be likely, for good or evil, to govern the way the nation approached future calms or crises. Like Canadians and New Zealanders, Australians now had to take more independent control of their destinies than ever before. Especially in the fields of strategy and defence, national economy, and culture and society would the established national identity be under strain, scrutiny and sometimes radical redefinition.

After 1945, many ambitious socioeconomic developments and national projects appeared to herald a new era of self-possession. Among these were an aggressive immigration scheme, the massive Snowy River irrigation and hydro-electric project, the founding of the Australian National University, the creation of the Joint Coal Board, and the nationalisation of Qantas airlines and overseas telecommunications. These years also saw the advent of television, which soon became a powerful purveyor of political, commercial, cultural and educational information and images. Labor's defeat in 1949 inaugurated over twenty-three years of Liberal–Country coalition government, led for sixteen of these years by Prime Minister Sir Robert Menzies. Neither Canada nor New Zealand experienced anything like the Australian Labor 'split' of the 1950s, but it was paralleled in the politics of many European countries by movements concerning rival ideologies in process of change, for example Catholics versus Communists. The conservatives were assured of a long tenure of office, but the process of 'nation-building' continued, largely along the time-honoured lines, in a time of economic expansion and continued centralisation.

By the time of the Korean War (1950–3) it was clearer than ever— as, with the usual interesting variations, was the case with New Zealand and Canada—that the balance of Australia's security alliance had swung definitively from the United Kingdom (from which, however, migration was running at an all time high) to the United States. The Australia–New Zealand–United States Treaty (ANZUS) was signed in 1951, and the less long-lasting SEATO regional pact in 1954. Australia's historic 'search for security' against the French, the Russians, the Japanese, the Chinese, the Indonesians, or whoever was seen as the current menace, has always had a high priority in national self-perception, but her strategic posture has been variously interpreted (Meaney, 1976; Hudson and Sharp, 1988).

Such gestures as participation in the Korean and Vietnam conflicts were perceived by some as a sign of national immaturity and evidence for the essentially 'colonial' nature of at least the Australian elites. For others they were a shrewd 'nationalist' strategy, token contributions to guarantee against an ever possible American withdrawal into isolationism. The twentieth century, no less than the nineteenth, was destined to be not merely an era of rampant nationalism, but of grand alliances (Eddy and Schreuder, 1988; Millar, 1978). The international map of military and economic groupings polarised in a time of 'Cold War', further compounding traditional tensions.

Vietnam was, in Australia as elsewhere, an unpopular as well as an unwinnable war, and other disturbing developments loomed. There was increasing criticism of American and Japanese economic 'imperialism', fear of an expanding Asian immigration which threatened 'White Australia', and unease over a perceived decline in personal and social standards when challenged by the excesses of 'materialism'. The moral agenda of the community, its religious background and the manifestations of the Australian 'soul' received a good deal of attention. With the passing of the sectarianism which had embittered a good deal of Australian social discourse in the nineteenth century and the advent of fresh streams of migration, some maintained that Australia was a notably, perhaps uniquely secular post-Christian society. Others noted the religious and cultural baggage of the new migrants, and the continued influence and impact of even organised denominations in the life of the community and the regularly enthusiastic, if cyclical, church attendance (Mol, 1985; O'Farrell, 1986).

In 1967, a more socially conscious generation overwhelmingly supported a referendum to enable the Commonwealth to legislate for the Aborigines. This added another important area to its growing responsibilities, already augmented by its post-war prominence in trade, banking, social welfare, health and educational matters. Eventually internal discord as well as disagreement over economic strategies so plagued the Liberal–National coalition that a revitalised Labor Party under Gough Whitlam, with a mandate for change, won a majority of seats at the election of December 1972.

The last twenty years have witnessed the process of Australia's integration into the wider world, often at breakneck speed. Traditional economic and social patterns remain very stubbornly entrenched, but the 'colonial' remnants are gradually yielding to the 'cosmopolitan' requirements of the age of technology. The field of national debate widened in the 1970s to encompass all the global issues. Japan loomed larger than ever before in Australia's consciousness, but in this she was not unique. Major resource development created boom periods dependent on market demand and was often accompanied by costly mega-projects such as hydro-electric dams and oil or gas pipelines. The States took on new importance, in the style of Alberta and British Columbia in Canada, and their bureaucracies expanded accordingly. Resource-rich territories demanded more say in national planning, while warning voices told of the perils in becoming an open quarry for a greedy planet. Australian entrepreneurs cut a swathe in the world of international commerce and finance, until the cold winds of the late 1980s cut them down. The national survival was now seen to depend rather on being a 'clever' than a 'lucky' country (Horne, 1989). Questions concerning Aborigine land claims and other 'ethnic' rights became prominent, as did serious environmental concerns. There were fears that 'multiculturalism', however defined, would transform and destroy community consensus. New educational and social attitudes were pursued. The bicentennial year, 1988, generated a surfeit of discussion on national identity in a climate of change. Similar veins were opened up in New Zealand and Canada. As in Canada, constitutional revision was a topic of serious study and debate. The energy crises of 1973 and after forced a great deal of rethinking.

Whitlam's experience of power was shorter than that of his contemporaries: Pierre Trudeau in Canada and Harold Wilson in Britain. His form of messianic leadership, 'crash through or crash', was afterwards repudiated by the Fraser (1975–83) and Hawke governments (1983–) as careless and ineffectual, as well as electorally unwise. But at the time it caught the public imagination and seemed in itself to herald an era of new and heightened national aspiration or decline. His symbolic first actions included recognition of China, the withdrawal of Australian troops from Vietnam, the end to compulsory military service, the offering of free university education, and plans for more ambitious universal health and education measures. All involved more power at the centre (Whitlam, 1985).

Other community attitudes changed perceptibly. Australians had long been lampooned as 'male chauvinists'. From the 1970s, in a move taking place throughout the wider world, formal acknowledgement of the 'role of women' was promoted officially. Such names as Caroline Chisholm, Miles Franklin, Daisy Bates, Christina Stead, and Mary McKillop—to say nothing of the contemporary Germaine Greer and Ita Buttrose—were added to the national roll of honour. At a deeper level there were shifts in employment patterns of women and in family habits which vastly changed the Australian 'way of life' which had been inherited from generations of pioneers, through 'Dad and Dave', to the 'Australian Dream'—proper to the 1940s and 1950s—of kangaroos, meat pies, a Holden car, rabbit-proof fences and a suburban home.

Not surprisingly, Whitlam's domestic agenda created as much agitation and applause as his 'new nationalism'. As Trudeau discovered in Canada, the lot of reform governments is to disclose the flinty nature of the underlying national identity. Visions are not easily rendered into reality, especially in view of the essentially conservative or at least cautious nature of Australian political response. The constitutional issues and divisions occasioned by Whitlam's 'Dismissal' in 1975 still remain to be resolved, but the event itself has entered powerfully into the national mythology.

By the 1980s Australia felt itself to be, and was seen to be, essentially an experienced, modern, self-confident democracy, willing to play forward roles in international initiatives, with respect to such diverse arenas as South Africa or Cambodia. As always there were critics and Cassandras who pointed to rocks ahead. Debates raged about the uncertain prospects for a community deeply affected by major shifts in the world's economic balance, where wool and wheat and minerals were no longer trumps. There was a new consciousness of the 'Pacific Rim' and talk of an 'Asian future' (McQueen, 1982). In 1986 the federal treasurer Keating exhorted national restructuring so that Australia would not become a 'banana republic'. Others spoke darkly of 'the poor white trash of Asia'. Yet the nation's core identity seemed formed, with its patterns and characteristics well established. The challenge would now be to express that identity, to learn from the Australian past, and from others' successes and mistakes, so that responses to new demands would not endanger national democracy and individuality on the one hand (as the pessimists feared) or fail to meet them appropriately and leave Australia adrift, an object of international markets rather than a subject and an independent agent.

Other countries, even those closest in demographic and political composition, as for example New Zealand, would find their own solutions to similar dilemmas. The Lange government fell out with the Americans over the question of nuclear weapons, and opted for different economic recipes. Canada engaged in an earnest 'repatriation' of the Constitution, and a new bout of federal tinkering. Compared with these, Australian redefinition has been undramatic. Continuity with a real or imagined past is an essential element in any nation's discourse. The Hawke administrations have tried to build their national consensus on politically moderate reforms and have made full and enthusiastic use of those elements of the national memory which seem to assist the maintenance of morale and nerve necessary for the nation to reform, restructure, and regroup in a rapidly changing world without undergoing an 'identity crisis'. This book outlines some vital areas where the 'state of the nation' is compared with that of her contemporaries. Australia's past suggests, with the necessary caution, that she can draw upon sufficiently rich social experience and historical development to cope with both continuity and change.

REFERENCES

Alomes, S. (1988) *A Nation at Last* Sydney: Angus and Robertson

Attwood, B. (1989) *The Making of the Aborigines* Sydney: Allen & Unwin

Bolton, G. (1981) *Spoils and Spoilers* Sydney: Allen & Unwin

———— (1990) *The Oxford History of Australia, 5, The Middle Way, 1942–88* Melbourne: Oxford University Press

Butlin, N.G. (1985) *Our Original Aggression* Sydney: Allen & Unwin

Carroll, J. (1982) *Intruders in the Bush. The Australian Quest for Identity* Melbourne: Oxford University Press

Clark, C.M.H. (1962) *A History of Australia*, 1, Melbourne: Melbourne University Press

———— (1980) 'The Quest for an Australian Identity' in *Occasional Writings and Speeches* Melbourne: Fontana/Collins

Clarke, F. (1977) *The Land of Contrarieties* Melbourne: Melbourne University Press

———— (1989) *Australia* Melbourne: Oxford University Press

Conway, R. (1978) *The Land of the Long Weekend* Melbourne: Sun

Denoon, D. (1983) *Settler Capitalism* Oxford: Oxford University Press

Eddy, J.J., and Schreuder, D.M., eds (1988) *The Rise of Colonial Nationalism* Sydney: Allen & Unwin

Grant, B. (1983) *The Australian Dilemma* Sydney: Macdonald Futura

Goldberg, S.L., and Smith, F.B., eds (1988) *Australian Cultural History* Cambridge: Cambridge University Press

Hancock, W.K. (1961 edn) *Australia* Sydney: Jacaranda

Harper, N. (1987) *A Great and Powerful Friend* Brisbane: University of Queensland Press

Hirst, J. (1983) *Convict Society and Its Enemies* Sydney: Allen & Unwin

Hodgins, B., Wright, D., eds (1978) *Federalism in Canada and Australia; the Early Years* Canberra: Australian National University Press

Hodgins, B., Eddy, J.J., eds (1989) *Federalism in Canada and Australia; Historical Perspectives 1920–88* Peterborough: Frost Centre, Trent University

Horne, D. (1964) *The Lucky Country* Sydney: Penguin

———— (1989) *Ideas for a Nation* Sydney: Pan

Hudson, W. and Sharp, M. (1988) *Australian Independence* Melbourne: Melbourne University Press

Hughes, R. (1987) *The Fatal Shore* London: Collins/Harvill

Inglis, K.S. (1988) 'Multi-culturalism and National Identity' Canberra: Annual Lecture, The Academy of the Social Sciences in Australia

Jupp, J. (1988) *The Australian People* Sydney: Angus and Robertson

La Nauze, J.A. (1972) *The Making of the Australian Constitution* Melbourne: Melbourne University Press

Macintyre, S. (1985) *Winners and Losers* Sydney: Allen & Unwin

McLachlan, N. (1989) *Waiting for the Revolution. A History of Australian Nationalism* Melbourne: Penguin

McQueen, H. (1982) *Gone Tomorrow* Sydney: Angus and Robertson

Mandle, W. (1977) *Going It Alone* Melbourne: Allen Lane

Mathews, R. ed. (1982) *Public Policies in Two Federal Countries: Canada and Australia* Canberra: Australian National University Press

Meaney, N. (1976) *The Search for Security in the Pacific* Sydney: Sydney University Press

———— (1989) *Under New Heavens* Melbourne: Heinemann

Millar, T.B. (1978) *Australia in Peace and War* Canberra: Australian National University Press

Miller, J.D.B. ed. (1987) *Australians and British* Sydney: Methuen

Mol, H. (1985) *The Faith of Australians* Sydney: Allen & Unwin

O'Farrell, P. (1987) *The Irish in Australia* Sydney: New South Wales University Press

———— (1986) *The Catholic Community in Australia* Sydney: New South Wales University Press

Power, J. (1989) 'The Modernization of Australian Federalism', (mimeo), Canberra: Centre for Research in Federal Financial Relations, Australian National University

Reynolds, H. (1987) *The Law of the Land* Sydney: Penguin

Rickard, J. (1988) *Australia; A Cultural History* Melbourne: Longman Cheshire

Serle, G. (1973) *From Deserts the Prophets Come* Melbourne: Heinemann

Seton-Watson, H. (1977) *Nations and States* Oxford: Oxford University Press

Shaw, G. (1983) 'Writing Australian History' in *Current Affairs Bulletin*, 60/4, September

Sinclair, K. (1986) *A Destiny Apart. New Zealand's Search for National Identity* Wellington: Unwin Hyman

———— ed. (1988) *Tasman Relations* Auckland: Auckland University Press

———— (1990) 'Patterns of Identity' in *Times Literary Supplement*, 2 February

Statham, P. (1989) *The Origins of Australia's Capital Cities* Melbourne: Cambridge University Press

Tsokhas, K. (1986) *Beyond Dependence* Melbourne: Oxford University Press

White, R. (1981) *Inventing Australia. Images and Identity 1688–1980* Sydney: Allen & Unwin

———— (1990) 'Memories of Anzac' in *Journal of the Australian War Memorial*, 16, April

Whitlam, E.G. (1985) *The Whitlam Government 1972–75* Melbourne: Viking

3 Managing ethnic diversity: how does Australia compare?

JAMES JUPP

Public debate on ethnic diversity in Australia often proceeds as though Australia were unique. Australia is sometimes described as 'the most multicultural country in the world', which is quite untrue. It *is* amongst the societies with the highest overseas-born proportions and the highest proportionate intake of immigrants (Jupp, 1988; BIR, 1990). Australia has a very recent monocultural past and much public policy and administration is still conducted as though everyone were culturally similar. This is the opposite, and equally inappropriate, extreme. At the crudest level, public debate on Australian multiculturalism often proceeds as though the ethnic conflicts so important in other, usually less developed societies, are inevitable in Australia. Yet it is a basic proposition in the social sciences that valid generalisations can only be made by comparing societies which possess many common features. Even then, such comparisons must be grounded in an understanding of differing historical and social experiences. Australia is not like Sri Lanka or Fiji. It is more like Britain, Canada or the United States, but is certainly not the same as them. There are common approaches with New Zealand, Sweden and The Netherlands and there is a rather different situation in West Germany, which serves as an interesting contrast as it does not officially accept multiculturalism.

Whatever the ethnic composition of their populations, whatever their traditions of nation-building and whatever the specific character of their institutions and practices, the English-speaking and the north European democracies surveyed here (Australia, Britain, Canada, the United States, New Zealand, Sweden, The Netherlands and West Germany) all accept that ethnic diversity presents a challenge. The concept of the nation state, to which all subscribe to a degree, assumes common values and attitudes. Yet it has historically been extended to embrace the notion of common origins, most horrifically in the case of Nazi Germany. Thus one challenge is the extent to which national unity

and sense of purpose can be preserved when citizens come from a variety of cultural and ethnic backgrounds and may subscribe to values
which are not uniform. A further challenge is posed by the observable
fact that human beings in many social situations tend to feel prejudice
towards those who are not similar in appearance or customs. A potential
threat to social harmony is always present where ethnic cleavages correspond to other social and economic cleavages, for example in the persistence of 'ethnic underclasses' based on race in the United States, or
in the dilemma of equalising the life chances of aboriginal peoples in
Australia, New Zealand, the United States or Canada.

Democratic systems must give equal rights to all citizens while at
the same time acknowledging a degree of prejudice against minorities
among mainstream voters. Settler societies need policies which will integrate new arrivals into society and make them feel part of the national
enterprise. Older societies, while depending on immigrants for economic reasons, may be reluctant to accept them as permanent residents
and potential citizens. All of these challenges impel democratic systems
to devise means for lessening social tension, for equalising rights, for
integrating those of minority culture and for managing ethnic diversity.

ABORIGINAL, INDIGENOUS AND IMMIGRANT MINORITIES

Ethnic and cultural minorities are recognised in various ways in official
statistics, in legislation and in administrative programmes (ABS, 1984;
Kee, 1986). They are minorities in the numerical sense, varying from
the 'co-founding' French Canadians down to statistically insignificant
groups like the gypsies. In all the surveyed societies there are majority
core communities: English-speaking in Australia, Britain, New Zealand, the United States and Canada; Germanic-speaking in Germany,
Sweden and The Netherlands. These majority linguistic communities
(as small as 62 per cent in Canada) include within them considerable cultural variety and have assimilated individuals from a wide
range of origins (Statistics Canada, 1984). In The Netherlands official
policy has for long recognised religious differences (Lijphart, 1968),
while elsewhere the emphasis is on ethnicity, culture and 'race' (physical appearance). The social and economic situation of minorities varies
enormously in developed societies. Many are disadvantaged—often as
with Australian Aborigines or Black Americans very seriously so. Some
are much better off than the national average—as with Jews, Asian
Americans or Asian Australians. Within ethnic communities there is
also much variety.

There is no necessary reason to suppose that ethnic minorities will
be seriously disadvantaged or need protective public policies. All these

democracies are officially committed against ethnic and racial discrimination and social disadvantage. Their policies range widely, from the interventionist Swedish and Dutch welfare states to the greater reliance on pluralist and individual solutions in the United States. While there is often no overt distinction made between different ethnic categories, it emerges from studying local situations that there are *de facto* differences in the treatment of different groups. One difference is in the prevention of racial discrimination, where special attention is paid to groups felt most likely to suffer. The other tends to distinguish between aboriginal, indigenous and immigrant minorities. There are overlaps between these categories, but they are useful for understanding the politics of ethnic minority policy.

An aboriginal minority is one based on hunter/gathering or subsistence economies which existed before European arrival. Such societies were very vulnerable and all suffered at the hands of those more technologically advanced with ruthless and profit-oriented cultures. The ultimate social consequences have been the same in most instances, though less disastrous for the 15 000 Swedish Lapps than for all others. These consequences include: the collapse of social, economic and religious systems; dependence on public funds; low levels of employment and skill; poor health; low levels of esteem; high rates of crime; and inability to reach standards of equality with the majority. All relevant governments have, in consequence, treated their aboriginal peoples as a special category, even after the extension of full civil rights in recent years (Rowley, 1970).

Indigenous minorities are of more recent creation and approximate more closely to the cultures and skills of the majority. Some, such as the Canadian Metis, are created by intermixing immigrant and aboriginal peoples. Some, like the Gaelic Scots or the Welsh, were established before the majority arrived, but are not aboriginal in the sense used above. Indigenous minorities in settler societies were created by past immigration but most or all of their members were born in the country of residence and know no other. Most Black Americans originated between 1660 and 1830 through slave importation from Africa. French Canadians were created as an ethnic group between 1630 and 1760 and have not been replenished by significant immigration from France. Indigenous groups may still be culturally distinct after many generations. In Australia such groups include Queensland Pacific Islanders, Barossa Germans and (on the religious dimension) Irish Catholics. As with many similar minorities in Canada or the United States, such groups are often strongly attached to their country of residence but insist that they have different origins from the majority. New Zealand is unique as its largest ethnic minority is the aboriginal Maoris (Spoonley et al., 1984).

The third basis for ethnic variety is immigration (Piore, 1979; Rao, Richmond and Zubrzycki, 1984). Some indigenous minorities have been able to replenish themselves through subsequent immigration and the boundary between indigenous and immigrant groups may be vague. Australian Jews straddle the division, while American and Canadian Jews have mainly made the transition to being an indigenous minority. Many immigrant communities, such as the Vietnamese in Australia, the United States and Canada, are completely new and had no local presence until very recently. In due course immigrant groups become indigenised but this is not necessarily the same as becoming assimilated. Already in Australia such European communities as the Greeks, Italians or Dutch are passing into the second or third generation as immigration drops off. In Germany and other European societies, the principle of *jus sanguinis* (nationality through descent), makes it very difficult for alien minorities to become indigenised. They are treated as temporary guest workers and naturalisation is very difficult unless complete cultural assimilation has taken place (Castles and Kosack, 1973; Castles et al., 1984). This eventually creates tensions, as with German-born Turks, who do not belong anywhere. English-speaking societies, in contrast, accept the notion of *jus solis* (nationality through birthplace) which extends citizenship to those born within the country regardless of ethnic origin (Elles, 1980). Immigrant minorities suffer various disadvantages not shared with the indigenous in most cases. Many of them are not citizens and cannot participate directly in the political system. However, immigrants are often young, well educated and enterprising and should not be seen as always in a disadvantageous position comparable to Aborigines or to alienated indigenous minorities like Black Americans. Nor do they necessarily cause social upheaval. There is a far longer history of ethnic conflict involving indigenous minorities in Northern Ireland or the United States than there is of violence against recent immigrants.

Although public policy does not clearly distinguish between the three categories outlined above, in practice there are often differing approaches to them. All relevant states have separate legislation and administration for their aboriginal people. All states have acknowledged political pressure from indigenous minorities, though this has been weakest and least important in Australia and Sweden. Where such minorities are disadvantaged, as with Black Americans, gypsies or Hispanic Americans, specially targeted programmes have been common. The right to use a minority language has been grudgingly conceded in many cases, though even in Canada with official bilingualism a number of towns have recently declared themselves to be 'English-only'. Most legislation relating to immigrants concerns their right to enter and to remain. The trend is to extend rights available to indigenous minorities to immigrants. While immigrant languages are less frequently recognised than indigenous languages, they are widely used in public information programmes in Australia, Britain, Canada, Sweden, The

Netherlands and the United States. Immigrants in the European Community have the right to mother tongue instruction for their children, as they do in fifty languages in Sweden.

OFFICIAL DEFINITIONS OF ETHNICITY

Different political and social situations have prompted governments to adopt differing definitions of minority groups in their populations. In Australia the definition of Aborigines was shaped by ideas of 'pure' and 'mixed' descent. This led to forced segregation on reserves, to the breaking up of families and to different legal rights and prohibitions for classes of Aborigine. A similar policy was adopted towards American Indians. In Canada the signing of numerous treaties with Indians and the existence of a strong Meti community in Manitoba and Alberta, has led to the creation of three categories—Status Indians, non-Status Indians and Metis. Membership of these categories involves various privileges, including residence on reserved lands and access to the product of their development. The Inuit (Eskimos) are also recognised as a distinct community though coming under the same Federal department as Indians.

In New Zealand Maoris also have recognised status under the Treaty of Waitangi (1840). This status has included (since 1867) a distinct representation of four seats in parliament. As Maoris are a legal and constitutional entity their definition is important. The census term 'Maori' is used for those of pure or half Maori descent and these two groups are separately listed. But under the Maori Affairs Amendment Act (1974) the definition is extended to include anyone of Maori descent. The Australian census definition of an Aborigine, based on descent, self-acknowledgement and recognition by others, has led to oscillations of the numbers of Aborigines enumerated in the 1976, 1981 and 1986 censuses comparable to similar variations in New Zealand. However, rights to land for Maoris, Aborigines, Canadian Indians and many Native Americans depends on recognised membership of an appropriate clan or its equivalent. The right to vote and nominate for the representative level of the newly created Aboriginal and Torres Strait Islander Commission depends on Aboriginality, denial of which may be challenged in the courts.

The definition of aboriginal peoples is of considerable importance as they have rights and privileges (and in the past disabilities) and are able to utilise departmental services and government funds specifically allocated for their ethnic group. Other ethnic groups are also defined where special services are directed towards them, although not usually so rigorously. In Australia no group other than Aborigines and Torres Strait Islanders has a carefully defined status. However Commonwealth and State policy recognises those of non-English-speaking birth or origin (NESB) as a special case for equal employment opportunity programmes. Actual ability to use English is not tested in most such programmes. This means, of course, that there is a very wide range of social experience in the NESB category which, at its widest may embrace 25 per cent of the population. An administrative category of 'newly arrived groups' is often used by the Department of Immigration to focus grants and programmes more narrowly on those assumed to need them most.

Other societies have defined ethnic groups in ways which more effectively target disadvantage or discrimination. In Britain the term 'ethnic group' in official publications refers only to what are also called New Commonwealth with Pakistan (NCWP) immigrants and their immediate descendants. Thus the large European and Irish immigrant communities are simply included under 'white' with the majority. The assumption is that all identifiable 'coloured' people are likely to be disadvantaged or to suffer discrimination (Layton-Henry, 1984). In practice some grants to organisations also go to other disadvantaged groups such as gypsies, Irish or Turks.

European mainland states have not subscribed to the notion of a common citizenship regardless of origin, which dominated policy in the British Commonwealth until the 1970s. They use the term 'alien' to distinguish those born overseas. Citizenship requirements are strict except in Sweden which has liberalised its policy. As not all aliens are disadvantaged, there are further definitions for special programmes. Guest workers are the subject of various national and European Community requirements. In The Netherlands a special group of the disadvantaged was defined by the Ministry of Welfare in 1983. This included gypsies and travellers, Moluccans, Surinamese and Mediterranean immigrants (including North Africans) (Netherlands, 1983). A similar classification has been followed in Sweden, bringing together those characterised by multiple disadvantage but otherwise having no common citizenship or ethnic character.

The United States now recognises three minority classifications: Black Americans, Hispanics and Native Peoples. Only the latter have a federal department responsible for them, but the other two groups number more than 17 per cent of the American people and are very important for the allocation of funds and for equal opportunity programmes. Black Americans are defined in terms of descent from some-one of African origin. There is an overlap with Hispanics, as some Spanish-speaking Blacks come from the Caribbean through recent immigration (Handlin and Thurstrom, 1980). Black Americans were the first beneficiaries of programmes designed to eliminate ethnic disadvantage. Hispanics are defined by surname and by self-description and 'may be of any race'. A high proportion are recent Latin American immigrants, though they include Puerto Ricans (who are American citizens) and long-established indigenous populations in the southwest. In recent years many of the measures designed for Black Americans have been extended to Hispanics. By definition many Hispanics are not native speakers of English and the 1980 census showed that over 5 per cent of Americans normally used Spanish.

In Canada the power of indigenous ethnic minorities is of political significance (Porter, 1975; Dahlie and Fernando, 1981). French Canadians totally dominate Quebec, the second largest Canadian province. Canadian federalism cannot be understood without accepting the importance of this fact. Canada, like other states, also recognises the possibility that 'visible minorities' such as Asians or Blacks may be subject to discrimination and prejudice. These groups, as defined by the report *Equality Now!*, include aboriginal natives, Asians and Canadians of African descent (Canada, 1984).

Several issues arise from the varied definitional practices of governments. It is necessary to define any class of persons to whom legally binding rights are extended, such as land rights. Non-aboriginal groups in society, numbering far more than the aboriginal natives, rarely have a legal definition. There is no definition in the United Kingdom of English, Welsh, Scots or Irish. Special services are extended to those who use the Welsh or Gaelic languages. They must individually choose to benefit from such services which may sometimes also be used by those for whom the language is not a mother tongue. Canadian law extends language rights to all French-speaking Canadians, whether living in Quebec or not, but not to any other minority language. Rights can be exercised by anyone speaking French, but French Canadians are not defined as a legal entity.

Black Americans do not enjoy rights which were not previously available to white Americans. The whole thrust of United States policy has been away from the legal definitions which restricted the rights of Black Americans in the past. Hispanic Americans have no special rights, though they may press for the use of their language in educational systems or the courts. The official definition of ethnic minorities in democracies (other than for aboriginal natives) has been anomalous or determined by political expediency. Policy has been guided by 'common sense' ideas of what constitutes an ethnic minority. To establish legally defined groups could create a legal nightmare which all governments including the Australian have sought to avoid. This contrasts with the approach of states like the Soviet Union or South Africa in which ethnic entities are given official recognition. In immigrant societies like Australia there has been considerable ethnic mixing which makes rigid definition impossible and undesirable. Instead a vague category such as non-English-speaking-background forms the basis of much public policy.

ADMINISTRATIVE AND CONSTITUTIONAL ARRANGEMENTS

The United Kingdom, New Zealand, Sweden and The Netherlands are unitary systems: Australia, the United States, Canada and West Germany are federations. In all of them immigration is a national power, although this power was not generally assumed by the Australian Commonwealth until 1921 and concurrent power over immigration remained with the Canadian Provinces under the British North America Act (section 95). The United States Constitution contains a power to prohibit 'migration or importation' (Article 1, section 9) into any of the States, but this was not fully implemented until 1921. In Britain and New Zealand the control of immigration is left to ordinary legislation and was first made effective in Britain in 1905 with the Aliens Act. Like the earlier Australian Immigration Restriction Act 1901, this was designed to give administrative power to prohibit or remove 'undesirable aliens'. The immigration power has frequently been used to determine the ethnic character of societies. It is now used quite deliberately to do so in Britain, West Germany and The Netherlands, though no longer in Australia, Canada and the United States (Hawkins, 1989).

Apart from constitutional differences, there are differing administrative arrangements in each country for dealing with ethnic diversity. In Australia a smaller role is taken by local government than elsewhere, although this is starting to change in Sydney and Melbourne. As there is a heavy concentration of NESB immigrants in only ten per cent of Australian local authority areas, there is considerable room for targeting such populations through those authorities. In the unitary United Kingdom, local authorities are closely linked with the Community Relations Councils on which local councillors serve and for which the authorities provide accommodation and support. Authorities are obliged to institute equal employment opportunity programmes and to avoid any staffing or other policies which could be construed as discriminatory. They also, at one level, control education and can experiment with various methods of teaching immigrant children or with the maintenance of language and culture. In the United States most multicultural programmes are made effective at the local level, in the absence of any national policy commitment.

INSTITUTIONAL ARRANGEMENTS: THE NATIONAL LEVEL

In all the reviewed societies there are various levels of government and government agency which deal with ethnic diversity. In many instances there are also subsidies or other forms of official support to voluntary agencies. At the national level government controls immigration and thus the future ethnic composition of its people. In Australia the major relevant institutions are the Office of Multicultural Affairs within the portfolio of the Prime Minister; the Department of Immigration, Local Government and Ethnic Affairs; and the Department of Aboriginal Affairs (now converted into a commission). A major responsibility also lies with the Department of Employment, Education and Training, especially for the National Policy on Languages, and the Special Broadcasting Service. In Canada the major institution is Multiculturalism Canada, located in the portfolio of the Minister of State for Multiculturalism and maintaining twenty-four regional and local offices in all provinces. This operates and funds a number of special assistance programmes aimed at cultural integration, cultural enrichment, group development, writing and publications, ethnic studies, intercultural communication and performing and visual arts. Immigration is a distinct function located in the Department of Labour. In contrast to Australia, Canada has never had a close administrative link between immigration and multicultural policy.

The Australian and Canadian systems are close in many respects and there has been considerable interchange between them on multicultural and immigration policy. At the national level in the United States both the Federal government and the Supreme Court have taken major roles, with the judicial arm much more important than in other states. Many issues, which would be treated administratively or through legislation elsewhere, have been enforced by court decisions in America. Most advances in rights of American minorities in the past thirty years have arisen through interpretations of the Constitution. In the United Kingdom much responsibility ultimately lies with the Home Office, which has a wide range of functions including police, immigration control and race relations. The most important institution answerable to the Home Office is the Commission for Racial Equality established under the Race Relations Act 1976. The Commission is responsible for monitoring the Act and for conciliating (and if necessary prosecuting) breaches of it, a function close to that of the Australian Human Rights and Equal Opportunity Commission.

National government responsibilities in West Germany, The Netherlands, Sweden and New Zealand reflect differing priorities and concepts. It is not officially acknowledged that Germany is a multicultural society. National policies for some years have been based on three principles: integration and coexistence for those who have settled permanently; an end to immigrant recruitment; and subsidised repatriation for those willing to leave. Immigrants are subject to the Foreigners' Law of 1965 which denied the right to permanent residence and to a wide variety of organisational and political rights enjoyed by German citizens. At the Swedish national level major responsibility rests with the Minister for Immigration Affairs. The goal of legislation in the 1970s was equality of opportunity and the emphasis was initially on language learning. In 1975 parliament established three goals for immigrant and minority policy—equality, freedom of choice and cooperation.

In The Netherlands ethnic minorities are the responsibility of the Home Secretary and the Minister of Welfare, Public Health and Cultural Affairs. In 1980 the Home Secretary was appointed coordinating minister for minorities policy and a single management unit was set up in the department to coordinate and innovate policy both interdepartmentally and between national and municipal levels. The Ministry of Welfare has developed a target category of 'minorities' which is not based on birthplace or nationality but includes such criteria as: Mediterranean migrants, Surinamese and Moluccans, refugees, gypsies and caravan dwellers. Research on immigrants and minorities has been conducted by the Scientific Council for Government Policy, an autonomous public agency. Current policy, based on research begun in 1978, produced the White Paper on Minorities of 1983 covering a wide range of issues in labour market, welfare and human rights areas.

New Zealand, as the smallest and most unitary of the states, concentrates most relevant functions at the national level. The Human Rights Commission was established under the UN International Covenant on Human Rights in 1978 within the portfolio of the Minister of Justice. It includes a Race Relations Conciliator and has powers under the Race Relations Act 1971. The Commission also engages in research and publication and has regional offices in the major cities. The Department of Maori Affairs supports programmes and a network of community officers. Its functions were extended to cover immigrant Polynesians, but these are now supervised by a separate department. The effectiveness of existing programmes towards Maoris and other Polynesians was questioned by the Human Rights Commission in its report, *Race against Time*, published in 1982 (Tauroa, 1982).

INSTITUTIONAL ARRANGEMENTS: REGIONAL AND LOCAL

Multiculturalism developed in Australia mainly through the immigration power of the national government (Australia, 1986). However, largescale settlement in some States and municipalities has led them to develop their own mechanisms. There are Ethnic Affairs Commissions (or equivalents) in five States and divisions within other departments in the ACT, Tasmania and the Northern Territory (EAC of NSW, 1978). In South Australia the structure and functions of the commission have been extended through an amending Act of 1989 stressing a State commitment to multiculturalism. There are divisions or ministries responsible for some aspects of Aboriginal affairs, which are most important in Queensland, the Northern Territory and Western Australia. However many functions have been transferred to the federal government since 1967 and State or Territory policy is most important in the educational area. At the local government level, a small number of metropolitan municipalities have appointed officers with a responsibility for ethnic affairs. The municipal franchise has been extended to non-citizen permanent residents in South Australia and Victoria but not elsewhere.

Power over education is also important in Canada, where the provinces have responsibility for tertiary institutions, including those teaching in French (inside and outside Quebec). Quebec has a particular concern with the status of the French language and has passed legislation which elevates French, contrary to the national policy of bilingualism. Ontario has an extensive heritage language programme which is publicly funded and free for young children at weekends. There are advisory bodies on multiculturalism in such provinces as Ontario and Saskatchewan. At the local level education is provided by school boards which have adopted a variety of approaches to multicultural and bilingual education. Municipalities with high minority populations employ officers with a responsibility for community relations and also operate equal employment opportunity programmes, especially for 'visible minorities'. The most elaborate provision is made by Metropolitan Toronto. Many cities have mayoral committees on multiculturalism which provide consultative and coordinating services for ethnic minority groups.

Multicultural and ethnic minority policies in the United States are extremely varied and depend on State or local political situations to a large extent. There is no national policy towards cultural pluralism, despite the long 'melting pot' tradition of creating Americans from a multiplicity of origins. In reaction to the rise of Hispanic influence, a number of States and localities have adopted English as an official language through referendum, especially in California and Florida. Elsewhere, for example in New York, publicly funded education is available in Spanish and there is public support for Indian languages in Minnesota. There is thus no overall policy towards cultural pluralism and some contradiction between the constitutional guarantees of liberty and the political realities in particular areas. This contradiction is not as acute as it was prior to the civil rights gains of the 1960s and the national protection of Black minority rights. At all levels of government and in private corporations, policy may be affected by Federal contract compliance practices which enforce certain obligations on those in receipt of national funds. Similar policies are pursued in Canada.

Local government is used most effectively in Britain and Western

Europe, which have long traditions of administering welfare at a local level. In the United Kingdom there are offices of central government concerned with a range of services to Scotland, Wales and Northern Ireland, which are not responsible to locally elected politicians but to national ministers. The Scottish and Welsh education offices have a special interest in Gaelic and Welsh teaching and language maintenance. The Northern Ireland Office has responsibility for equal opportunity and anti-discrimination legislation specific to Northern Ireland and based on religion rather than race or ethnicity. At the local government level specific obligations are imposed by the Race Relations Act (section 71) which requires special arrangements to eliminate racial discrimination and to promote equality of opportunity and good community relations (CRE, 1982).

Local government involvement in ethnic affairs is most advanced in The Netherlands (Penninx, 1984), where foreign born residents have been allowed to vote in local elections since 1986 if they have resided for more than three years. Responsibility for primary immigration welfare was transferred to local councils in 1987, with appropriate funding. The most developed programmes have been those of Amsterdam city council. In Sweden foreign nationals have been entitled to vote since 1975 and also to contest elections, a right of most benefit to Finns (Hammar, 1985). In West Germany immigrants are without the vote, except for Aliens' Committees attached to city councils to advise on all matters relating to foreigners and their families.

EDUCATION AND LANGUAGE POLICY

All the states have had public education systems for over a century, with Sweden and Germany being pioneers. All previously had systems provided by the churches and these have continued in various forms. The American Constitution (First Amendment of 1791) forbids public support for religion, which prevents parochial schools from receiving state aid. In Canada, by contrast, the entire system of Quebec was parochial until 1964, with the Protestant schools teaching in English and the Catholic in French. The tertiary system of Canada was eventually nationalised and universities belonging to various denominations were brought into the public system. Several of these, including three outside Quebec, teach wholly or partly in French. In the United States private universities play a major role and there are Catholic (Notre Dame), Jewish (Brandeis), Black (Howard) and Mormon (Brigham Young) universities of national renown as well as a whole range of Bible colleges. The North American tertiary systems are thus more multicultural than any of the others under review.

The inheritance of the past century of public education is a confusing one and the confusion is increased by the intense debates on the purposes of education which have raged for the past twenty years. Systems are now much more tolerant towards minority languages than in the past and this has extended to bilingual education for Maoris, Aborigines and American Indians. It is recognised that immigrant children need to be inducted into the system gradually. Bilingual teachers' aides are now quite common. Multicultural education and education to combat racism are widely accepted, though there is considerable doubt about their effectiveness. The Australian federally-funded multicultural education programme was abolished in 1986 (Foster and Stockley, 1988).

The extremely varied origins of modern immigrants makes it particularly difficult to develop uniform approaches which will have equitable outcomes. 'Ethnic pecking order' has been heavily researched in the United States, where Asian and Jewish students do much better than Anglos, while Blacks usually do worse. Some similar work has been done in Britain. The American findings prompted the Head Start programmes which aimed to assist the education of disadvantaged minorities. In Australia such research is at an early stage, though there is reason to suppose that Greek, Jewish and Asian students do much better than average. If the education system discriminates, as many critics have claimed, it does not do so consistently against all ethnic minorities.

A by-product of universal education has often been the suppression of minority languages. In many societies the domination of the majority language has led to the decline of all others. French Canadians have always feared the reduction of their language in the face of English and have fought back politically and with much success. Spanish Americans and Hawaiians saw their languages reduced to second class status in their ancestral homelands. The proportions speaking Welsh have declined from the great majority in Wales in the 1870s to less than one-fifth today. The majority of Aboriginal languages spoken in 1788 are now extinct. Most Aborigines and Maoris speak English, often as their only language. Yet languages persist where they are given institutional support within the educational system. State responsibility for maintaining indigenous minority languages is now widely recognised.

While there is now widespread acceptance of indigenous languages, this is less true for immigrant languages which have been in use for only one or two generations. Mother tongue maintenance for immigrants and their children is most widely accepted in the European Community and Sweden. Practical convenience has demanded bilingual tuition at primary school level in England, the United States and Canada, as well as in the major cities of Australia. This rarely extends to the secondary level except for Spanish-speakers in the United States. Governments are reluctant to commit themselves to the indefinite maintenance of immigrant languages. In continental Europe the right to mother tongue maintenance is seen as encouraging the return home of immigrants and their families. Elsewhere the assumption is that immigrant children are in transition to becoming fluent in the majority language.

Language policy is in a state of flux in many countries, as immigration has introduced a wide variety of languages and minority nationalism has raised the profile of indigenous languages. The maintenance of immigrant languages has relied on three factors: the need to begin teaching children in their mother tongue; the efforts of voluntary organisations and foreign governments; and the acceptance of languages into the formal curriculum where there is effective demand. None of this commits public funds to the indefinite support of languages in the same way as is true for such long-established indigenous tongues as Welsh. In Australia, as elsewhere, official policy is likely to be that enshrined in the Lo Bianco report (*National Policy on Language*, Canberra, 1987), namely support for international languages, for the most widely spoken immigrant languages, and for indigenous (in this case Aboriginal) languages. Otherwise most policy, while prepared to pay small subsidies for the maintenance of 'heritage', does not envisage a major input into language maintenance where there is no massive demand. The largest 'heritage' commitment is currently in Canada (Canada, 1969).

CONCLUSIONS

Factors which need to be taken into account when comparing Australia with other situations include: the high level of employment and opportunity (which is now less apparent); a relatively egalitarian distribution of resources and prestige (which has recently changed); an industrial arbitration system which is fairly successful in preventing exploitation and 'wage poverty'; a low level of population density even in urban areas and a modern housing stock; official policies of multiculturalism designed to sustain self-esteem amongst minorities; an immigration policy based on permanent settlement; a high (though not outstanding) level of general education; a refusal by most public figures to engage in racist politics; an electorate sufficiently varied to modify majority pressures on politicians favouring assimilation; the absence of any ethnic minority large enough to appear threatening; and a consensual belief in intellectual and educational circles that Australia should be a liberal and egalitarian society. All these tend to make the ethnic situation in Australia fairly benign at present, despite an undercurrent of hostility to mass Asian immigration. Racist organisations are probably weaker in Australia than in any of the other societies surveyed. Ethnic militancy is also very muted and Aborigines have been far more politically active than any immigrant group.

Most of the societies reviewed have attempted to focus attention on groups which are distinguished both by their ethnicity and by social disadvantage and discrimination (Rose et al., 1969; CRE, 1982). Apart from Aboriginal policy, Australia has been reluctant to do this (AIMA, 1982; Australia, 1986). In the USA, the largest such groups are the two American categories of Blacks and Hispanics, making up seventeen per cent of the total population (Lieberson and Waters, 1988). The British NCWP group (with descendants) comprise about four per cent. In Sweden and The Netherlands the targeted groups include gypsies and travellers as well as more recent immigrants and are only one per cent of the population. In West Germany aliens account for seven per cent; in New Zealand Maoris and Polynesian immigrants are twelve per cent; and in Canada 'visible minorities' (including aborigines) are fewer than five per cent (Canada, 1984). All these groups are characterised in various ways by multiple disadvantage and some are also marked by consistently anti-social behaviour.

In Australia the NESB I and II group tends to be treated as a single entity. It comprises fourteen per cent in the first generation, over twenty per cent with locally-born children and about twenty-five per cent altogether (though this ancestry group is often very mixed and assimilated). Aborigines and Torres Strait Islanders make up 1.5 per cent. Categories such as refugees get very little distinct treatment once they have arrived. Non-Europeans are not officially regarded as distinctive. Australian public policy is rightly wary of stigmatising whole groups, such as 'Asians', in the fear of sustaining majority prejudices. This reluctance does not fully address such issues as the very high unemployment rates among certain ethnic groups or recent refugees, or the low educational levels and English skills among others. The NESB category is very varied and the possibility that particular ethnic communities may be relatively disadvantaged and may pass this on to their children has hardly been considered, except for Aborigines where the problems are obvious.

Australian public policy has concentrated on minimal satisfaction of ethnic community demands for recognition and cultural maintenance; improving access and equity in public services; protecting 'social harmony' in the light of overseas experience of race relations; defending universalism in immigration policy; and subsidising welfare activity directed specifically towards ethnic minorities (Jupp, 1989; OMA, 1989).

Policy has been confused by the contradiction between egalitarianism, which is essentially assimilationist, and liberalism, which is tolerant of multiculturalism. There has not been the bipartisan agreement on policy in recent years which characterises Canada, Sweden or The Netherlands. But neither is there the sharp-edged and sometimes violent racial tension which is found in Britain, West Germany or the

United States. Policy is, therefore, not made in an atmosphere of impending crisis. It is ameliorative and cautious, attempting to bridge the sometimes incompatible expectations of the majority and the minority. Local critics of Australian multiculturalism have presented it as threatening social harmony. In comparative perspective, however, Australia has been relatively successful in integrating millions of recent arrivals into a democratic society, though less successful in achieving equality for its Aborigines.

ACKNOWLEDGEMENT

The research for this chapter was funded by the Office of Multicultural Affairs.

REFERENCES

Australian Bureau of Statistics (1984) *The Measurement of Ethnicity in the Australian Census of Population and Housing* Canberra: Australian Government Publishing Service

Australian Institute of Multicultural Affairs (1982) *Evaluation of Post-Arrival Programs and Services* Melbourne: AIMA

Berry, J.W., Kalin, R. and Taylor, D.M. (1977) *Multiculturalism and Ethnic Attitudes in Canada* Ottawa: Minister of Supply and Services

Bureau of Immigration Research (1990) *Australia's Population Trends and Prospects 1989* Canberra: Australian Government Publishing Service

Canada House of Commons (1984) *Equality Now!: Report of the Special Committee (Task Force) on Visible Minorities in Canadian Society* Ottawa: Queen's Printer

Canada Royal Commission on Bilingualism and Biculturalism (1969) *The Cultural Contributions of Other Ethnic Groups (Book Four)* Ottawa: Queen's Printer

Castles, S. and Kosack, S. (1973) *Immigrant Workers and Class Structure in Western Europe* London: Oxford University Press

Castles, S. et al. (1984) *Here for Good: Western Europe's new ethnic minorities* London/Sydney: Pluto Press

Commission for Racial Equality (1982) *Local Government and Racial Equality* London: CRE

Community Relations Commission (1983) *Urban Deprivation, Racial Inequality and Social Policy: a Report* London: Commission for Racial Equality

Dahlie, J. and Fernando, T. eds (1981) *Ethnicity, Power and Politics in Canada* Toronto: Methuen/Canadian Ethnic Studies Association

Department of Immigration and Ethnic Affairs (1986) *Don't Settle for Less: Report of the Committee for Stage I of the Review of Migrant and Multicultural Programs and Services* Canberra: Australian Government Publishing Service

Elles, D. (1980) *International Provisions Protecting the Human Rights of Non-Citizens* New York: United Nations

Ethnic Affairs Commission of New South Wales (1978) *Participation: Report to the Premier June 1978* Sydney: EAC of NSW

Foster, L. and Stockley, D. (1988) *Australian Multiculturalism: a Documentary History and Critique* Clevedon (UK): Multilingual Matters

Hammar, T. (1985) *Election Year '85: Immigrant Voting Rights and Electoral Turnout* Stockholm: Swedish Institute (Svenska Institutet)

Handlin, O. and Thurstrom, S. eds (1980) *The Harvard Encyclopedia of American Ethnic Groups* Cambridge (Mass.): Harvard University Press

Hawkins, F. (1989) *Critical Years in Immigration: Canada and Australia Compared* Montreal: McGill University Press/Sydney: New South Wales University Press

Jupp, J. ed. (1988) *The Australian People* Sydney: Angus and Robertson

————— ed. (1989) *The Challenge of Diversity: Policy Options for a Multicultural Australia* Canberra: Australian Government Publishing Service

Kee, Poo-kong (1986) *Conceptualising and Measuring Ethnic Origin and Identification: the Australian, Canadian, American and British Experience* Melbourne: Australian Institute of Multicultural Affairs

Layton-Henry, Z. (1984) *The Politics of Race in Britain* London: George Allen and Unwin

Lieberson, S. and Waters, M.C. (1988) *From Many Strands: Ethnic and Racial Groups in Contemporary America* New York: Russell Sage Foundation

Lijphart, A. (1968) *The Politics of Accommodation: Pluralism and Democracy in The Netherlands* Berkeley: University of California Press

Netherlands Ministry for Home Affairs (1983) *Summary of the Policy Document on Minorities* The Hague: Ministry for Home Affairs

Office of Multicultural Affairs (1989) *National Agenda for a Multicultural Australia* Canberra: Australian Government Publishing Service

Penninx, R. (1984) *Migration, Minorities and Policy in the Netherlands; Recent Trends and Developments* Rijswijk: Ministry of Welfare, Public Health and Cultural Affairs

Piore, M.J. (1979) *Birds of Passage: Migrant Labour and Industrial Societies* Cambridge: Cambridge University Press

Porter, J. (1975) *The Vertical Mosaic; An Analysis of Social Class and Power in Canada* Toronto: University of Toronto Press

Rao, G.L., Richmond, A. and Zubrzycki, J. (1984) *Immigrants in Canada and Australia* Toronto: York University Press

Rose, E.J.B. et al. (1969) *Colour and Citizenship: a Report on British Race Relations* London: Oxford University Press/Institute of Race Relations

Rowley, C.D. (1970) *Aboriginal Policy and Practice* Canberra: Australian National University Press

Spoonley, P., Macpherson, C., Pearson, D. and Sedgwick, C. eds (1984) *Tauiwi: Racism and Ethnicity in New Zealand* Palmerston North: The Dunmore Press

Statistics Canada (1984) *1981 Census of Canada, Population, 1, Ethnic Origin* Ottawa: Statistics Canada

Tauroa, H. (1982) *Race Against Time* Wellington: Human Rights Commission

4 Are Australian families like others?

GEOFFREY McNICOLL

Australian families, we are told and have come to believe, are in trouble. The signs are to be seen in rising divorce rates and numbers of one-parent families, in people choosing cohabitation over marriage, in greater voluntary childlessness, and more people living alone—the stuff of innumerable magazine articles and op-ed pieces and the staples of campaign politics. The trends, for the most part, are indisputable; their interpretation and implications are not. Looking at the ways in which Australia's experience of family change is distinctive and the ways it mirrors or even lags the experience of other countries can deepen our understanding of the Australian situation and provide a sounder basis for debate on an important part of social policy. That international comparison is the subject of this chapter.

The big differences among families, or family systems, in the world—to do with matters such as lineage and conjugality—are among very broad cultural regions: Europe (and its overseas offshoots such as ourselves) compared to, say, East Asia or Sub-Saharan Africa. Clearly, Australian family patterns would be incidental in any such comparison. We must seek a narrower universe. For some purposes—for example assessing comparative economic competitiveness—Australia's geographical region would supply apt international contrasts. However, for the family, indeed for questions of social organisation in general, our peer group is better defined by cultural than geographical nearness. The countries chiefly relevant for viewing our society in comparative perspective are the industrialised English-speaking nations, notably the United Kingdom (for statistical convenience often truncated to England and Wales), Canada, and the United States; and a number of continental European countries. France, Italy and Sweden are the three chosen here.

Comparing families is less simple than it seems. Within any given society, families are of all sorts; average values of a particular family

55

characteristic often don't convey much information. Families, like the individuals that compose them, have a life cycle: the distribution of families in a population at a single time—the usual kind of data produced by censuses and surveys—tells us little about the processes of family formation and dissolution. Moreover, the distribution of family forms is changing over time. Apparently substantial differences in family structure revealed by international comparisons may represent only a few years' lag along the time dimension. And there are changes that may be affecting statistics more than realities: taking the analogy of family with firm, there is a family counterpart to the growth of the black economy (and for some of the same reasons). This is not just a measurement difficulty; it is a part of what is or might be happening to the family—a statistical withering away that leaves actual relationships more or less intact but no longer operating under state conferral of legitimacy.

MARRIAGE

Marriage is later, less frequent and less permanent than it was a generation ago, both in Australia and in each of the comparison countries. Although the comparison with the marriage patterns of the 'baby boom' years of the 1950s and 1960s—a period that saw a temporary resurgence of marriage—exaggerates the differences, the present patterns appear to be moving onto genuinely new ground.

Delayed marriage can be seen in the rising proportion of single women in the age group twenty to twenty-four years: around 40 per cent in the 1960s, 60 per cent in the 1980s (in Sweden, 60 per cent and 90 per cent). Trends in the proportion never marrying at all must be gauged from much older women. The fraction was quite high for women born at the turn of the century (above 20 per cent in the European countries and 10 to 15 per cent in Australia, Canada and the USA), falling to 4 to 7 per cent among women born in the 1940s. This level, however, will likely be a trough, the non-marrying share rising again in the subsequent 'birth cohorts' (the term demographers use to describe a group of people born in the same period) as the patterns seen at young ages start to show up. Peter McDonald (1984a) projects that 11 per cent of women in the Australian birth cohort of 1951–56, and, more speculatively but in line with some predictions for the USA, 20 to 25 per cent of both men and women now at young adulthood, will never marry.

Rising divorce rates operate in complementary fashion to reduce the proportions married in the population. Figure 4.1 charts the trends in terms of one simple index, annual divorces per 1000 population. The

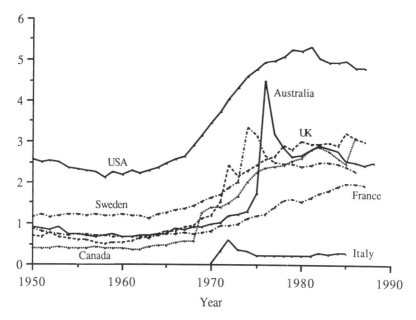

Figure 4.1 Annual divorces per 1000 population

dramatic Australian peak corresponds to the passage of the Family Law Act of 1975; similar liberalisations elsewhere tended to be more gradual. Under the demographic conditions of these countries, the proportion of marriages that would end in divorce were the rate to persist, can be estimated roughly by multiplying this index by ten (see Preston, 1987: 34). With the fairly constant divorce rates that have been experienced in Australia, Canada, the United Kingdom and Sweden in the 1980s, around 25 to 30 per cent of marriages would end in divorce. France is edging up to this range. The USA and Italy, however, are outliers: the USA consistently much higher (now nearly one in two marriages ending in divorce), Italy with essentially no divorce prior to the 1970s and very low rates since.

Cohabitation, or common-law marriage, offsets some of the recent shifts in formal marital patterns. Official data on this are somewhat dubious, with results sensitive to the (fast-rising) normative acceptability of the practice and to the precise wording of survey questions about it. As Dirk van de Kaa (1987: 17) has remarked, 'once cohabitation has shed its deviancy, cohabitation without marriage becomes a social institution'. Sweden (together with other Scandinavian countries) is

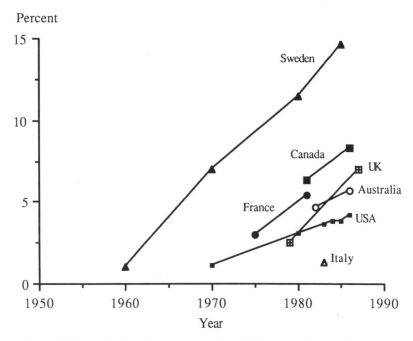

Figure 4.2 Unmarried couples as a proportion of all couples (per cent)

famously in the forefront here: in 1981, two-fifths of Swedish couples
under thirty-five years of age were reported to be cohabiting (Bozon,
1988: 216). Comparative estimates are assembled in figure 4.2, the erratic
coverage reflecting the data situation. While far less extreme than
Sweden in disavowal of marriage, the other countries in the group, with
the striking apparent exception of Italy (though we have only a single
data point for it), all show a strong upward trend.

   In hindsight, explanations for these changes are not hard to find.
Greater desire for independence among the young, combined with freer
sexuality and the economies offered by joint residence, promote cohabitation. Readier divorce, by making marriage less of a commitment,
paradoxically may remove one reason for marriage in the first place.
New patterns of behaviour, once they are common enough, generate
new norms and a new array of informal sanctions. The role of house-
wife, for example, becomes inadmissible. Reforms in legislation, typically lagging behavioural change, do the same with formal sanctions.

   In what sense are cohabitors a family? The answer hinges on definitions and little hinges on the answer. Clearly, though, if there are children of one or both partners present we have something comparable to

Percent

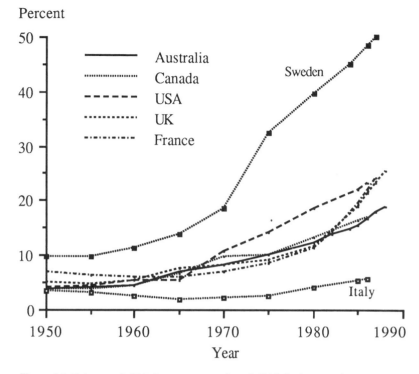

Figure 4.3 Extra-marital births as a proportion of all births (per cent)

a marital family. Increasingly, children *are* present. The proportion of children born outside formal marriage has risen steadily (figure 4.3). Sweden reached 50 per cent in 1987. The USA, UK and France are over 20 per cent, and Canada and Australia not much lower. Italy again stands out; its births overwhelmingly occurring within marriage. Beyond some level, long achieved in Sweden, the state bows to the inevitable and starts to remove the legal and administrative distinctions between marriage and cohabitation. 'Illegitimacy' as both a term and a concept disappears.

The number of people living alone parallels the rise in cohabitation and perhaps results from some of the same cultural and economic changes. In Australia, the 1986 census recorded almost a million such people: single-person households made up one-fifth of all non-institutional households. The comparative situation is seen in figure 4.4. The trends and the inter-country differences are in part a reflection of the ageing population: 40 per cent of Australians living alone in 1986 were sixty-five or over, most of them women (ABS, 1989: 14). But there

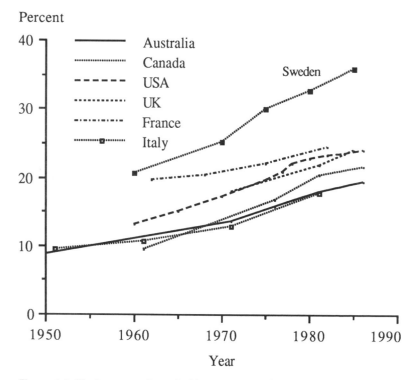

Figure 4.4 Single-person households as a proportion of all households (per cent)

are increasing numbers of single-person households at younger ages too. Some will be little different from cohabiting relationships—a partner temporarily absent or who chooses for one or other reason not to be reported to officialdom; others represent welcomed independence in living arrangements, where once that would have signified eccentricity; and still others contribute a net rise in the quantum of loneliness. David Popenoe (1988: 195), writing of the thus-far extreme case (in 1985 36 per cent of Swedish households were single-person; one in five Swedes aged sixteen to sixty-four lived alone), asks some relevant questions:

> What is the ultimate psychological impact of many years of living alone and not having to adapt on a regular basis to at least one other person? What sort of residential environment results, in terms of its social atmosphere and communal nature, when the majority of residents are unattached? What are the consequences for public social services when so many people have no one immediately available to them for care and sustenance?

CHILDREN

Families are about children. The family may be statistically elusive but children are entirely tangible, documented in elaborate detail by governments that explicitly espouse protection of the innocent and little less under those that pursue a hard-headed distancing of their affairs from the business of parenting.

For more than a century virtually all Western countries have been experiencing fertility decline, from total fertility rates (roughly, the average number of children ever born per woman over her life) of around six in the mid-nineteenth century to a little below two today. The story has an interruption in the 1950s, when post-World War II young adults married and bore children at much higher rates than had their parents: a combination of a bunching of deferred events, people's responses to newfound prosperity and optimism after the stringency of the Depression and war years, and a resurgence and spread of middle-class family values. The 'baby boom' was especially pronounced in Australia, Canada and the United States, with total fertility rising from prewar levels well below 3.0 children per woman to above 3.5 (and in New Zealand, another settler nation but one that is not part of this comparison, where it rose above 4.0). In the 1960s the decline resumed, until mostly levelling out in the 1980s. Currently, total fertility is 1.8 in Australia (1988), and virtually the same in each of the comparison countries except Italy and Sweden. In Italy, remarkably (given its very 'traditional' patterns of marriage and divorce), fertility continued to drop in the 1980s to 1.3 in 1986–88, equalling the lowest national level of any country. (West Germany has hovered in the range 1.3–1.5 since the 1970s; Denmark and The Netherlands are nearly as low.) Sweden's total fertility, after being at 1.6 in the early 1980s, has recently shown an upturn to near 2.0 (see figure 4.5). The fluctuations in this index to some extent are effects of variations in the timing of births rather than in ultimate numbers: fertility rates calculated for birth cohorts would trace a smoother path. Short-term trends, even reversals, should be interpreted with caution.

In Australia, and in each of the other countries, childbearing continues to be spread fairly widely over the reproductive ages. Substantial contributions to total fertility are made by women in their 30s, both those having larger-than-average families and those who have deferred their first births. Fertility at very young ages differs more: in the USA, around fifteen per cent of births are to women below age twenty, around twice the proportions for Australia, Canada, and the UK, which in turn are twice those of France, Italy and Sweden. The USA is also exceptional in not showing a strong downward trend for this age group. For individual women, however, childbearing has become more bunched,

Children
per women

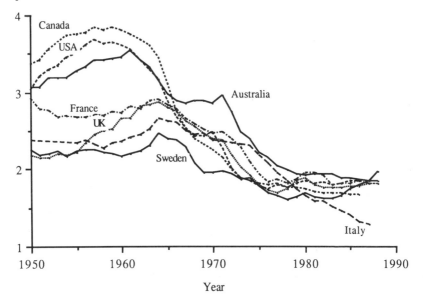

Figure 4.5 Total fertility rates, 1950–88

reflecting lower family size intentions, better contraception and high opportunity costs of absence from the labour market.

A simple comparison of family size outcomes among countries can be made in terms of the distribution of women of a given birth cohort by the number of children they have borne. Table 4.1 presents such distributions for women born in the 1940s, who had therefore essentially completed their childbearing years when surveyed in the mid-1980s. In each of the countries considered, between half and two-thirds of these women had either two or three children. The remainder were roughly evenly split (10 to 15 per cent each) among zero, one, and four-or-more children.

What of the time trends in these distributions? The two most evident changes, comparing women born in the 1920s, 1930s and 1940s, have been a drop in proportions of those having four or more children and a concentration on the two-child family. Together, these have left the proportions of three-child families rising slightly and then falling slightly. One-child families and childlessness declined over the earlier birth

Table 4.1 Percentage distribution of women aged around 40 by number of children they have borne, and average number of children per woman, birth cohorts of mid or late 1940s

Country and year of birth	Age at survey	Children per woman	Children ever born					
			0	1	2	3	4+	0+
Australia 1946–51	35–40	2.4	12	11	39	25	13	100
Canada* 1941–46	35–40	2.2	15	12	36	22	15	100
USA 1944–48	40–44	2.1	15	15	35	21	14	100
UK** 1947	41	2.1	13	14	43	20	10	100
France 1947	39	2.1	9	19	40	32		100
Sweden 1947	38	1.9	12	16	45	26		100

Notes: * Assuming never married women to be childless
** England and Wales
Sources: National statistical reports
Data for Italy unavailable

cohorts (the parents of the baby-boom generation) and began to rise again in the 1940s cohorts.

The countries we are comparing show remarkable similarities in these patterns and time trends. One might well have expected them to display more distinctive distributions of family sizes, reflecting their specific economic conditions, institutional configurations, and cultural traditions. At least for this group that has not been the case. Sweden shows somewhat greater concentration at two children than the other countries and correspondingly fewer families of three and above, but the difference read as a time lag is less than a decade. (The Australian childlessness data needs treating with some caution since some 6 to 7 per cent of women in most cohorts in the 1986 census were recorded as 'not stated' on the question of number of children. In table 4.1 these women are distributed pro rata among family sizes; it is possible they were disproportionately childless.)

What eventual distributions of family size will be generated by the birth cohorts of the 1960s, still in their peak reproductive years? Expectations as recorded in surveys have proven generally unrealistic, reflecting social norms and individual hopes rather than hard reality. Charles Westoff (1987: 165), commenting on survey data for the USA in the early 1980s that show over 60 per cent of childless women aged twenty-five to twenty-nine still expecting two or more births in their lifetimes, remarks that 'childlessness—and perhaps to a lesser extent having an only child—is a status that women tend to back into as the "costs" (age, job considerations, lifestyle) of making the actual decision to have a child loom larger'. The consensus among American demographers seems to be that USA childlessness will reach or even somewhat exceed 20 per cent in the 1960s cohorts. Similar figures are bruited for the UK and Australia. Of British women born in 1952, 19 per cent were still childless in 1987—that is, at age thirty-five. While this fraction would not be unprecedented (it was the typical outcome for birth cohorts prior to the 1920s) it probably reflects deliberate choice of lifestyle to a much greater extent than before.

With 20 per cent childless, and the remaining distribution of completed family size unchanged from that of Australian women born in 1946–51 (table 4.1), average children per woman would drop to just below two, which is the likely outcome for the birth cohorts of the 1960s. Radically lower fertility, for example levels like the 1.3 children per woman implied by present rates of childbearing in Italy, would most likely see both higher proportions childless and lower proportions of 'large' families. A distribution taken from recent German urban populations, yielding total fertility of 1.4, shows the majority of women having at most one child:

No. of children	0	1	2	3	4+	Total
Per cent of women	26	31	23	11	9	100
(Le Bras and Tapinos, 1979)						

PARENTS

Demographers, like most other people, depict families from the standpoint of adults who choose living arrangements, sexual partners, and numbers of children. The distributions of women by completed family size, discussed above, exemplify that perspective. In assessing the implications of particular family patterns, however, the perspective of the child is just as important.

There is an essential asymmetry here: everyone comes from a family but not everyone goes back to one. Most children, moreover, necessarily are born into families that are larger than average: the number of children in the family from which the average child comes is substantially higher than the number of children that the average woman has. (How much higher depends on the variance of the distribution of children among families.) In the case of the Le Bras-Tapinos distribution just mentioned, 80 per cent of children are born to mothers who have families of two or more children, but those mothers make up only 43 per cent of the cohort of women.

Such differences are not just a statistical curiosity. Disproportionately, children come from poorer and less educated parents—in some part,

from parents made poorer or hindered from gaining education by having children. Blau and Duncan (1967: 328–330), in their classic study
of intergenerational mobility, argued that a large family dilutes the
resources available for investment in each child, limiting the child's
educational attainment and chances of occupational success. Thomas
Sowell (1983: 255) traces the transmission of disadvantage also through
the differential quality of the home environment, with economic pressures tending to push fertility below replacement among the very groups
best able to instil the values and patterns of life that make for economic
success.

The potential effect of family size distribution on intergenerational
economic mobility is probably roughly similar across low-fertility
countries—except, arguably, for the USA, whose 'underclass' seems to
present a self-perpetuating situation without close parallel elsewhere in
the industrialised world. Responses to the problem, and thus actual
outcomes, are more variable. Policies to promote upward economic
mobility between generations by removing social barriers and by encouraging human capital investment in children from disadvantaged
families have sharply differing priorities among governments. Assessment of mobility outcomes is an important research topic. (See Broom
et al., 1980 and Rowland, 1989 on the Australian case.)

While children in larger families may on the whole be worse off, their
parents have a ready-made support network in their old age. That at
least is the idealised picture, and one that appeals also to governments
faced with steeply mounting social security costs. The pace of population ageing (set out in table 4.2) is slower than often supposed for the
countries we are concerned with, particularly in Australia, Canada and
the USA. But as the relative size of the old age population increases, so
does the proportion of those elderly who have no children or only one
child—that, after all, is the principal reason for population ageing. De-
signing an equitable and politically feasible social security system is

Table 4.2 Population 65 years and over as a percentage of the total population,
1950–2020: estimates and UN medium-variant projections

	1950	1960	1970	1980	1990	2000	2010	2020
Australia	8	8	8	10	11	12	13	16
Canada	8	8	8	10	11	13	14	19
USA	8	9	10	11	13	13	14	17
UK	11	12	13	15	15	15	16	19
France	11	12	13	14	14	15	16	19
Italy	8	9	11	13	14	17	18	21
Sweden	10	12	14	16	18	18	19	23

Source: United Nations (1989)

difficult in a notionally family-free population; recognising the distribution of family structures and the differential incidence of childraising costs and benefits adds greatly to the complications.

ECONOMICS AND IDEOLOGIES

Whatever one's theory of the family, undeniably families are responsive to their economic environment. Decisions on seeking employment, on how many children to have and who is to care for them in their early years, and on expenditure on education and health are altered in predictable directions by shifts in income-earning opportunities and relative prices. This is the family as miniature firm. And as with the firm there is a level of analysis that discards the fiction of single economic entity, and looks at the interests and strategic behaviours of individual members—at the games people play. (One such game is that played in the market for partners, prior to the setting up of the family.)

The feature of the economic environment that has most to do with family behaviour is the labour market, particularly the opportunities it presents for women. The middle-class values that spread along with industrialisation included the idea that women should find full-time occupations as child-raisers and household managers, an aspiration achieved and rationalised as families came to be left more to themselves, shorn of the help of live-in or nearby kin and servants. With less time needed for childrearing as fertility fell, and diminishing economic security offered by marriage as divorce rates rose, women again entered the labour market. The causal link worked the other way as well: marriage and fertility patterns responded to greater labour market commitment by women—resulting, for example, from their better education and growing awareness of forgone earnings—and to wider employment opportunities as gender discrimination abated.

For the western industrialised countries over recent decades, there is a fairly consistent trend over time in patterns of female labour force participation (see OECD, 1988). Initially, the schedule of age-specific participation rates (the proportion of each age-group that is in the labour force) shows a single peak at ages twenty to twenty-four and a decline at later ages as women leave the labour force on marriage or childbirth. Subsequently a second, broader peak develops in the age range thirty-five to fifty-five years, reflecting re-entry of women to the labour force as their children grow up. Finally, the saddle between the peaks disappears, yielding an inverted U-shape schedule that roughly parallels the schedule for males—resulting from very low fertility rates and policies that seek to make market work and childrearing more compatible. All the countries we are considering had passed the first stage by the 1960s; Canada, France, Italy, Sweden and the USA have essentially reached stage three, though with variations in the height of the schedule (part-time work is a complication) and in the steepness of the fall-off at later labour force ages. Australia and the UK still indicate significant withdrawal of women from the labour force during the peak childbearing ages.

Other major economic influences on the family where international differentials might be expected would be taxes and transfer payments and housing. Countries have not deliberately sought to make children inaffordable—quite the opposite in some cases—but many widely pursued policy directions tend to have that consequence and attempted remedies through the tax system tend to be trivial or to have been eroded away by inflation. The tax exemption per family member in the USA was doubled by President Reagan, to a level of $2000 in 1989. As Senator Moynihan (1986: 167) has pointed out, however, to offset the same proportion of average personal income in 1984 as in 1948 (when income-splitting was introduced), the exemption would have had to be raised to more than $5000. Over the same period, family allowances in Australia, never as generous, have declined to virtual inconsequence except for those at the bottom of the income distribution (see Young, 1989: 46–9).

Housing costs are a popular explanation for deferring marriage or childbearing: the large increases in housing demand that came with the entry of the baby boom cohorts into adulthood could have generated various responses, but resulted most often in price rationing and unprecedented calls on disposable income. (In Australia, vigorous immigration has maintained the scarcity.) Once the family is ensconced, however, albeit greatly in debt, other effects may come into play. The style of the housing may influence behavioural patterns (low-density suburbia sustaining traditional familism in North America and Australia; high-density apartment living undermining it in Europe—argued by Popenoe, 1988); and home ownership itself may re-establish a yeoman-like conservatism—a tenet, for example, of Mrs Thatcher.

The forces for convergence that might yield the observed similarities in family trends among these countries are not only economic; they may also be cultural. Witness choice of family size. For the great majority of couples, rich and poor, in the industrialised countries today, the domain of choice in family size extends from zero children (still conveying, where voluntary, a tinge of yuppie selfishness) to three (verging upon irresponsible excess). One can imagine shifts over time among those choices, perhaps like fashions or fads in other kinds of consumption behaviour, but hardly a breakout to higher numbers. In fact, a further closing in of the upper boundary—towards making the three-child option seem somewhat eccentric rather than merely excessive—is quite possible.

Among the cultural forces that plausibly make for the convergence of family behaviours across countries the most obvious would be the images of family life (and, perhaps more important, of alternative lifestyles) purveyed by television (soap operas particularly—see Taylor, 1989), newspapers, and popular magazines and novels. The effect of continual and virtually subliminal exposure to these messages seems likely to generate or reinforce the patterns and boundaries of socially legitimate behaviours, just as the sanction of kin and neighbour within the local community once did. Unlike the gossip-based coercion of the distant past, however, the media pressures of today are increasingly transnational: crossing the English-speaking world, and, only slightly less readily, extending well beyond it.

This may, however, be too literal and confined a route of cultural influence. Familial values are closely associated with the broader moral and political orientations of individuals: their strength of religious belief, degree of 'postmaterialism', and place on the political spectrum (Lesthaeghe and Surkyn, 1988). Movements such as feminism and environmentalism take root in country after country, profoundly altering people's perceptions of society and the values brought to it. Distinctive national profiles in beliefs about the division between the public and private realms, the limits of individual autonomy, the scope of government, the work ethic, and so on, are attenuated, differences in family values along with them.

Whatever the broad family similarities among countries, there will hardly be a total convergence. Cultural traditions have great inertia. Social institutions acquire staying power from the interest groups or the tangible infrastructure to which they have given rise. And the processes of local cultural innovation will continue, as at least a modest countervailing force for distinctiveness.

POLICIES

Is Australian family policy like others? A cynic might rule the question irrelevant to the topic of this chapter on the grounds of inconsequence. The political rhetoric does not vary much from Canberra to Ottawa, or Stockholm to Rome: families are good things; governments should support them. The policy substance, however, does vary, although with effects that have more to do with welfare than with behaviour.

Although all political parties are pro-family, family policy has acquired a somewhat rightist tinge. This may be in part because of the anti-feminist line of 'getting women back to the kitchen' taken by curmudgeonly proponents, or because fiscal incentives, to be effective across the income distribution, have to be 'regressive'—set in proportion to income rather than to need. As governments change in the predominantly two-party states we are discussing, there are small course corrections affecting family policy. When large budget items or tax expenditures are at issue—serious support for day care of children, for instance—governments of all stripes (even Sweden's incipiently?) can agree on their inaffordability.

Family policy and immigration policy are both concerned with the recruitment and induction of new members of society, with the supply of human capital and cultural feedstock. In low-fertility situations, a balance between the two policy domains is usually struck. Some countries—Japan most prominently—put their policy emphasis almost wholly on the creation of native human capital. In others—and Australia is the exemplar—the balance is far towards the side of immigration. (UN estimates for average net immigration per 1000 population per year in the late 1980s are: UK, 0.5; France, 0; Italy, 0.7; Sweden, 0.7; USA, 1.8; Canada, 2.2; and Australia, 4.6 [UN, 1989].) Since family policy, broadly construed, has no simple budget line or, in most countries, a single ministerial locus, and since it is so bound up with distributional issues, there is no ready way for the policy tradeoff to be made explicit in political debate.

Only France among the countries under discussion has seriously sought to increase its birth rate as a matter of public policy, and it none too successfully. In Australia, Canada and the USA fertility has not been low enough for long enough to present imminent prospects of population decrease. In Europe, further economic integration and emerging east–west links are radically altering market size and are likely to defer worries about low fertility for the time being. In both regions, migration may seem anyway a simpler and probably cheaper way of governing population numbers if latent ethnic tensions can be contained.

FUTURES

From this discussion it appears that, to a good first approximation at least, Australian families are much like others. If the family is in danger, we are far from alone in that state. The conclusion is of course weakened by the 'others' being chosen to be economically and culturally quite similar societies. In this company, Australia is not at the forefront of change but follows along, tracing a moving average that stops somewhat short of extremes and is sedately lagging by a few years. Of course, I have mentioned only fairly simple aspects of the family, principally demographic ones. More detailed exploration would no doubt unearth substantive and attitudinal factors in which Australia has a distinctive profile. Proof of that distinctiveness, however, would likely require more sophisticated comparisons than the sort I have presented or that would be appropriate here. But if broadly alike today, will these countries remain alike? What does the comparative perspective suggest might be their medium-term future? In the best traditions of demography I will sketch out three scenarios, each supportable on the evidence.

1 The most upbeat is the future that might be described as change but no change. It is the picture broadcast by the Australian Institute of Family Studies. McDonald (1984b: 14) writes: 'marriage and family are losing their significance in the public sphere but taking on a far greater relevance in the private'. There is a wider spread of family forms, and more recourse to the options of not marrying or not having children, but no reason for alarm. Michael Bracher and Gigi Santow (1989: 19), on the basis of early results of the Australian Family Project at the Australian National University, concur: 'Thus, the picture for the 1990s is not radically different from that of the 1970s and 1980s. Rather, it is one of increasing diversity, with a greater variety of familial and non-familial states, and with individuals more likely to experience this greater variety in their own lives'. Katja Boh (1989), summarising a comparative study of the European situation, writes of a 'convergence to diversity'. An incidental consequence of such a future might well be greater differences among countries. With a series of acceptable family and non-family lifestyles, there need be no strong central tendency, no cross-national pressures for conformity.

2 A different future would see a recovery to something closer to the mid-century familism, perhaps modified by freer sex roles. There are forces that may induce an upturn: children come from families, disproportionately from large ones, and may be predisposed to create their own; the society collectively may reassert its reproductive interests in the face of its ageing and its demographic marginalisation in a crowded world, and find subtler promotional routes than Stalin's 'hero mothers'; a sociobiological residue of familism may be exposed. Some American demographers are predicting a fertility rebound in the 1990s as members of the small birth cohorts of the 1970s reap the economic benefits of being few. Migrants from Third World countries, an increasing presence in the low-fertility west, may bring familial values with them. Or fashions and values may simply change: as Paul Demeny (1987: 352) writes, semi-seriously:

> In a Herman Kahn-like exurbanised super-affluent future, the tedium
> of working at home at one's computer terminal may be relieved by
> rediscovery of the fun of having children around. Visiting faraway places
> will no longer be appealing and distracting, since Bali will look much the
> same as Westchester County. Throw in a pro-family religious revival and
> rediscovery of "traditional values," and the Nixonian worry of where to
> put the next hundred million Americans may reassert itself.

3 Or again, the family may indeed in some sense be withering away. The forces tending to restore a semblance of traditional family pat-

terns may simply not be strong enough. Childbearing would of course continue, but childraising would decreasingly take place in continuing nuclear or quasi-nuclear groupings. David Popenoe, in one of the best recent books on the family, has seen the future and it is Sweden. 'Sweden should . . . be viewed not as an exception but a pacesetter' (1988: 254). There the 'postnuclear family' is already virtually in place, the family's former triple functions—pair-bonding, sexual activity, and the procreation and socialisation of children—decisively unbundled. Children routinely experience a variety of parenting, with the state (no kibbutz) providing a safety net of sorts.

> Sweden's fertility, now somewhat higher than the European average, has perhaps been sustained by generous public expenditures and transfer payments. Its government's share of GDP, at 56 per cent in 1988, is well above Britain, France and Italy (37 to 44 per cent) and far in excess of Australia, Canada and the USA (around 30). Where the welfare state is less advanced, or has already retreated, or has lighted upon the environment as a worthier cause than the family, fertility may sputter at levels radically below replacement. Workers have greater discretionary income and discretion may advise against buying children. Labour shortages can be remedied by immigration, up to (and sometimes beyond) the limits imposed by the society's tolerance of ethnic and cultural diversity. Any absolute decrease in population can probably be made slow enough to be politically innocuous; besides, governments can plausibly claim that there are no proven measures that would restore fertility levels.

To a considerable degree, which of these projections is favoured may depend, as has been remarked of the future of marriage, 'on whether one subscribes to linear or to cyclical theories of social change' (Espenshade, cited by Westoff, 1987: 161). The large inherent unpredictability in future societal trends beyond a relatively few years, even in a matter as rooted in stolid demography as the family, argues for a close watching brief on developments both here and elsewhere. To the extent the past is a guide, the range of experience represented by the countries of Europe and North America is likely to continue to define the bounds within which Australian family trends will lie.

REFERENCES

Australian Bureau of Statistics (1989) *Census 86: Australian Families and Households* Canberra
Blau, Peter M., and Duncan, Otis Dudley (1967) *The American Occupational Structure* New York: Wiley
Boh, Katja, et al. eds (1989) *Changing Patterns of European Family Life: A Comparative Analysis of 14 European Countries* London: Routledge
Bozon, Michel (1988) 'Cohabitation et classes sociales en Suède', *Population* 43, pp. 216–221

Bracher, Michael, and Santow, Gigi (1989) 'The family histories of Australian women', paper presented to the IUSSP General Conference, New Delhi, September 1989

Broom, Leonard et al. (1980) *The Inheritance of Inequality* London: Routledge and Kegan Paul

Demeny, Paul (1987) 'Pronatalist policies in low-fertility countries: patterns, performance, and prospects', in Kingsley Davis et al. eds *Below Replacement Fertility in Industrial Societies* Cambridge: Cambridge University Press

Le Bras, Hervé (1986) *Les Trois France* Paris: Seuil

Le Bras, Hervé and Tapinos, Georges (1979) 'Perspectives à long terme de la population française et leurs implications économiques', *Population* 34, pp. 1391–1452

Lesthaeghe, Ron and Surkyn, Johan (1988) 'Cultural dynamics and economic theories of fertility change', *Population and Development Review* 14, pp. 1–45

McDonald, Peter (1984a) 'The baby boom generation as reproducers: fertility in Australia in the late 1970s and the 1980s', in *Proceedings of the Australian Family Research Conference* (Melbourne: Institute of Family Studies), 1

—— (1984b) 'Can the family survive?' Discussion Paper No. 11, Institute of Family Studies, Melbourne

Moynihan, Daniel P. (1986) *Family and Nation* San Diego: Harcourt Brace Jovanovich

Organization for Economic Co-operation and Development (1988) *Employment Outlook* Paris

Popenoe, David (1988) *Disturbing the Nest: Family Change and Decline in Modern Societies* New York: Aldine de Gruyter

Preston, Samuel H. (1987) 'The decline of fertility in non-European industrialized countries', in Kingsley Davis et al. eds *Below Replacement Fertility in Industrial Societies* Cambridge: Cambridge University Press

Rowland, D.T. (1989) 'Who's producing the next generation? The parentage of Australian children', *Journal of the Australian Population Association* 6, pp. 1–17

Sowell, Thomas (1983) *The Economics and Politics of Race: An International Perspective* New York: Morrow

Taylor, Ella (1989) *Prime-Time Families: Television Culture in Postwar America* Berkeley: University of California Press

United Nations (1979) *Demographic Yearbook 1979: Historical Supplement* New York

United Nations (1989) *World Population Prospects 1988* New York

US Bureau of the Census (1988) *Statistical Abstract of the United States* Washington, DC

Van de Kaa, Dirk J. (1987) 'Europe's second demographic transition', *Population Bulletin* (Population Reference Bureau, Washington, DC) 42

Westoff, Charles F. (1987) 'Perspective on nuptiality and fertility', in Kingsley Davis et al. eds *Below Replacement Fertility in Industrialised Countries* Cambridge: Cambridge University Press

Young, Christabel (1989) 'Population policies in developed countries: how do Australia's policies compare?', *Journal of the Australian Population Association* 6, pp. 38–56

Data sources for tables and figures: principal sources are UN Demographic Yearbooks and the statistical offices of the individual countries. Details are given in a longer version of this chapter available from the Demography Program, Research School of Social Sciences, Australian National University.

5 Are Australian attitudes to government different?: a comparison with five other nations

CLIVE BEAN

COMPARING ATTITUDES

The political, social and economic choices we as a society make for ourselves and our future are influenced in no small part by our attitudes on significant policy issues. Indeed, public attitudes are crucial components of the fabric of Australian and other modern societies alike. Seen in this light, it is not only of considerable importance to study social and political attitudes, it also becomes of great interest to see whether a country such as Australia has distinctive patterns of attitudes which set it apart from other nations. Such distinctiveness may both reflect and help explain other features of political and social life that make Australia unique in the world. On the other hand, there is also the question of how far we are all part of the one global society and of the extent to which people in different countries feel much the same about social and political matters.

As a preliminary to explaining attitude differences between countries, the major task is to establish their form and nature. Yet attitudes are so personal and varied that to measure and evaluate them accurately is by no means easy. Different approaches can lead to conflicting results and sometimes, alas, even similar approaches do. The answer to the question of whether or not, in cross-national comparative terms, the attitudes of Australian citizens are different or distinctive will depend very much on the approach taken and the specific topic addressed, as any brief survey of relevant research will reveal.

Indeed, it is possible to build up a sizeable collection of evidence for the distinctiveness of certain Australian attitudes on the one hand and an equally sizeable pile of evidence pointing to the similarity of many Australian attitudes (and/or their consequences) to those in other countries, on the other. Let us take just one or two brief examples from the realm of politics, starting with a case of where Australia appears to be different. Australia is renowned for being an exception to the phenomenon of declining levels of political partisanship (that is, the extent to which individuals feel an allegiance to one political party over others) among the mass public that has occurred in many other western democracies (Aitkin, 1982; Dalton, 1988). While elsewhere fewer and fewer citizens express a general party identification, and for those who do, its importance to their voting behaviour diminishes, in Australia partisanship remains both extremely pervasive among voters and far and away the predominant electoral influence.

On the other side of the ledger, Australia sits very much in the international mainstream in terms of general levels of public interest in politics (Aitkin, 1982; Jones, 1989) and also in terms of the rise in levels of interest that has been evident over the last twenty or more years in many countries (Bean, 1988; Dalton, 1988). Furthermore, the effects of attitudes such as political interest and strength of party identification (irrespective of which party the identification is with) on participation in different political activities display remarkably similar patterns in Australia to those found in a wide variety of different countries (Bean, 1989; Verba et al., 1971; 1978). In Australia and elsewhere, interest in politics facilitates all kinds of orthodox political activity, whereas strong party identification encourages participation in identifiably partisan activities, such as election campaigning, but has little or no impact on nonpartisan kinds of political participation, such as working to solve local community problems.

The fact that we have been able to use the same attitude variable, political partisanship, both to exemplify cases where Australia is similar to other nations and where it is different illustrates an important point. It is not merely the case that investigating different attitudes will inevitably lead to different answers. Whether Australia stands out as distinct or merges in with the international crowd will often come down to a choice of what one wishes to emphasise and in what context the findings are to be evaluated. One aspect of the context that can make a difference is which other variable or variables are being considered in relation to the attitude in question, as we have seen in the case of partisanship. Another important contextual dimension is the set of countries available as cross-national referents. On any particular attitude, the pattern in Australia may look different from some countries and similar to others. These are considerations that need to be borne in mind as the analysis proceeds.

CROSS-NATIONAL RESEARCH USING ATTITUDE SURVEYS

There are at least two avenues we could follow in addressing the question of the distinctiveness or otherwise of public attitudes in Australia. Each would contribute something to the discussion. The first method would involve taking a general, broad-brush sweep across the array of pertinent literature (basically, expanding the brief examples given above). While providing a broad picture, a piecemeal approach of this sort is nonetheless fraught with pitfalls since it is very difficult to synthesise accurately or represent fairly the individual findings from such a wide variety of different studies. The other way is to be very specific and focus rather narrowly on a particular set of comparable attitude data which in themselves will give more systematic results than the broad-brush approach. One thus sacrifices breadth of coverage in favour of internal coherence and more substantial analysis. At the end of such an exercise it may be possible to attempt some broader generalisations. It is this latter approach that we adopt here.

A big advantage of systematic cross-national research is that it helps to overcome the problem of 'parochial' interpretations in social research—of, for example, viewing Australian research findings purely in terms of Australian experience. In the past comparable evidence from other countries was so scarce that it was often not possible to evaluate Australian data in an international light. More recently, however, a considerable body of comparative data has been generated by cross-national attitude surveys, in particular through the European and Australian Values Surveys of the early 1980s and the International Social Survey Programme (ISSP) and also, in a less systematic way, through political attitudes/election surveys which, although conducted for the most part as separate projects in different countries have increasingly contained a large core of common questions, thus facilitating cross-national analysis.

Opinion surveys of this kind, which collect data from a representative sample of the adult population, provide the best available method by which we can systematically address questions such as the extent to which attitudes of the Australian mass public may be different or distinctive. Of course, in addition to its intrinsic interest, one benefit of investigating such questions is that isolating what is distinctive or different about Australian attitudes (and identifying what is not) can help point towards fruitful lines for further, more in-depth, enquiry.

The data used in this chapter come from the International Social Survey Programme's first Role of Government survey, conducted in 1985–86.[1] Six countries—Australia, West Germany, Great Britain, the United States, Austria and Italy—participated in this the inaugural

ISSP survey. The respective sample sizes are 1528 for Australia, 1048 for West Germany, 1530 for Great Britain, 677 for the United States, 987 for Austria and 1580 for Italy.

ATTITUDES TO CIVIL LIBERTIES

About a third of the 100-plus attitudinal variables collected in the 1985–86 ISSP role of government survey have been selected for examination in this exercise. They comprise three groups: attitudes to civil liberties, attitudes to social welfare and attitudes to government intervention in the economy. The latter two groups are less distinct than the first, both conceptually and in terms of the presentation of the relevant items to the survey respondents. They are therefore discussed together, in the next section.

Initially, however, we turn to a comparison of attitudes to certain aspects of civil liberties in Australia, West Germany, Great Britain, the United States, Austria and Italy. Figure 5.1 shows that views on whether newspapers should be allowed to publish confidential government documents, acquired by some unspecified means, differ much more according to the subject matter of the documents than by country. In all six countries, most people are against allowing publication of such documents if they are about defence plans but a majority is in favour of allowing publication if the documents are about economic plans. For example, only 16 per cent of Australians believe that a newspaper should be allowed to publish the documents if they relate to defence plans whereas 60 per cent would allow publication of economic documents.

This latter response is very similar to that from all five other nations (the range being from 56 per cent in Austria to 64 per cent in Italy) while the former is the lowest national proportion favouring publication, but still very much in line with the collective sentiment expressed in most of the other countries. Thus, in Australia, more than three times as many citizens think confidential economic plans are fair game for publication in the media as think the same about defence plans and these ratios are similar in most of the other countries. Austrian citizens show the smallest amount of variability between their views on the two questions. In general the issue seems to be not the confidentiality of government documents, but rather how vital the contents of the documents are thought to be.

The data in figure 5.2 show that large majorities of citizens in all nations think that 'orthodox' forms of political action such as organising public meetings and publishing pamphlets to protest against government actions should be allowed, especially in Australia and Britain, and

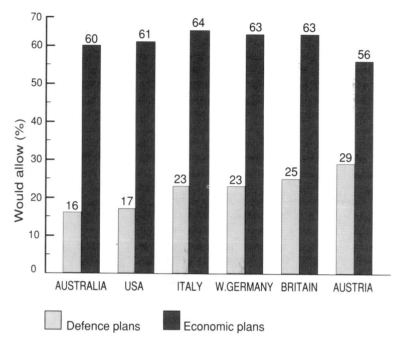

Figure 5.1 Percentages saying newspapers should be allowed to publish confidential government papers, in six nations

Source: International Social Survey Programme Role of Government Survey, 1985–86.

in Germany on the first question. Respondents in the United States, on both questions, and Austrians and Germans on the second are somewhat less in favour of allowing such protests. On the question of whether organising protest marches and demonstrations should be allowed, there is a sharp split between the Germanic countries, in which only a third say yes, and the other four countries, in which around two-thirds say yes. It is possible that we are seeing a legacy of the Nazi regime among the German and Austrian respondents who may associate 'protest marches and demonstrations' with the Nazi rallies of the Hitler era.

Turning to the more 'radical' forms of protest shown in the bottom half of the figure, there is very wide agreement among citizens in all countries that protesting by occupying a government office and stopping work there for several days is going too far and should not be allowed and citizens are virtually unanimous against protests that would seriously damage government buildings. In Australia, the United States and to a lesser extent Great Britain, organising a nationwide strike of all

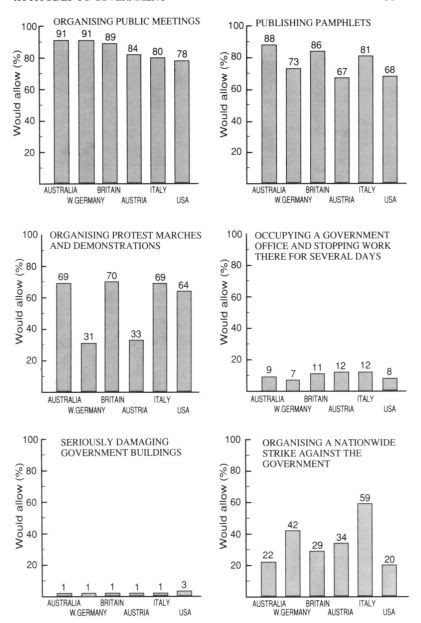

Figure 5.2 Percentages who would allow different forms of political protest, in six nations

Source: International Social Survey Programme Role of Government Survey, 1985–86.

workers against the government is also unacceptable to the large majority, while fewer Germans and Austrians are antagonistic and a clear majority of Italians believe such action should be allowed. One tentative explanation for this division of opinion might lie in differing 'political cultures'. The political scientists Almond and Verba (1963) have argued for example, that the Anglo–American democracies have political cultures which emphasise constructive or positive action, and a general strike which would result in widespread disruption to the 'innocent' public might thus be seen as less appropriate in these nations than elsewhere.

Overall, however, the dominant impression from these measures of attitudes to civil liberties' issues—bearing in mind that they cover but a small set of topics that would constitute civil liberties broadly defined—is one of similarity in the views of citizens of the six nations in the survey. In particular Australia appears not to be especially distinctive on any one of these questions but to display attitudes that are similar to at least some of the other countries in every case.

ATTITUDES TO WELFARE AND ECONOMIC INTERVENTION

This conclusion does not hold to anywhere near the same extent when it comes to attitudes to social welfare and government intervention in the economy, however. Table 5.1 contains data on questions concerning the responsibilities of government in the social services and other areas. Although a small majority of Australians believe the government should take responsibility for providing jobs for those who want them, providing a decent standard of living for the unemployed and reducing income differences between the rich and poor, these are relatively low numbers compared with the citizens of all five other countries except the United States, the public of which displays (comparatively speaking) a consistent aversion to government intervention in any of the spheres addressed in the survey.

By contrast with Americans, Australians' views are not consistently antigovernment intervention by any means. Australians are overwhelmingly in favour of the government taking responsibility for keeping prices under control, providing health care for the sick, providing a decent standard of living for the old and assisting the growth of industry. In this they are certainly not unique, however, with very large numbers in almost all the other countries holding the same opinion, led by the near international and intranational unanimity in the belief that health care and care of the aged are government responsibilities. However, even on these questions the United States displays less certainty that it should be the government's role, as does Germany on the

Table 5.1 Cross-national attitudes on areas of government responsibility

Per cent in agreement	Australia	West Germany	Great Britain	United States	Austria	Italy
It should be the government's responsibility to:						
provide a job for everyone who wants one	53	82	72	35	84	89
keep prices under control	88	76	93	76	93	98
provide health care for the sick	93	98	99	83	98	100
provide a decent standard of living for the old	96	97	98	88	99	99
provide industry with the help it needs to grow	87	54	95	63	75	84
provide a decent standard of living for the unemployed	59	85	86	50	68	85
reduce income differences between rich and poor	54	67	75	39	78	84
It is the responsibility of the government to reduce the differences in income between people with high incomes and those with low incomes	43	56	52	30	66	67
Those with high incomes should pay a larger proportion of their earnings in taxes than those with low incomes	65	90	70	59	n.a.	86

Notes: n.a. No available data.
Sources: International Social Survey Programme Role of Government Survey, 1985–86

questions of price control and industry assistance. Italians, on the other hand, are the most consistently in favour of the government taking responsibility, followed by the British and the Austrians.

Figure 5.3 looks at the role people believe the government should play in five different industries, two that are generally regarded as public utilities and three others that are usually thought of as large-scale commercial enterprises. Predictably, fewer in each country believe that electricity and local public transport—industries traditionally run by government—should be privately run (specifically, that the government should neither own nor control their prices and profits) than believe that the steel, banking and insurance and automobile industries should be run by private enterprise.[2]

There is, in other words, something of a 'reality principle' operating here. People tend to endorse the status quo. Yet there is a certain amount of variability in the extent to which reality and opinion match. Citizens of the Anglo–American countries are more likely to favour private ownership and control of electricity and public transport than citizens in the continental European nations, but Australia lags considerably behind the United States and Britain, where privatisation of formerly government industries is much further advanced. Australia, however, is to the forefront in being against government involvement in the other three industries, surpassing the United States in the number believing that the car industry should be run by private enterprise (68 per cent compared with 61 per cent). Again the Italians display a consistent and quite distinctive preference for all of these industries to be run with at least some form of government involvement, either ownership or control—and in fact for each industry a substantial majority favours government control of prices and profits rather than actual ownership. The Austrians, and to a lesser extent the Germans, err towards a similarly corporatist stance.

Table 5.2 looks at respondents' views on a series of economic policy measures the government might take. On the first four items listed, Australian attitudes are very much in the middle of the wide range of views across countries on each of the issues. Again, Italians are consistently 'for government involvement and Americans fairly consistently against. The Australian pattern, on the other hand, is not particularly distinctive, although further down the list it stands out as having the largest numbers in favour of less government regulation of business and government support for industry to develop new products and technology. Australia, along with the United States, has the smallest proportion favouring a reduced working week to create more jobs. The stances of Australians on some of these questions appear somewhat contradictory, perhaps more so than in other countries. Broadly speaking, Australians favour wage and price controls but they want less government regulation of business; yet they believe the government should provide

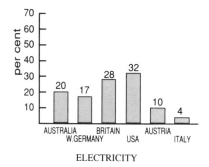

ELECTRICITY

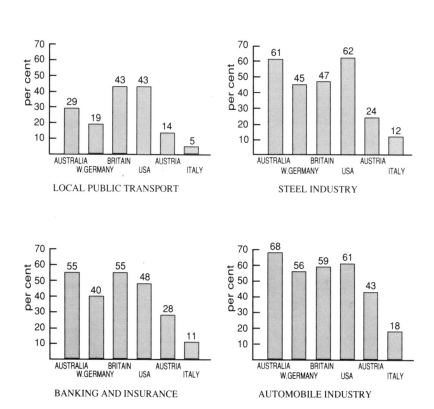

LOCAL PUBLIC TRANSPORT

STEEL INDUSTRY

BANKING AND INSURANCE

AUTOMOBILE INDUSTRY

Figure 5.3 Percentages favouring different industries being run privately rather than by the government, in six nations

Source: International Social Survey Programme Role of Government Survey, 1985–86.

Table 5.2 Cross-national attitudes to government economic action

Per cent in agreement	Australia	West Germany	Great Britain	United States	Austria	Italy
Things the government might do for the economy:						
control of wages by legislation	54	28	32	23	58	72
control of prices by legislation	69	56	60	38	87	90
cuts in govt spending	75	77	38	82	82	68
govt financing of projects to create new jobs	77	71	88	69	72	91
less govt regulation of business	61	41	54	52	47	41
support for industry to develop new products and technology	92	75	90	72	66	84
support declining industries to protect jobs	49	58	50	51	46	74
reducing the working week to create more jobs	26	51	49	27	36	63

Source: International Social Survey Programme Role of Government Survey, 1985–86

financial assistance for industry although they also want cuts in government spending.

Australia does display a fairly distinctive (and consistent in this case) pattern of attitudes towards specific areas of government spending, reflecting a utilitarian and rather conservative approach to the types of things on which members of the public think governments should spend their taxes (figure 5.4). These data tend to endorse the impressionistic views of earlier commentators as to the nature of Australian political culture (for example, Hughes, 1973). The essential message is that when it comes to government spending Australians support the status quo and have little taste for cutting traditional areas in order to shift funding into new ones.

Thus the Australian sample strongly endorses spending on the police and law enforcement (67 per cent would like to see more government spending), education (64 per cent), health (63 per cent) and to a lesser extent old age pensions (55 per cent), but it shows little liking for government spending on culture and the arts (only 10 per cent want more spending) or unemployment benefits (13 per cent). The environment is also viewed as a relatively low priority (32 per cent), particularly by comparison with the countries of continental Europe where, in Austria and West Germany, it is way out in front as the top spending priority. Of course, since the Australian survey was conducted, in late 1986, environmental concerns have become increasingly prominent on the national political agenda and so it is quite conceivable that the environment would currently be viewed more highly as a spending priority. On the other side of the coin extra spending on the military and defence, although favoured by less than half of the Australian respondents (46 per cent), receives much greater backing than it does in any of the other countries, where it is either the bottom priority (by a very large margin in Italy) or second-to-bottom.

The 'no frills', pragmatic approach of the Australians to government spending priorities stands out from the patterns in other countries. While more spending on health is endorsed by majorities everywhere (and by much larger majorities in Britain and Italy than in Australia) and the same is true with respect to education, except in the Germanic countries, Australia is alone in the extent of its concern over the police and law enforcement. The top spending priorities elsewhere (remembering that the priority rankings are inferred from the data rather than being elicited explicitly) are the environment in Germany and Austria, health in Great Britain and Italy and education in the United States. The pre-eminence of health care in Britain and environmental protection in West Germany as spending priorities is confirmed by data from a different source presented by Dalton (1988).

At the opposite extreme from Australia, Italy stands out as having a much more 'culturally imaginative' approach to government spending.

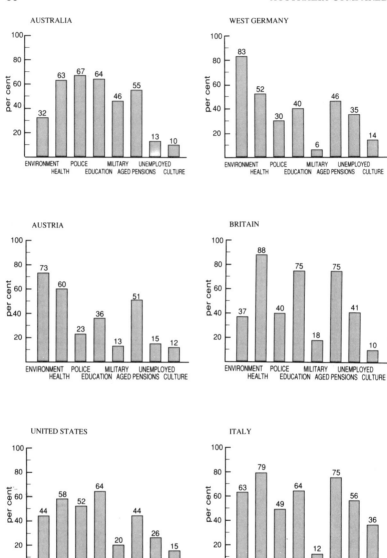

**Figure 5.4 Percentages favouring increases in different areas of government
spending, in six nations**

Source: International Social Survey Programme Role of Government Survey, 1985–86

As well as strongly endorsing spending on the environment, over a third Italians support more spending on culture and the arts, which is more than twice as many as in any other country. Italy is also the only nation in which a majority favours increased spending on unemployment benefits. In fact, in contrast to those surveyed in other countries, whose collective responses indicate that they perceive limits to the amount of money available for government spending and a consequent need to set priorities, Italians only favour lower spending on the military and defence.

Government spending is another area where the reality principle might conceivably apply. OECD data on government expenditure around the time the survey data was collected provides some evidence of opinion reflecting actual government practice in that spending on education is lower in Germany and Austria than elsewhere, thus matching the low levels of endorsement of extra government spending in those two nations. But the education data does not show a close match between government spending levels and public opinion in the remaining countries and for other areas of expenditure systematic patterns of association between reality and opinion appear for the most part to be absent. A partial exception is health, where something of an 'inverse reality principle' seems to apply: the countries with the lowest overall levels of government spending on health (Great Britain and Italy) are the two whose respondents stand out as most wanting increases in this area. In general, however, the reality principle appears to be a rather tenuous one: public opinion is not merely an artifact of political reality.

A DEEPER LOOK AT HOW AUSTRALIA COMPARES

Unlike the data on civil liberties, the impression conveyed by the examination of attitudes to welfare and government intervention in the economy is of much greater cross-national variability. Australian attitudes appear more distinctive in some of the areas surveyed than in others. But cross-national comparisons based purely on marginal distributions of variables are unsatisfactory for a number of reasons. Such distributions are sensitive to sampling fluctuations and measurement error and can be quite unstable. Furthermore, the exact measure chosen as the basis for comparison can affect the results of the comparison (for example, comparing the per cent who agree strongly with a proposition may suggest different implications from comparing all those who agree in some manner).

So with this kind of data we can only make comparisons at a very general level and it is unwise to focus too closely or place much weight on individual variables. Moreover, while comparing attitudes in different countries may be interesting, what makes it important to do so (indeed what makes it important to study attitudes at all) is that attitudes help explain significant social and political behaviours. And, as Verba (1969) argued some twenty years ago, serious cross-national comparisons require variables to be embedded in their contexts; that is, we should study not just the distributions of attitude variables but relationships between variables, while controlling for background factors that may bear some relation to those attitudes.

It is thus time to move away from frequency distributions and apply techniques that help overcome the inherent problems of measurement error in single attitude items, as the first step towards grounding the variables in their contexts and examining the explanatory power of attitudes. The appendix to this chapter shows the results of factor analyses which identify a number of distinct attitude scales in the Australian data among the variables we have been discussing.[3] Three separate dimensions emerge from among the civil liberties and from the welfare variables and four from the economic intervention variables. A single scale is constructed for each dimension identified (the scales are simple additive indexes each of which is assigned a minimum score of nought and a maximum of one).

The mean (or average) scores for these new variables—each of which represents a more general concept underlying the several individual variables which combine to construct it—are shown in figure 5.5. In themselves, these scores are more reliable comparative measures than the individual items in the earlier figures and tables because much of the measurement error has been 'ironed out' in their construction. Nonetheless, as we would expect, figure 5.5 gives a broadly similar picture to the earlier tables.

On the civil liberties questions cross-national similarity is still the main story. The contrast between the broad consent given to more orthodox forms of political protest and the widespread unpopularity of more radical protest styles is particularly evident. With respect to welfare, Australia scores low on the extent to which government should take responsibility for employment and on the desirability of wealth being redistributed from the rich to the poor, along with the United States in both cases (see also Castles, 1989). In the realm of government economic intervention, Australia shows through as being relatively anti-postmaterialism (as measured by attitudes to government spending on the environment and cultural activities),[4] somewhere in the middle on whether government should control wages and prices and on the privatisation (rather than government ownership or control) of public utilities and, finally, at the pro-private enterprise end of the distribution (along, again, with the United States) on the question of what the government's role should be in commercial business enterprises.

There is no good reason at all to expect the distributions of variables to relate to their effects (see Bean and Mughan, 1989). The fact that views on the right of newspapers to publish confidential government papers is relatively uniform across all six nations under study, for instance, does not necessarily imply that such views will have the same implications for, say, political party support cross-nationally. Nor does the fact that in the United States and Australia similar proportions favour private control of big business suggest that this variable should impact on party support equally in these two countries. By the same token, if distributions among some variables are observed to differ across countries, this should not of itself lead to an expectation of differing effects.

The final stage, then, of grounding the attitude variables in their contexts in order to make more rigorous comparative judgments and to demonstrate their importance, comes by way of a multivariate analysis of the influence the ten attitude scales have on that key variable in any modern democracy, political party support. The regression analysis controls for the effects of a wide range of potentially important background social structural variables and also for attitudes to the power of trade unions, a political orientation known to have a strong effect on party preference in Australia and elsewhere (see Kelley, 1988). The results are presented in table 5.3 and in a less technical form in figure 5.6.[5] Since all of the variables are scored between nought and one the unstandardised regression coefficients (bs) can be interpreted as the percentage difference (omitting the decimals) in support for right as opposed to left parties between those at either extreme on the attitude scales.

First, let us take an example by way of illustration. In the Australian equation, the unstandardised (b) coefficient for the scale labelled 'government responsibility for jobs' is -0.16. What this means is that for two hypothetical people who are the same on all the other variables in the equation (that is, they are the same age, same sex, have the same education, religion and so on, and the same attitudes to civil liberties and to economic intervention and to other aspects of welfare) but who have opposite attitudes on whether the government should take responsibility for employment, the one who believes the government should definitely take responsibility is 16 per cent more likely to support the Labor Party, as opposed to the Liberal or National coalition parties, than the one who strongly believes that employment should not be a government responsibility. Or, put another way, there is a 16 per cent difference in party support between those with the most extreme views on this issue. The minus sign simply tells us that believing the government should take responsibility for employment goes with support for Labor, as we would expect, rather than the coalition. (A positive sign would mean those favouring government responsibility were more likely to support the coalition.) Finally, the coefficient is significant at the .05 level. That means we can be confident that the relationship is real

CIVIL LIBERTIES

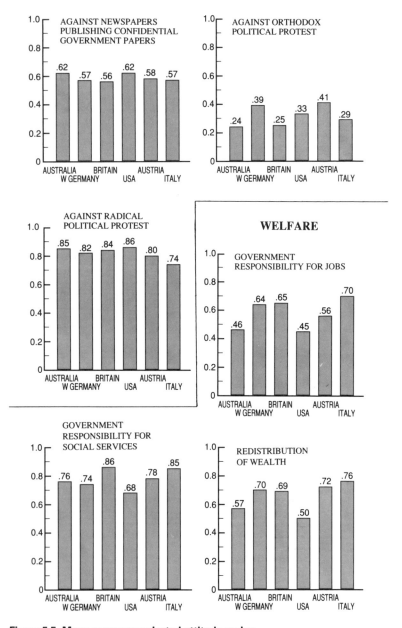

Figure 5.5 Mean scores on selected attitude scales

ECONOMIC INTERVENTION

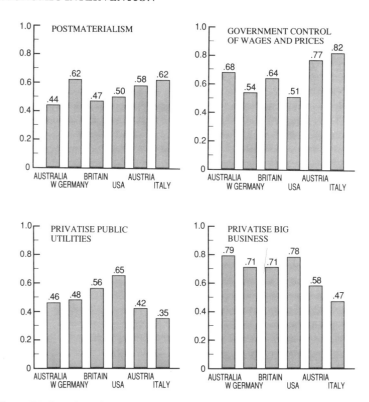

Figure 5.5 (continued)

Source: International Social Survey Programme Role of Government Survey, 1985–86

Figure 5.6 Percentage effects of attitudes on party indentification

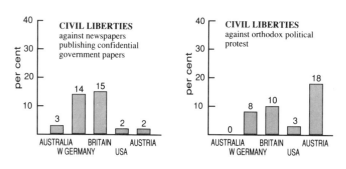

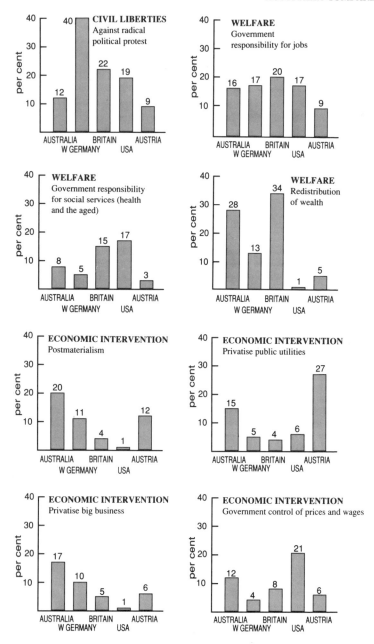

Figure 5.6 (continued)

Note: [a] See table 5.3 for the direction of effects and further methodological details.
Source: Table 5.3

Table 5.3 Multiple regression analyses showing effects of attitude scales on party identification

Variable	Australia		West Germany		Great Britain		United States		Austria	
	b	beta	b	beta	b	beta	b	beta	b	beta
Civil liberties										
Against newspapers publishing confidential govt papers	.03	.02	.14	.12**	.15	.13**	.02	.02	−.02	−.01
Against orthodox political protest	.00	.00	.08	.04	.10	.06	.03	.02	−.18	−.11*
Against radical political protest	−.12	−.05	.40	.16**	.22	.10**	.19	.09	.09	.04
Welfare										
Govt responsibility for jobs	−.16	.07*	−.17	−.07	−.20	−.09*	−.17	−.09	−.09	−.04
Govt responsibility for social services (health and the aged)	−.08	−.02	−.05	−.01	−.15	−.04	−.17	−.08	.03	.01
Redistribution of wealth	−.28	−.14**	−.13	−.06	−.34	−.18**	−.01	−.01	.05	.02
Economic intervention										
Postmaterialism	−.20	−.08**	−.11	−.04	.04	.01	.01	.00	−.12	.05
Government control of prices and wages	−.12	−.06*	−.04	−.02	.08	.04	−.21	−.12*	−.06	−.03
Privatise public utilities	.15	.10**	−.05	−.03	.04	.03	−.06	−.04	.27	.16**
Privatise big business	.17	.09**	.10	.06	.05	.03	−.01	−.01	.06	.04
R²	.31		.34		.40		.20		.29	

Notes: * Significant at $p < .05$ ** Significant at $p < .01$
The analyses control for: age, sex, urban–rural residence (not available for West Germany), education, self-employment, government worker (not available for Austria), trade union membership, subjective social class, catholic, no religion, church attendance and attitudes to trade unions. All attitude scales are scored from 0 to 1; 0.5 for centre parties and no party preference.

Source: International Social Survey Programme Role of Government Survey, 1985–86

and not just an artifact of sampling fluctuations (specifically, there is less than a 5 per cent probability that the effect does not in reality exist).

Turning now to examine the results in detail, by and large they present a picture of considerable dissimilarity across the five countries able to be subjected to the multiple regression analysis. Despite some overlaps, each nation has a unique set of significant attitudinal effects on party support. Even among the civil liberties variables the pattern of uniformity disappears to a large extent. Attitudes to orthodox political protest are insignificant except in Austria, but the impact of views on radical protest varies markedly, from being highly important in Germany, such that people who are against radical protest are more likely to support parties of the right, to having a negative (though not significant) effect in Australia. Attitudes towards the publication of confidential papers have a similarly moderate effect in Germany and Britain but no impact elsewhere.

The extent to which people believe the government should take responsibility for jobs and the jobless produces the most consistent effect across nations (even though it is statistically significant only in Australia and Britain) despite the balance of opinion on the issue differing more from country to country than it does on many of the other attitudes (see figure 5.5). Attitudes to the redistribution of wealth have the strongest effect of all the variables under examination on Australian political party preference (as they do also in Britain), such that someone strongly in favour of redistribution is some 28 per cent more likely to be a Labor party supporter than someone who strongly opposes the redistribution of wealth.

In Australia none of the civil liberties variables matters while all of the economic intervention ones do (in Britain and West Germany a pattern close to the reverse is true). Strong postmaterialists, as defined here in terms of attitudes to government spending, are 20 per cent more likely to support Labor (as opposed to the Liberal or National parties) than those who are very antagonistic to postmaterialist aims. Staunch advocates of government control of prices and wages are 12 per cent more likely to support Labor while those who like public utilities and big business to be run privately are 15 and 17 per cent more inclined to support the coalition parties respectively. Only in the United States (where the wage price control variable is important) and Austria (where attitudes to privatising public utilities have a big impact) are any of the four economic intervention scales significant outside Australia. What this data suggests, therefore, is that government intervention in the economy is an issue with partisan political implications in Australia in a way that it is not elsewhere (on the impact of economic attitudes in Australia, see also Kelley, 1988).

We can relate the regression effects back to the distributions of attitudes to see how their potential consequences vary from country to country. For example, the sizeable impact of attitudes to the redistribution of wealth in both Australia and Britain has substantially different implications for the partisan balance in the two countries because the British are in general considerably more in favour of redistribution than are Australians (see figure 5.5). Thus the Labour Party in Britain is more likely to benefit from this issue being important than is the Labor Party in Australia. In another case, the fact that Australia is the country whose citizens give the strongest endorsement to private control of big business is the more significant because it is also the only country in which such attitudes influence partisanship. By contrast, although Americans stand out as more in favour than other citizens of having public utilities run by private enterprise, the importance of this distinction is reduced because these attitudes appear not to matter for political party support in that nation.

DISCUSSION

In sum, it could probably be said that Australia is both 'a little bit similar and a little bit different' to the other five countries with which it has been compared on attitudes to the role of government. Although in some of the instances where Australian attitudes clearly differ from elsewhere they can be seen to form a quite distinctive pattern (most notably on priorities for government spending), this is not always the case. In some instances Australian attitudes simply appear to be different without being particularly distinctive (for example, with respect to government actions for the economy). Of all the nations, Italy in particular and also the United States appear to possess the most distinctive patterns of attitudes across the range of topics covered.

However, if there is one country in this group of six that Australian attitudes are more similar to more of the time than others it is probably the United States. Yet, overall, the notion of a distinctive Anglo–American political culture (Almond, 1956) receives scant empirical support in these data, for there are very few instances indeed where attitudes to the role of government in Australia, the United States and Britain form a distinct 'block'. Indeed, a stronger case can almost certainly be made that Australia and the United States together betray the legacy of having been 'settler societies'. The concept of what constitutes a 'fair go' in these nations appears to revolve around individual endeavour with a smaller emphasis than elsewhere on the government playing a major role and a greater endorsement of private wealth and of not imposing on the wealthy to share their riches.

Lastly, an interesting question that this research raises is the extent to which observed cross-national differences reflect not so much differences between countries, but rather different political, economic and social situations in the countries at the time. In the British data, for example, we see some evidence of a reaction against the hard-line conservative economic policies of the Thatcher government. Thus the British sample from the mid 1980s is exceptionally opposed to further cuts in government spending generally, while large majorities call for more spending in the key areas of health, education and old age pensions. The British respondents are also strongly in favour of government assistance to industry and the needy. At the same time the fact that the British are comparatively favourable towards the idea of privatising public utilities may indicate that some of the flavour of the prevailing ideology has penetrated into the minds of the public with positive effects. Yet, caution must be exercised with this line of argument, since evidence from elsewhere (for example, Castles, 1989) and indeed a good deal of the evidence in this chapter suggests that there need not be much relationship between public perceptions and current social or political realities at all.

ENDNOTES

[1] The ISSP was begun in the mid-1980s by established academic survey organisations in a number of countries with the aim of conducting annual high quality precisely comparable cross-national attitude surveys of the mass public on selected topics of importance in the social sciences. The membership has now grown to over a dozen countries and its expansion is continuing. The Australian participant is the National Social Science Survey (NSSS), conducted in the Department of Sociology, Research School of Social Sciences, Australian National University. The data, which are publicly available, were supplied by the Zentralachiv fur Empirische Sozialforschung, University of Cologne, West Germany, through the Social Science Data Archives, Australian National University. The ZSSP module itself is always conducted as a self-completion questionnaire, additional to each organisation's regular social survey (usually by mail, as in the case of the Australian NSSS, or as a 'leave-behind' supplement), but apart from that the sampling and survey methods vary across countries (they are described in detail in the codebook which accompanies the data file and in Kelley et al., 1989, for Australia, which also contains the exact question wording of all the attitude items in this analysis). For further details on the ZSSP see Davis and Jowell (1989).

[2] The other two answer categories are that the government should own the industry, or control its prices and profits but not own it.

[3] Factor analysis is a statistical technique which helps identify underlying patterns among sets of variables. Items that reflect the same underlying conceptual dimension 'load' together on one factor and can then be combined to form a single scale (that is more analytically reliable than any one item on its own) representing that concept. For example, in the appendix to this chapter, the first three political protest variables from figure 5.2 form a single dimension (as

can be seen by their high loadings on the first factor—around 0.7 or 0.8) which we have labelled 'orthodox protest'. For further details about factor analysis, see Kim and Mueller (1978).

[4] Note that this is not the conventional way that postmaterialism, as conceived by Inglehart (1977), is measured. For the more conventional application of this concept and a discussion of its meaning, see the chapter by Papadakis in this volume.

[5] The results from an ordinary least squares regression analysis show the separate effect on the dependent variable (in this case party identification) due to each independent variable when the potentially confounding influences of other variables in the equation have been accounted for. For an introduction to multiple regression, see Lewis-Beck (1980). Following convention, in the analysis party affiliation is scored 1 for parties to the right of centre, 0 for parties of the left and 0.5 for minor parties of the centre and for respondents with no party preference. All the attitude scales are also scored between 0 and 1. Missing data are deleted pairwise. Party identification is used in preference to actual voting behaviour because the British data have no measure of the latter variable. In practice the two measures produce very similar results. Unfortunately the analysis cannot be performed for Italy since no measure of party support at all is provided in the Italian data.

ACKNOWLEDGEMENT

Some of the attitude scales used in this chapter were derived from earlier analyses performed by Jonathan Kelley, for which I express gratitude.

REFERENCES

Aitkin, Don (1982) *Stability and Change in Australian Politics* 2nd ed., Canberra: Australian National University Press

Almond, Gabriel A. 'Comparative Political Systems', *Journal of Politics*, 18 (1956), pp. 391–409

Almond, Gabriel A., and Verba, Sidney (1963) *The Civic Culture: Political Attitudes and Democracy in Five Nations* Princeton, New Jersey: Princeton University Press

Bean, Clive (1988) 'Politics and the Public: Mass Attitudes towards the Australian Political System' in Kelley, Jonathan and Bean, Clive (eds) *Australian Attitudes: Social and Political Analyses from the National Social Science Survey* Sydney: Allen & Unwin, pp. 45–57

———— (1989) 'Orthodox Political Participation in Australia', *Australian and New Zealand Journal of Sociology*, 25, pp. 451–479

Bean, Clive and Mughan, Anthony (1989) 'Leadership Effects in Parliamentary Elections in Australia and Britain', *American Political Science Review*, 83, pp. 1165–1179

Castles, Frank (1989) 'Australia's Inequality Paradox', *Australian Society* November, pp. 44–45

Dalton, Russell J. (1988) *Citizen Politics in Western Democracies: Public Opinion and Political Parties in the United States, Great Britain, West Germany and France* Chatham, New Jersey: Chatham House

Davis, James A. and Jowell, Roger (1989) 'Measuring National Differences: An Introduction to the International Social Survey Programme (ISSP)' in Jowell, Roger, Witherspoon, Sharon and Brook, Lindsay (eds) *British Social Attitudes: Special International Report* Aldershot: Gower, pp. 1–13

Hughes, Colin A. (1973) 'Political Culture' in Mayer, Henry and Nelson, Helen (eds) *Australian Politics: A Third Reader* Melbourne: Cheshire, pp. 133–146

Inglehart, Ronald (1977) *The Silent Revolution: Changing Values and Political Styles Among Western Publics* Princeton, New Jersey: Princeton University Press

Jones, F.L. (1989) 'Changing Attitudes and Values in Post-war Australia' in Hancock, Keith (ed.) *Australian Society* Cambridge: Cambridge University Press, pp. 94–118

Kelley, Jonathan (1988) 'Political Ideology in Australia' in Kelley, Jonathan and Bean, Clive (eds) *Australian Attitudes: Social and Political Analyses from the National Social Science Survey* Sydney: Allen & Unwin, pp. 58–77

Kelley, Jonathan, Bean, Clive and Evans, M.D.R. (1989) *Study Description NSSS 1986–87: Role of Government* Canberra: National Social Science Survey, Research School of Social Sciences, Australian National University

Kim, Jae-On and Mueller, Charles W. (1978) *Introduction to Factor Analysis: What It Is and How to Do It* Sage University Paper series on Quantitative Applications in the Social Sciences, 07–013, Beverly Hills and London: Sage Publications

Lewis-Beck, Michael S. (1980) *Applied Regression: An Introduction* Sage University Paper series on Quantitative Applications in the Social Sciences, 07–022, Beverly Hills and London: Sage Publications

Verba, Sidney (1969) 'The Uses of Survey Research in the Study of Comparative Politics: Issues and Strategies' in Rokkan, Stein, Verba, Sidney, Viet, Jean and Almasy, Elina *Comparative Survey Analysis* The Hague and Paris: Mouton, pp. 56–106

Verba, Sidney, Nie, Norman H. and Kim, Jae-On (1971) *The Modes of Democratic Participation: A Cross-National Comparison* London and Beverly Hills: Sage Professional Papers in Comparative Politics

———— (1978) *Participation and Political Equality: A Seven-Nation Comparison* Cambridge: Cambridge University Press

Appendix Varimax rotated factor loadings, from a principal components analysis with unities on the main diagonal, identifying attitude scales for Australia

A Civil liberties	Orthodox protest	Radical protest	Publish confidential papers
Newspaper publish:			
defence plans	−.05	.20	.79
economic plans	.17	−.06	.81
Forms of protest:			
public meetings	.88	−.04	.02
publish pamphlets	.87	−.01	.05
protest marches	.73	.29	.11
occupy govt office	.12	.82	.08
damage govt buildings	−.17	.74	−.01
nationwide strike	.32	.62	.12

B Welfare	Govt responsible for health and aged	Redistribution of wealth	Govt responsible for jobs
Govt reduce work week to create more jobs	.01	.18	.59
Govt spending on unemployment benefits	.14	.06	.81
Govt's responsibility to provide jobs for all	.32	.38	.45
Govt's responsibility to provide for unemployed	.23	.14	.77
Govt spending on health	.64	.06	.05
Govt spending on old age pensions	.63	.04	.24
Govt's responsibility to provide health care for sick	.77	.20	.06
Govt's responsibility to provide for the old	.78	.11	.14
Govt's responsibility to: reduce income differences between rich and poor	.18	.76	.34
reduce differences between high and low incomes	.15	.82	.15
High income earners should pay more tax	.03	.72	.05

Appendix (cont)

C **Economic intervention**	Privatise big business	Govt control of wages/prices	Privatise public utilities	Post-material-ism
Govt spending on:				
the environment	.09	.02	.05	.91
culture and the arts	−.02	.00	.04	.82
Govt control wages	.01	.83	.06	−.01
Govt control prices	.14	.90	.05	.01
Govt's responsibility to keep prices under control	.28	.71	−.03	.04
Govt's role in:				
electricity	.14	.00	.88	.04
local public transport	.18	.07	.86	.06
steel industry	.82	.15	.14	.03
banking and insurance	.80	.11	.16	.03
automobile industry	.86	.14	.08	.04

Source: International Social Survey Programme Role of Government Survey, 1985–86

PART II POLICIES

6 How much are Australia's economy and economic policy influenced by the world economy?

R.G. GREGORY

The trading links between Australia and the rest of the world seem to be very different from the typical OECD economy. Perhaps the most noticeable difference is that international trade is only a small fraction of economic activity. It is not widely known, but in terms of exports as a fraction of GDP, the USA is the most inward looking of all the OECD countries, Japan is second and Australia is third. For the USA and Japan, exports are less than 11 per cent of GDP, and for Australia the proportion is 16 per cent. Some smaller OECD countries, such as Belgium, export as much as 70 per cent of output and larger countries, such as France, export around 30 per cent (table 6.1). Another noticeable difference is that most Australian exports are mineral and rural products. During 1988 coal accounted for 12 per cent of exports, wool for 8 per cent, gold for 6 per cent and iron ore for 4 per cent. The manufacturing share of exports was quite small, somewhere around 33 per cent. For most OECD countries manufacturing products dominate exports and mineral and rural products are inconsequential (table 6.1). Finally, Australian export prices fluctuate more than export prices of other OECD traders. Primary and mineral export prices fluctuate more over the economic cycle and more in response to special factors such as droughts and wars. It follows, therefore, that the Australian terms of trade—export prices divided by import prices—vary more than the terms of trade of most OECD countries.

This different trade structure for Australia leads naturally to questions which are the subject of this chapter. What is the relationship between Australian economic cycles and world economic fluctuations? Since exports are such a small fraction of GDP, are Australian economic cycles largely independent of the rest of the world? Or do fluctuations of export prices and other factors compensate for the small international trade share and perhaps magnify the impact of world economic cycles?

Table 6.1 Export shares: selected countries, 1988

Country	Export share of GDP[1] %	Shares of exports[2]		
		Manufacturing %	Food/raw materials %	Energy %
Australia	16	34	46	20
UK	24	84	9	8
Germany	29	93	6	1
France	31	78	19	2
Italy	20	89	9	2
USA	9	82	15	3
Japan	11	98	1	0

Source: 1. National Accounts, Main Aggregates, vol 1, 1960–1988, OECD 1990
        2. OECD data bases

Although we cannot respond precisely to this set of questions, it is important to develop some feel for the answers, because they are crucial building blocks in the analytical foundations of a second set of questions. Have Australian policies led to economic outcomes different from those of other countries with similar income levels? Can it be said, for example, that Australian economic management is better or worse than average? After discussing the basic data in the next section we address these questions by examining the experiences of the three governments since 1972: the Whitlam Labor Government 1972–75, the Fraser Liberal–National Party Government 1975–83, and the Hawke Labor Government from 1983 onwards. In the remaining sections we change the focus slightly to discuss the importance of labour market institutions and then offer some summary conclusions concerning the way in which Australia's economic performance is linked to the world economy.

THE BASIC DATA

Most Australian exports are directed towards the Pacific Rim. In 1989 these countries accounted for over seventy per cent of Australian exports and it would be natural to relate fluctuations in export receipts and the Australian economy to growth variations in these economies. Instead, we begin by comparing Australian economic cycles with those of the European Economic Community which accounts for only 14 per cent of Australian exports.[1] We adopt this methodology rather than the standard cross-national comparison of many countries for the following reasons. First, we compare Australia to a group of countries

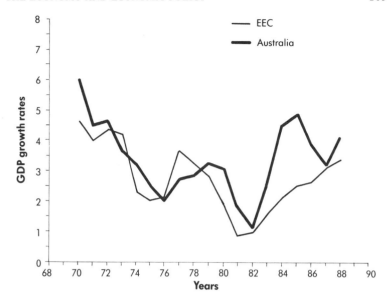

Figure 6.1 GDP growth rates: Australia and EEC, 1969–89

Note: Three year moving average of GDP growth rates
Source: OECD Economic Outlook, June 1990, table R1

to emphasise the importance of world cycles and not to become over conscious of changing outcomes of individual countries. Second, we choose the EEC because in terms of direct economic links the EEC is only weakly tied to Australia and consequently EEC–Australian correlations will more clearly identify the effects of a general and diffused world economic cycle. Finally, towards the end of the chapter the contrast between EEC and the USA outcomes can be used to illustrate an important economic debate.

We focus on three measures of macro economic performance; the rate of growth of output of goods and services in constant prices (Gross Domestic Product), inflation and the unemployment rate.[2] Other important measuring rods such as the growth of labour productivity, real wages and household incomes are put aside (but see Dowrick, chapter 7).

Figure 6.1 plots the rate of growth of Gross Domestic Product (GDP) for Australia and the EEC. To focus on the business cycle, rather than individual year to year fluctuations which may be produced by random factors or measurement errors in the national accounts, we smooth the series by subjecting them to a three year moving average. Thus, the rate of growth of GDP during 1969, 1970 and 1971 will be added together, divided by three and then placed in figure 1 opposite 1970, then the GDP growth of 1970, 1971 and 1972 will be averaged and placed against 1971 and so on. This smoothing technique is very useful and none of the important movements in the series is lost.

A number of noticeable features are obvious in the GDP data and the most important is the similarity of the two series. Fluctuations in Australian growth rates look much the same as fluctuations in EEC growth rates. Both data series reveal high growth rates during the 1960s which gradually decline to reach a trough during the mid 1970s which was the first major world recession since the 1930s. To explain this slowdown some commentators place particular emphasis on the commodity boom of 1972–73 and the oil price shock of 1973, when oil prices trebled. It is evident, however, that the slowdown had begun well beforehand. It is interesting in this regard to note that commentators often argue that Australia gains from commodity booms and upward oil price shocks because it does not import significant quantities of oil and is a net energy exporter. The Treasurer, for example, made similar arguments in 1990 as the oil price increased in response to the Iraqi invasion of Kuwait. By a similar argument the EEC loses in these circumstances as, on balance, it is a net energy importer. However, any such income redistribution between energy importing EEC and energy exporting Australia, which might be expected to affect relative GDP growth rates, is not obvious in the data.

After the 1975 recession there is a mild recovery in Australia and the EEC until the early 1980s when another recession occurs, again following an oil price shock. Finally, there has been a long expansion since 1982 as growth rates have steadily increased, but not to mid 1960s levels. Australia experienced strong growth relative to the EEC in 1984 and 1985 but since then growth rates have been much the same.

The similarity of GDP growth rates translates into the utilisation rate of human resources. A moving average of Australian and EEC unemployment rates is given in figure 6.2 and again the similarity is remarkable. During the 1950s and 1960s the Australian economy constantly produced one of the world's lowest unemployment rates which typically varied between 1 and 2 per cent of the workforce. Unemployment in the EEC was higher than this, typically varying between 2 and 3 per cent. Then, beginning around 1975, in response to the world recession and slow growth rates, unemployment drifted upwards in both Australia and the EEC. There was a pause in the rate of increase during the late 1970s and then, in response to the recession in the early 1980s, the three year moving average of unemployment increased to 11 per cent in the EEC and 9 per cent in Australia. The strong GDP growth since 1983 has prevented unemployment from increasing further, as Austra-

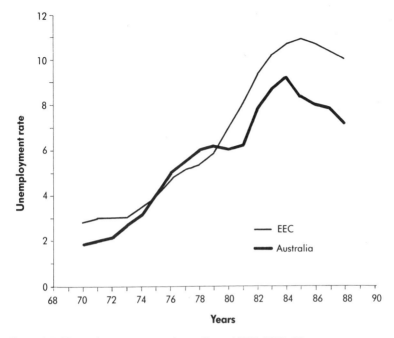

Figure 6.2 Unemployment rates: Australia and EEC, 1969–89

Note: Three year moving average of unemployment rates
Source: OECD Economic Outlook, June 1990, table R18

lian unemployment has fallen by about 40 per cent but the EEC reduction has been quite small. The seemingly inexorable increases in
unemployment in the 1970s and early 1980s in Australia and the EEC,
whereby unemployment increased quickly in each recession but only
slowly fell afterwards, or not at all, and then increased to higher levels
in the next recession, has led to the application of the term *hysteresis* to
the unemployment rate. Hysteresis suggests that each increase in unemployment moves the equilibrium unemployment rate to a new higher
level and the term expresses the pessimism that generally prevails in
Europe and Australia with regard to prospects of reducing unemployment to 1950s and 1960s levels. In 1990 unemployment was increasing
again in Australia and exceeded 7 per cent.   The outlook of unemployment in the EEC is more confusing as the EEC economies were
about to enter a downswing which now looks as if it could be short-lived
as a result of the general stimulus provided by the liberalisation of East-
ern Europe.

Finally, we turn to inflation. Governments regard high inflation rates as undesirable because they redistribute income, usually away from the poor and those on fixed incomes, make planning difficult for investors, and as a result of interactions with the personal income tax system and its non symmetric treatment of interest received and paid, there are significant biases between real after tax interest rates received by lenders and paid by borrowers. All countries set low inflation rates as an economic objective. For example, The Reserve Bank Act of Australia, 1959, stated that:

> It is the duty of the Board, within the limits of its powers, to ensure that the monetary and banking policy of the Bank is directed to the greatest advantage of the people of Australia and that the powers of the Bank . . . are exercised . . . [to] best contribute to the stability of the currency of Australia; the maintenance of full employment in Australia; and the economic prosperity and welfare of the people of Australia.

The inflation rate experience of Australia and the EEC is given in figure 6.3. After the early 1950s, when inflation from the Korean War abated, Australia became a low inflation country until the end of the 1960s when inflation began to increase quickly to reach a peak at 15 per cent around 1975. Since then the rate has fallen until in 1990 it was about 7 to 8 per cent. Once again the similarity between Australia and the EEC is remarkable, especially until 1982, after which inflation falls more quickly in the EEC and is currently proceeding at around 3 to 4 per cent.

To sum up the economic performance of Australia and the EEC has been virtually identical until the mid-1980s since when Australian GDP has grown marginally faster in the upswing, unemployment has fallen more and inflation fallen less.

THE CONTRIBUTION OF ECONOMIC POLICY

All governments seem to believe that economic policy matters and that they have a large degree of control over their economic affairs. The Australian government is no exception. Furthermore, some governments acquire reputations for good economic management, for example, the Menzies Liberal–Country Party Government during the 1950s and 1960s was widely regarded as a successful economic manager, with the exception of the events leading to the 1961 credit squeeze. Others have acquired reputations for bad economic management, for example, the Whitlam Labor Government, 1972–75. What do comparisons of the previous section suggest as to the relative performance of recent Australian governments?

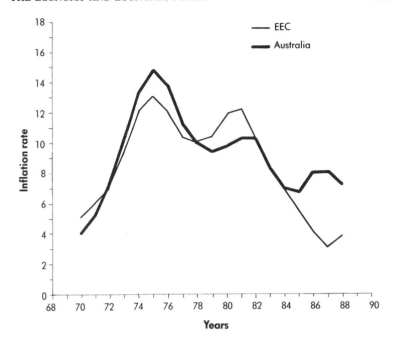

Figure 6.3 Inflation rates: Australia and EEC, 1969–89

Note: Three year moving average of inflation rates
Source: OECD Economic Outlook, June 1990, table R11

To begin to answer this question it is first necessary to understand why output growth rates of Australia, with its specialised exports mainly to Japan, Asia and North America are so similar to the EEC? Among possible answers are the following:

1 the similarity of experience was an accident,
2 world economic influences are so pervasive and important relative to economic policy that it does not matter much what policies are followed,
3 economic policy is important, but Australian policy reactions to pervasive world economic influences were much the same as other EEC governments with similar GDP growth rates being the result.

It is fairly easy to discount the possibility that similar GDP outcomes were an accident. If the comparison is extended further back, the relationship between EEC and Australian GDP fluctuations would still be

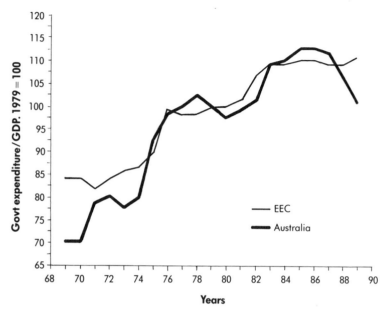

Figure 6.4 Government expenditure/GDP: Australia and EEC, 1969–89

Source: OECD Economic Outlook, June 1990, table R15

close. There are just too many similarities in the cycles for the correlations to be fortuitous. Although it is not easy to assess accurately the independent impact of policy, I would suggest, on balance, that the correct answer is somewhere between 2 and 3, the similarity of GDP experiences is predominantly the result of pervasive world influences, and, although these influences lead to similar policies being followed in most EEC countries, the policy contribution is usually a minor part of the outcome.[3]

There are a number of ways that the similarity of broad economic policies can be demonstrated. For example, we can measure fiscal policy in terms of variations in government expenditure as a proportion of GDP (figure 6.4). Although the increase in government expenditure until recently has been greater in Australia, once again the experience of fluctuations has been similar in the EEC and Australia as government expenditure increased significantly during the mid 1970s in a Keynesian policy attempt to offset the recession. Government expenditure also increased in response to welfare payments generated by higher unemployment rates. Expenditure increased again in response to the 1981 recession, but, since then governments have attempted to reduce expenditure as a proportion of GDP with limited success in the EEC, but considerable success in Australia.[4]

We could also measure the stance of fiscal policy by the balance between government expenditures and receipts. Since 1975 both country sets have experienced government deficits as tax receipts have not kept pace with expenditure. Again there is a broad similarity of outcomes, although recently Australia seems to have done a little better in turning the government deficit around. Despite these large deficits, it is evident from figures 6.1 and 6.2 that GDP growth and unemployment levels were not returned to earlier levels after the 1975 recession and it is now widely believed that Keynesian policies of increasing government expenditure to stimulate economic activity are not as effective as once thought. The links between increasing government expenditure and private sector responses are quite complex and the extent of crowding-out of private sector output by higher interest and exchange rates generated by government deficits has become a matter of debate (De Long and Summers, 1988).

Finally, the changing stance of monetary policy might be measured by fluctuations in a moving average of real interest rates (figure 6.5). Again experiences are similar in Australia and the EEC. Real interest rates fell in the early 1970s and became negative as nominal interest rates lagged behind inflation increases. During the 1980s there are historically high real interest rates as nominal interest rates increase and inflation rates decrease and, on average, real interest rates have been 2 to 3 percentage points higher in Australia.

This data on economic outcomes and policy responses suggests that world economic influences are pervasive and support our conjecture that policy responses, at least as measured in the broad aggregates of government expenditure, tax revenue and interest rates respond in a similar way in our set of economies. With this data base we can now look anew at the reputation of different governments as economic managers. We focus most of our attention on the Whitlam, Fraser and Hawke governments.

First, the Whitlam Labor government of 1972–75 was blamed for allowing inflation to increase to double digit levels. It has been argued that fiscal and monetary policy were not sufficiently tight during 1973 and, as a result, excess demand in labour and product markets in 1973 and early 1974 generated the highest rates of inflation since the Korean War. It does appear to be true from figure 6.3 that our relative inflation performance was perhaps 2 percentage points worse than the EEC, but if the EEC is regarded as a norm most of the acceleration of inflation could not be avoided. Furthermore, being an exporter of commodities for which price increases were greatest during this period, it may not have been possible to conform to EEC inflation standards. Consequent-

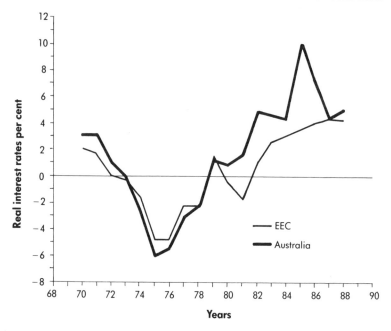

Figure 6.5 Real interest rates: Australia and EEC, 1969–89

Note: EEC—Long term interest rates for France, Germany, Italy and the United Kingdom adjusted for the rate of change of the consumer price index
Source: Norton WE, Garmston PM, Australian Economic Statistics, Occasional Paper No 8A, Reserve Bank of Australia, tables S12, S24

ly, although the Whitlam government may not have managed inflation well, it does not seem correct to blame it for the range of price increases from around 4 per cent when it took office to about 15 per cent when it left. Most of this change seems to be unavoidable world inflation. Secondly, the Whitlam Labor government was blamed for increasing unemployment, partly as a result of unemployment benefit increases, and as a reaction to tight monetary policy introduced to control inflation. It does seem that Australian unemployment slipped a little relative to the EEC towards the end of this period, but once again differences from the EEC seem slight. In any event monetary policy tightened throughout the world at this time and the Whitlam government had little choice as to how to respond to Australian and world inflation. Thirdly, the Whitlam Labor government was accused of being profligate by increasing government expenditure and creating government deficits. There is clearly some substance to this proposition as government expenditure has increased more in Australia than in the EEC, especially during the early years of the Labor Government. However, in response to the beginning of the 1975 recession, the Australian experience was much the same as the EEC, as were subsequent expenditure changes. On balance, therefore, Australia does seem to have done marginally worse during this period, but the overwhelming influence seems to have been economic developments in the world economy.

During the Fraser Liberal government years, 1975–82, the Australian performance was marginally better than the EEC, unemployment increases were less and inflation reduced more, but once again economic outcomes were dominated by similar changes in the EEC. The Fraser government was regarded, especially until its last year, as pursuing sound fiscal policies as it attempted to reduce the government deficit, and there is evidence of some degree of success relative to the EEC. However, in broad outline expenditure variations seem much the same as those of EEC governments just as the behaviour of the Whitlam government had been.

INFLATION AND UNEMPLOYMENT IN MORE DEPTH; THE ACCORD 1983–

During the 1950s and especially the 1960s, it was usual to talk of a trade-off between unemployment and inflation and to believe the economic system presented policy makers with a set of choices of inflation and unemployment rates. Good economic policy consisted of implementing policies to choose the best combination of these undesirable outcomes of the economic system. This way of thinking about macroeconomics is illustrated in figure 6.6, where AA plots the locus of inflation and unemployment generated by the structure of labour and product markets. This locus was named the Phillips curve after a New Zealander who subsequently held a Chair of Economics at the Australian National University. The relationship AA indicates that lower rates of unemployment are associated with excess demand in labour and product markets which produce higher rates of wage and price inflation. The curve BB maps the combination of inflation and unemployment that produces similar degrees of political satisfaction. Thus, for the degree of political satisfaction to remain constant at each point on BB, more inflation, which is politically unpopular, would need to be compensated with lower unemployment, which is politically popular. Good economic management consists of trying to locate the economy near a point such as C. Any other point will lie outside the BB set and therefore involve more inflation and/or more unemployment than necessary.

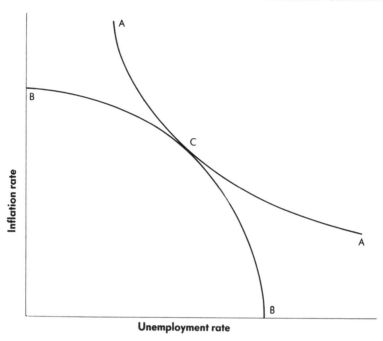

Figure 6.6 The Phillips curve

The second aspect of policy is to adopt labour and product market policies which will move the Phillips curve inwards towards the axis so the trade-off choice is improved.

The experiences of the 1970s and 1980s have shown that this conceptualisation of the relationship between macro policy and economic outcomes was far too simple. Figure 6.7 reproduces the actual inflation and unemployment data for Australia and the average of the EEC economies. The relationship does not look at all like a Phillips curve as during the early 1970s unemployment and inflation increased together, then from the mid 1970s until the early 1980s unemployment increased rapidly with only small reductions in inflation and now, if trade-offs exist, they lie far to the right of earlier experiences. As might be expected the theory of the Phillips curve has become more complicated in an attempt to explain this behaviour. This changing Phillips curve has had a profound effect on the attitudes of governments and has led to a greater divergence of economic policies.

During the Fraser years, the Labor opposition became increasingly interested in incomes policies as a third arm of policy, in addition to fiscal and monetary policy, to move the Phillips curve to the left to-

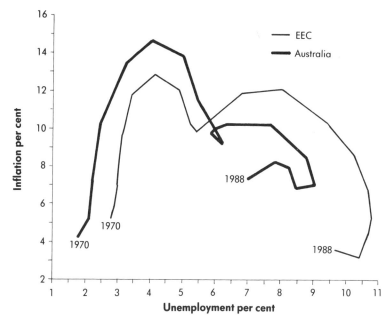

Figure 6.7 Inflation and unemployment: Australia and EEC, 1968–89

Note: Three year moving average
Source: OECD Economic Outlook, June 1990, tables R11 and R18

wards the position it held during the 1950s and 1960s. The Labour opposition became convinced that, if they could reach an agreement with the Australian Council of Trade Unions (ACTU) to exercise wage moderation, they might succeed, upon coming to government, to generate faster economic growth by traditional Keynesian means without rekindling nominal or real wages increases that would, of necessity, bring expansion to a halt. Just before coming to government in 1983 they signed the Prices and Incomes Accord with the ACTU. This is a fairly general agreement, the conditions of which have changed as problems facing the Labor government have altered.[5] For example, very early in the life of the government it became obvious that the economy could not be further stimulated by increases in government expenditure. Indeed policy would need to be directed towards reducing the government deficit and, if there was to be fast economic growth, it would need to come from the private sector. Consequently, the focus of the Accord shifted to moderate further and perhaps even reduce real wages to restore the profit share from its historical low levels during the

1970s to something approaching the levels of the 1950s and 1960s (Dowrick, chapter 7). A higher profit share should generate private sector investment and employment growth should follow.

Incomes policies similar to the Accord were widely used in Europe during the 1960s and 1970s to try and improve the unemployment–inflation trade-off, but gradually became less popular. It is generally thought that they contribute to inflation reductions for a while, but trade unions become quickly dissatisfied with the restraint placed upon them, the incomes policy fails and inflation accelerates to undo any temporary gains. Australian policy with respect to this instrument was moving in the opposite direction to most EEC countries.

In terms of figure 6.1, the Accord of the Hawke government may have impacted favourably on GDP growth in the early recovery years from the 1982 recession. The contrast with the 1975 recession is interesting in that, after that recession, Australia did not recover at a faster rate than the EEC. On balance, therefore, and relative to the EEC, the evidence might suggest the Accord stimulated economic growth perhaps lifting the level of GDP to 8 to 10 per cent higher than it might otherwise have been.

The largest potential effects of the Accord, however, seem to be apparent in figures 6.2 and 6.3, where differences in the pre- and post-Accord periods are quite marked. If the Accord has had an effect it has most likely prevented Australian inflation from falling as fast as EEC inflation but, on the other hand, it has reduced Australian unemployment much more. The widening gap between Australia and the EEC in these dimensions is evident in the last five points of figure 6.7, where almost all the improvement in Australian performance has been in terms of unemployment reductions and in the EEC, until recently, the improvement is mostly in terms of reductions in price inflation. This allocation of gains is what might be expected as the values of the Labor government tend to favour unemployment reductions relative to inflation reductions just as the values of the Liberal–National Party prefer more inflation reductions and are less concerned with unemployment (see Hibbs, 1977).

THE USA COMPARISON

The main theme of this chapter is the overall similarity of EEC and Australian experience, with perhaps some divergence apparent during the Accord period of the Australian Labor government. We are now in a position to re-emphasise why we undertook the comparison with the EEC rather than a comparison with Japan, the USA or an aggregate of countries from the Pacific Rim.

First, the juxtaposition of similar EEC and Australian outcomes

THE ECONOMY AND ECONOMIC POLICY

117

against the fact that direct links between the two regions are not particularly strong helps to underscore the point that the world economy is closely tied together in a vast number of ways other than through direct international trade flows. These links include international capital flows, second round effects of changes in trade between individual countries, policies of multi-nationals and the general spread of information and confidence as to the future path of the world economy. Increasingly we are living in a global village. Because the total effect of world links is so strong, world economic events are the predominant influence on Australia and to compare economic performances of different governments full account must be taken of the prevailing world economic outlook. A comparison of higher unemployment and lower inflation of the Fraser Liberal–National government 1975–83, for example, against the higher inflation and lower unemployment of the Whitlam Labor government years, 1972–75, is misleading. The world environment facing each government was very different and, as a consequence, so were the feasible domestic policy stances and their outcomes.

Second, the comparison with the EEC can be used to highlight an important economic debate. The gradual increase in unemployment in most countries over the last decade and a half has led to a questioning of the efficiency of different labour market structures and the view has evolved that perhaps Australian and EEC labour markets are not as efficient as they should be (Blanchard and Summers, 1986). The argument usually proceeds in two steps. The first step is that countries dominated by trade unions, without a high degree of centralised wage bargaining, do not have a sufficient degree of real wage flexibility to maintain full employment and stable prices when exposed to large economic shocks. Consequently, when subject to an upward oil price shock at the same time as high levels of excess demand—as occurred during the early 1970s—there are increases in real wages, inflation and unemployment which take a long time to unwind in these types of economies. Trade unions prevent the real wage falls that are necessary and keep nominal wage increases high. The second step in the argument is that the extensive development of the welfare state in Europe and Australia, relative to the USA, has gradually reduced labour market flexibility and individual incentives to leave unemployment in those economies. Consequently, when unemployment increases the duration of unemployment lengthens, hysteresis sets in and the equilibrium or long run unemployment rate increases.

At the broadest level, the evidence for these arguments has been based on a comparison of European and Australian outcomes— economies with strong unions and wage rigidities[6]—with those of the USA—an economy with few unions and wage flexibility. This is the methodology we will adopt in figures 6.8, 6.9 and 6.10. With regard to

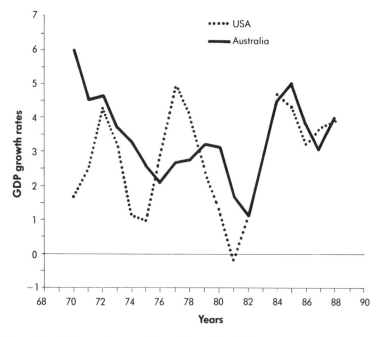

Figure 6.8 GDP growth rates: Australia and the USA, 1969–89

Note: Three year moving average
Source: OECD Economic Outlook, June 1990, table R1

growth, the Australian and USA variations of GDP growth rates have closely tracked each other since the first oil price shock, with perhaps the USA economy being more volatile (figure 6.8). Indeed the two countries almost appear as one and any differences in labour market structure over this period seem not to have affected the average output growth rates. Before the 1973 shock, however, Australian GDP growth rates were much higher than the USA, sometimes to the extent of 3 to 5 percentage points, but these differences were grouped together in the Vietnam War years, which may well explain the different outcomes. At this level of aggregation therefore there does not appear to be a difference in labour market flexibility which affects relative GDP growth rates. If labour market flexibility is important in the comparison of the USA and Australian outcomes, it will need to have more force with regard to other policy outcomes, such as unemployment and inflation.

Before 1975 unemployment in the USA was considerably higher than in Australia and the EEC, and was generally attributed to the wide

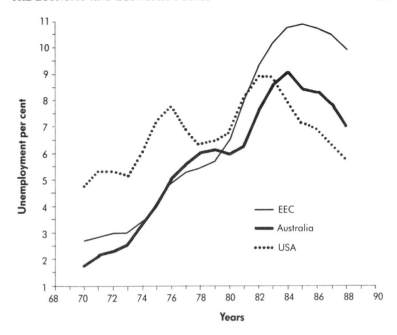

Figure 6.9 Unemployment rates: Australia, EEC and the USA, 1969–89

Note: Three year moving average
Source: OECD Economic Outlook, June 1990, table R18

diversity of regional labour market experiences combined with high
unemployment rates in the USA inner city areas. Since 1975, however,
the unemployment relationship between them has changed and, by
1982, unemployment in the EEC had surpassed that of the USA, as had
unemployment in Australia by 1983 (figure 6.9). By the end of the 1980s
the unemployment gap had widened further and the USA is now, in
relative terms, a low unemployment country with unemployment rates
only marginally above pre-1970 levels. Australia has slipped a long way
behind. Its position has deteriorated from unemployment rates, which
were about half those of the USA, to unemployment rates that are now
about 25 per cent higher. Almost identical GDP growth rates for
Australia and the USA since 1975 have not been sufficient to reduce
Australian unemployment relative to the USA. Australia needs to grow
faster than the USA to keep unemployment low.

The extent of the deterioration in Australia and the EEC is clearly
evident in unemployment duration (table 6.2). During the 1960s unemployment duration was not very different across most countries as few

Table 6.2 Proportion of unemployed exceeding twelve months duration

	1979 %	1981 %	1983 %	1985 %	1987 %
Australia	18	21	29	37	33
EEC	30	30	38	44	45
USA	4	7	16	12	10

Source: Employment Outlook OECD, various issues

people experienced unemployment beyond twelve months. By 1979, however, 30 per cent of the unemployed in the EEC had been unemployed for twelve months, 18 per cent in Australia and only 4 per cent in the USA. By 1983 these proportions had increased to 38, 29 and 16 per cent respectively. Since then unemployment duration has decreased markedly in the USA but has remained high in Australia and has continued to increase in the EEC.

The inflation history is a little more complicated (figure 6.10). All countries experienced increased inflation during the 1970s, but Australia and the EEC were the most severely affected during the 1974 boom. USA inflation rates seem to have caught up during the next upswing at the end of the 1970s, but since then EEC and USA inflation rates have fallen to levels below four per cent, which are comparable to inflation rates of the 1960s. Australia has failed to make further significant inroads in inflation since 1984. Relative to the USA, therefore, Australia has reduced both unemployment and inflation less over the last eight years and our performance is unambiguously worse in terms of these economic objectives. The EEC has matched the USA with regard to inflation outcomes but the unemployment record is very much worse.

Why is it that in terms of inflation and unemployment the USA economy has performed so much better than Australia? Can any of this better performance be attributed to superior economic policy? Fiscal policy has certainly been more expansionary under Reagan during the early 1980s, perhaps leading to faster economic growth. Monetary policy has also been a little tighter on average, perhaps reducing inflation, but most commentators attribute the better performance to a more flexible labour market. This flexibility of real and nominal wages seems not to affect relative GDP growth rates but to affect inflation, employment and unemployment. It appears, for a given rate of GDP growth, that more flexible labour markets seem better able to absorb unemployed workers, primarily as a result of slower labour productivity growth.[7]

It has been argued that, if an economy is dominated by strong unions, then it is better to centralise wage fixing rather than allow the trade unions to compete among themselves for higher real wage in-

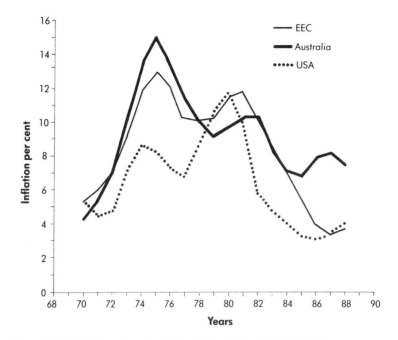

Figure 6.10 Inflation rates: Australia, EEC and the USA, 1969–89

Note: Three year moving average
Source: OECD Economic Outlook, June 1990, table R11

creases (Calmfors and Driffill, 1988). The Australian outcomes, relative
to the EEC, provide an example of this. The EEC countries, on average,
have been far less centralised than Australia under an Accord process
and Australia does seem to have performed better in all dimensions
except inflation. Centralised wage fixing, however, has not enabled
Australian outcomes to be better than the USA which is a relatively
free labour market.

CONCLUDING REMARKS

First, the overwhelming impression created by data presented in this
essay is the similarity of economic experiences of Australia, EEC and
the USA. This similarity, which we interpret to be the result primarily
of the pervasive influence of the world economy, and to a lesser extent
to similar policies pursued by governments of OECD countries, has the
important implication that the economic policy performance of Austra-

lian governments cannot be assessed without regard to the world environment. It appears, for example, as though the high inflation of the Whitlam years and increasing unemployment of the Fraser years were primarily the result of world influences. This does not mean that domestic policies are irrelevant, but that performance must be assessed relative to the prevailing world environment at the time. Looked at in these terms it is possible that governments with high inflation records, when world inflation is high, may be performing better than those with low inflation records, when world inflation is low.

Secondly, during the period of the Hawke Labor government, Australia's performance with regard to unemployment has deviated from EEC and USA patterns, suggesting that perhaps the Accord, with its centralised wage fixing processes, has enabled Australia to perform better than the EEC, at least with respect to output and unemployment, but worse than the USA. With respect to inflation Australia has done worse than both, suggesting perhaps that the price for a better unemployment record with this policy instrument is a higher rate of inflation.

Finally, it should be remembered that we have adopted a very broad brush approach and that many detailed aspects of policy have been ignored. Furthermore, some commentators suggest that it is too early to assess fully the ramifications of the Accord process and argue that it would have been better to have taken this opportunity to deregulate the labour market and begin the process of moving towards USA labour market institutions. These, however, are complicated issues which are not as yet fully understood.

ENDNOTES

[1] The European Economic Community consists of Belgium, Denmark, France, Germany, Greece, Ireland, Italy, Luxembourg, The Netherlands, Portugal, Spain and the United Kingdom. Greece, Portugal and Spain joined in the 1980s.

[2] A discussion of the importance of these economic objectives can be found in Maxwell, 1987.

[3] An exception to this proposition is the 1961 credit squeeze imposed after the Australian government liberalised import quotas. This major recession was not shared by the EEC.

[4] More recent data for Australia indicates further falls in government expenditure as a proportion of GDP.

[5] For a fuller discussion of the Accord and its effects see B.J. Chapman and F. Gruen, 1990.

[6] It is important to be aware of the quite considerable diversity in union density in these nations, with Denmark and Belgium having much greater membership than Australia, and countries like Turkey, Greece and Spain, far less. Nor, of course, do wage rigidities come from unions alone. For the EEC countries, a

common—and significant—set of rigidities stem from obligations under the Treaty of Rome.
[7] For further reading on this topic see, Bruno and Sachs, 1985.

REFERENCES

Blanchard, O.J. and Summers, L. (1986) 'Hysteresis and the European Unemployment Problem', in S. Fischer ed. *NBER Macro economics Annual* (1986) MIT Press pp. 15–78

Bruno, M. and Sachs, J. (1985) *The Economics of Worldwide Stagflation* Cambridge, MA: Harvard University Press

Calmfors, L. and Driffill, J. (1988) 'Centralisation of Wage Bargaining', *Economic Policy*, April pp. 14–61

Chapman, B.J. and Gruen, F. (1990) 'An Analysis of the Australian Consensual Incomes Policy: The Prices and Incomes Accord' in *Centre for Economic Policy Research*, Discussion Paper, 221

De Long, J.B. and Summers, L. (1988) 'How does Macro economic policy Affect Output', *Brookings Papers on Economic Activity* 2 pp. 433–495

Hibbs, D.A. (1977) 'Political Parties and Macroeconomic Policy', *American Political Science Review* 71 pp. 1467–87

Maxwell, P. (1987) *Macroeconomics* Sydney: Harper and Row

7 Has the pattern of Australian wage growth been unique?

STEVE DOWRICK

The last two decades have seen some major changes in Australian government attitudes and policies towards wages, moving from an interventionist approach aimed at increasing wages to attempts to restrain wages first through an adversarial approach and then through consensus. The aim of this chapter is to examine first the extent to which these aims have been achieved and secondly the extent to which both aims and outcomes have been conditioned by, or have deviated from, economic developments in the domestic and world economy. This latter objective makes this study an example of the way in which comparative analysis can be used as a testbed for hypotheses concerning the functioning of Australian economic and institutional structures. Viewing the Australian experience in isolation may incline us to the view that we are in some way unique. That may well be so in some areas, but can only be demonstrated by locating Australian patterns of development in cross-national perspective.

The institutional context of wage setting in Australia differs markedly from that in virtually all other advanced nations. Only New Zealand has had experience of a similar system of compulsory conciliation and arbitration, leading to wage decisions handed down by a quasi-judicial organ of the state. Since early this century Australia has possessed a set of institutions designed to regulate economic behaviour that are highly distinctive, and which have been claimed by some to offer particular advantages in permitting government control of the economy (Phelps Brown, 1969: 114).

A fascinating feature of the Australian wage setting system is the way in which it gives us insights into government attitudes towards economic policy in general and wages in particular, attitudes which are not necessarily articulated explicitly and publicly by governments in other countries. Wage cases heard by the Industrial Commission in Australia provide a forum in which governments may, if they so wish, present a public case for wages policy. The Commission's decisions can also significantly affect wage growth, though actual outcomes can, of course, differ from those which the government advocates or even from what the Commission recommends. Knowing the nature of the government's views as presented to the Commission allows us to make informed surmises as to its intentions in the wages policy arena. That, in turn, allows us to compare commonwealth government intentions with Australian wage outcomes as well as with wage developments in other nations in similar periods.

GOVERNMENT POLICY AND WAGE OUTCOMES 1972–89

The election of a federal Labor government in 1972 marks a watershed in recent Australian economic, as well as political and social, history. To the extent that previous conservative governments had intervened over the previous decade in National Wage Cases, it had been to advocate wage restraint, especially in the face of rising wage and price inflation in the early 1970s. The incoming Labor administration, however, pursued an active wages policy aimed at raising labour incomes.

The Whitlam government sought to achieve social and economic justice through reductions in perceived inequalities in income distribution, inequalities between labour and capital and also inequalities between women and men. This involved the government, or at least the Minister for Labour, Clyde Cameron, stating in a submission to the May 1973 National Wage Case that 'it is the Commonwealth's opinion that there is scope in the capacity and the flexibility of the Australian economy for an appreciable increase in wages without undesirable inflationary consequences'[1] (Nieuwenhuysen and Sloan, 1978: 112). A reasonable interpretation of this statement would be that the government was advocating a substantial redistribution of national income away from profits in favour of wage and salary earners. In addition to pursuing this aim through the Arbitration Commission the government acted through the Public Service Board to achieve major improvements in wages and conditions of work for its own employees, a policy widely interpreted as a deliberate attempt to set the pace for wage settlements in the private sector.

The government's commitment to shifting the distribution of wage income in favour of women was exemplified by its encouragement of the Board to implement equal pay immediately, rather than to exercise the option of phasing in pay increases. This latter option had been suggested by the Arbitration Commission in making the 1972 Equal Pay judgment.

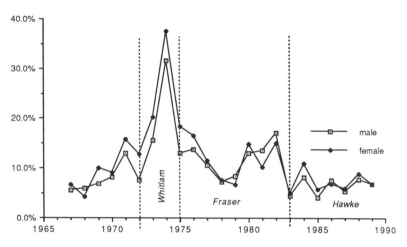

Figure 7.1 Australian nominal wage inflation, 1967–89

Source: ABS

The apparent impact of these policies is evident in that over the two years from October 1973 average weekly earnings rose by 43 per cent for men and by 60 per cent for women. Prices rose by 33 per cent, a substantial price inflation but not enough to erode fully the increase in purchasing power of wages. The rapid growth of nominal wages and the consequent rises in real earnings (on both an hourly and a weekly basis) are illustrated in figures 7.1–3. Real hourly earnings are also shown 'post-tax', reducing actual hourly earnings by the ratio of gross PAYE payments to total wage and salary income. 'Earnings' refer to total earnings including overtime payments.

It is evident that the rates of increase of both real and nominal wages under the benign patronage of the Whitlam government constitute an exceptional phenomenon of recent Australian economic history. The annual rate of increase of real wages over the previous decade had fluctuated around an average under 3 per cent, broadly in line with the rate of productivity growth in the economy. In other words, the share of wages and salaries in the cost breakdown of Australian economic activity had previously been fairly constant. The Whitlam era saw real hourly wages rise by an average of over 7 per cent per year, causing wage share to rise from 57 to 62 per cent of Gross Domestic Product (GDP),[2] or from 61 to 65 per cent of the non-farm component of GDP,[3] as real wage growth far out-stripped productivity growth.[4] Movements in both measures of labour share are illustrated in figure 7.4.

1980/81 $

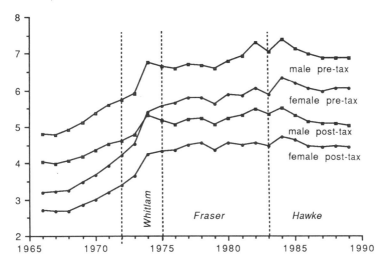

Figure 7.2 Australian real hourly earnings, 1966–89

Source: ABS

The previous constancy of wage and profit shares had been observed to hold not only in Australia but also in most advanced capitalist economies. One of the achievements of the Whitlam government was to upset this much beloved and extensively analysed 'stylised fact' of economics. One explanation of factor income shares centres around technical relationships in the production process which can, in the neo-classical economists' favoured world of competitive markets, determine the relative income shares of labour and capital. Alternative theories, following the pioneering work of Michael Kalecki, argue that factor shares are determined largely by the power of monopolistic firms to set prices as a mark-up on labour costs (Kalecki, 1971). This latter point does indeed highlight a puzzle. Why did Australian firms not raise prices to cover fully their increased labour costs? Nieuwenhuysen and Sloan (1978: 119) suggest that the establishment of the Prices Justification Tribunal served, at least in its first few years, to restrain profits while wages were pushed up. It appears that an active prices and incomes policy in the hands of a crusading government intent on redressing social and economic inequalities was indeed able to shift the functional distribution of income in favour of labour.

It is not surprising that the conservative government which came to

1980/81 $

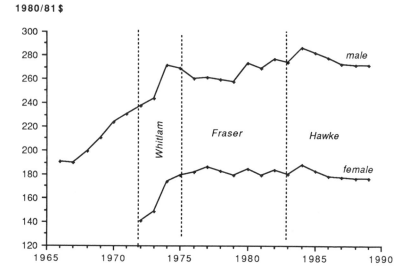

Figure 7.3 Australian real pre-tax weekly earnings all employees, 1966–89

Source: ABS 6304.0, 6401.0, est. 1989

power in 1975 should have sought to reverse the massive income redistribution which had occurred in the few years up to 1975. Covick (1983: 373–374) quotes from the government's statement number two to the 1976 Budget:

> . . . the increase in real wages . . . during 1974 in particular . . . shifting factor shares . . . has been preserved throughout the recession and . . . has contributed significantly both to its onset and its prolongation

and from the government submission to the Arbitration Commission's National Wage Case in May 1980:

> Previous Commonwealth submissions to National Wage Cases dealt with the need for a shift in the balance of factor income shares away from wages and towards profits . . . there is still a considerable way to go before the main income shares are restored to historically more normal levels . . .
> Accordingly, it is critical that the acceleration of wages is halted and preferably reversed so that the progress towards more appropriate shares can continue.

The previous figures illustrate the apparent success of the Fraser government in reversing the movements in income shares. Between 1975

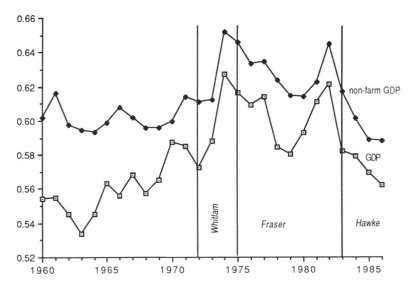

Figure 7.4 Wage share in GDP and non-farm GDP, 1960–86

Source: OECD and DX

and 1979 real earnings were held constant, so the benefits of productivity improvements in the economy accrued largely to capital and labour's income share fell to pre-Whitlam levels. The escalation of wage inflation and real wage growth which occurred during the 'resource boom' period of 1980–82 was sharply reversed by the wage freeze introduced in December 1982.

The return of a Labor government in March 1983 did not see any reversion to the expansionary wage policies of the Whitlam–Cameron type. The principal development was the institution of the Prices and Incomes Accord between the government and the Australian Confederation of Trades Unions. In return for promised tax concessions and efforts to reduce unemployment (which had peaked at over 10 per cent of the labour force in 1983), the ACTU agreed to urge their membership to restrain their wage demands. The extent of the ensuing wage restraint was remarkable especially considering that, despite its full title, the Accord involved no serious attempts at price control. There was a mild recovery of real wage levels in 1984, largely compensating for the reduction in purchasing power occasioned by the wage freeze of the previous year, but since then (up to 1989) real wage levels have undergone an unprecedented, sustained fall.

The extent of the real wage reduction occurring between 1984 and

1989 are illustrated in figure 7.2. Real hourly earnings for adult males, for example, fell 7 per cent over this five year period. This fall was not cushioned by tax reductions, rather the average rate of PAYE on wages and salaries rose from 25 per cent to 27 per cent, so real earnings after tax fell by some 9 per cent. By 1989, the purchasing power of the adult male hourly wage had fallen lower than at any time since 1973.

The share of wages in GDP is illustrated in figure 7.4 only up to 1986. We know, however, that it has fallen between 1986 and 1989 since real wages have fallen while productivity has continued to increase. We can infer, therefore, that the Hawke term of government has seen yet further redistribution of income away from labour. The apparent result of the Accord between the Labor government and the unions is that the share of national income accruing to capital is not only higher than at the time when Whitlam came into office, it is probably higher than at any time during the boom period of the 1960s (especially if we exclude the farm sector).

CAUSES AND CONSEQUENCES OF WAGE MOVEMENTS

The discussion so far has been couched in terms of the apparent influence of government policies on wages and factor shares. The record seems to be fairly straightforward in that the Whitlam government succeeded in bringing about a substantial shift in the distribution of income towards labour in general, and women workers in particular; Fraser's policies were eventually successful, after a major hiccough over 1980–82, in reversing the trend in factor shares in favour of capital; and the Hawke government has gone even further than Fraser in lowering real wages and restoring profit shares.

We have, however, to be careful first in attributing intentionality to government policies and secondly in attributing causality. While it certainly seems to be the case that the Whitlam government, at least in its first two years in office, did intend to redistribute in favour of labour, and it seems equally clear that the Fraser government was determined to reverse this redistribution, it is not so evident that the parties to the 1983 Accord foresaw or intended the cuts in real living standards and major redistribution which have in fact occurred. I would argue, however, that if the Labor government and the unions did not intend this result, they must have been extremely naive in hoping that productivity growth alone (or windfall improvements in the terms of trade) could furnish the restoration of business profitability which the Accord was designed to provide.

Given the assumed intentions of the Whitlam, Fraser and Hawke

non-farm   unemployment
wage   share   rate

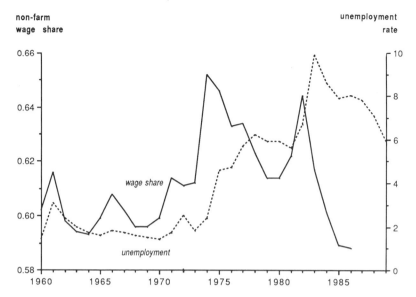

Figure 7.5 Wage share and unemployment

governments, and given that these intentions have in fact been realised,
can we infer that governments have actually had a significant impact on
wages and on income distribution? Or have government objectives and
policies merely reflected, and possibly facilitated, underlying social and
economic developments which would have eventually brought about
the same results? It can be argued that Australian wage outcomes reflect
the market forces of supply and demand for labour and the relative
bargaining strengths of labour and of employers. Seen from this perspective, government policies and the arbitration system merely mediate
the underlying economic forces. In particular, it is often claimed that
strong unions can push up wages, that profitability will fall and unemployment will rise in consequence, until the rise in joblessness restrains
union wage pressure.

It is possible that changes in the unemployment rate have been
driven by the changes in factor shares, as illustrated in figure 7.5. The
dramatic rise in wage share which occurred in 1974 was followed by an
equally dramatic rise in unemployment over the period 1975–78; the
1974–79 fall in wage share was succeeded by an improvement in unemployment 1979–81; the 1981–82 'wage breakout' saw unemployment
shoot up again in 1983; and the sharp fall in the share of income
accruing to labour since 1983 has been followed by a sharp downturn in

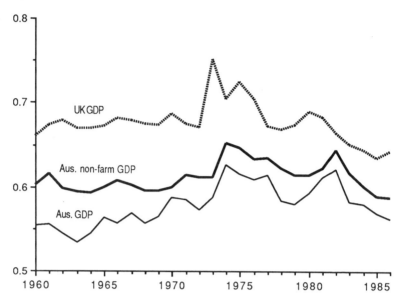

Figure 7.6 UK and Australian wage shares

unemployment. It can be argued, equally, that it is unemployment which is driving movements in the wage share, at least since the mid 1970s. Years of particularly rapid increases in unemployment, 1975 and 1983, have been followed by falling wage shares.[5]

The debate between the institutionalists, who argue that governments and institutions can and do affect wages and income distribution, and their opponents who argue for the primacy of the underlying economic forces, is still unresolved. A common failing of both sides, however, is that all too often they fail to consider the international environment in its economic, institutional and political dimensions. The following section attempts to redress this imbalance.

INTERNATIONAL MOVEMENTS IN WAGES AND FACTOR SHARES

A most illuminating comparison can be made between the experience of Australia and the UK with regard to wage outcomes and factor shares over the last two decades. Figure 7.6 illustrates this. The series move in a remarkably similar fashion.[6] In particular, the UK wage share rose sharply in 1973 after a decade of stability; it subsequently declined, with some temporary reversals, to 1983; and it has declined since 1983 to levels below that of the 1960s. It is of particular interest to note that during the 1980s Thatcherism in the UK and 'Hawkcism' in Australia have produced such similar movements in factor shares. Their ideological stances have appeared to be far apart, their attitude to trade unions and their records on unemployment have been widely different, but both approaches have resulted in, and have probably been motivated by, a major redistribution away from labour.

There are in fact strong similarities between the Australian wage experience and those of many other advanced capitalist economies, not just the UK. Table 7.1 illustrates this point, giving average annual rates of growth of real hourly earnings in manufacturing for twenty OECD countries[7] over the periods which have been of particular interest in examining the Australian record.

Australian real wage growth 1972–75 was, according to these OECD measures, somewhat higher than the unweighted average for the 'Big Seven' but only marginally higher than the average for the twenty countries for which series are reported. Many other countries reported higher wage growth. The small decline in Australian real wages 1975–79 was, however, almost unique; the only other country with negative wage growth was New Zealand. Taking these two periods together, Australian wage growth was somewhat below average. This pattern is repeated over the later two periods. Australian real wage growth was above average 1979–84, though not in a league of its own, and its negative growth 1984–89 was outdone only by Greece and New Zealand. It appears on this evidence that Australian wages have followed the medium term trends of most OECD countries. There have been short-lived deviations with above average (but not exceptional) wage growth for several years followed by retrenchment.

These comparisons of short and medium term trends in wages are likely to be dominated by patterns of productivity growth. Those countries, such as Japan and Italy, experiencing fast productivity growth can be expected to show relatively fast wage growth. Of more interest, perhaps, are comparisons of movements in the share of wages in GDP—a measure which corresponds roughly to the difference between wage growth and productivity growth. These comparisons are given in table 7.2. While the OECD supply data only on wage share in total GDP, the first line of the table gives an additional measure for Australia, wage share in non-farm GDP. This is probably a better measure for purposes of comparison since it excludes fluctuations due simply to changes in the relative size of the agricultural sector.

We now find that the 1972–75 surge in labour's share of domestic income was experienced throughout virtually all of the OECD. The

Table 7.1 Real hourly earnings in twenty OECD countries

Countries	1966–72	Annual average rates of growth 1972–75	1975–79	1979–84	1984–88
Australia	**2.9**	**4.9**	**– 0.2**	**2.3**	**– 1.8**
United States	1.5	– 0.6	0.7	– 0.9	– 0.7
Japan	9.2	3.8	2.1	1.3	2.4
Germany	5.1	2.9	2.3	– 0.1	3.3
France	5.1	5.4	3.1	1.4	0.4
United Kingdom	3.0	1.9	0.7	2.2	3.5
Italy		13.0	5.0	0.9	2.5
Canada	3.9	2.6	1.6	– 0.2	– 0.6
Weighted Average* Big 7		**2.4**	**1.8**	**0.4**	**0.6**
Unweighted average		**4.1**	**2.2**	**0.7**	**1.5**
Austria	5.2	5.9	2.2	0.2	2.1
Belgium	6.0	6.8	2.2	0.1	– 0.4
Denmark		7.3	1.1	– 1.0	2.1
Finland	5.8	4.2	0.1	1.3	2.6
Greece	6.2	3.1	7.7	3.9	– 7.5
Ireland	5.7	5.2	2.9	– 0.1	2.4
The Netherlands		4.9	0.6	– 1.3	1.7
Norway	4.0	5.8	1.7	– 0.5	2.7
Spain	7.2	9.2	6.7	2.5	1.7
Sweden		2.3	0.4	– 1.2	1.9
Switzerland		1.5	0.3	0.6	– 0.4
New Zealand	3.1	3.5	– 0.4	– 0.3	– 3.7
Weighted Average* OECD		**2.8**	**1.9**	**0.5**	**0.3**
Unweighted Average OECD		**4.7**	**2.2**	**0.5**	**0.8**

Notes: Hourly earnings in manufacturing, except Australia: adult males in all sectors, Japan: monthly earnings, France: hourly rates, UK: weekly earnings, Austria, Finland, Spain and NZ: total industry, The Netherlands: hourly rates
    * Country weights based on 1980 employment in manufacturing

Source: Historical Statistics and Economic Outlook

Table 7.2 OECD comparisons of growth in wage share

	Average growth rates (%) in the share of employees' compensation in GDP at factor cost					
	1960–72	1972–75	1975–79	1979–83	1983–86	1960–86
Australia 2	**0.1**	**1.9**	**– 1.3**	**0.1**	**– 1.6**	**– 0.1**
Australia 1	**0.3**	**2.5**	**– 1.5**	**0.1**	**– 1.2**	**– 0.1**
USA	0.4	– 0.1	– 0.1	0.1	– 0.4	0.1
Japan	0.9	4.8	– 0.2	0.9	0.0	1.1
Germany	0.3	0.4	– 0.2	– 0.2	– 0.5	0.1
France	0.8	2.6	0.4	0.7	– 1.5	0.6
UK	0.1	2.6	– 1.9	– 0.8	– 0.4	– 0.1
Italy	1.7	3.3	– 0.8	0.1	– 1.3	0.9
Canada	0.7	– 0.5	– 0.8	0.1	– 0.4	0.1
Big 7 average	**0.7**	**1.9**	**– 0.5**	**0.1**	**– 0.7**	**0.4**
Austria	0.8	3.2	0.3	– 0.7	– 0.3	0.6
Belgium	1.2	2.4	0.6	– 0.4	– 1.6	0.7
Denmark	1.0	1.5	0.4	– 0.5	– 0.5	0.6
Greece	0.9	0.2	4.1	1.3	– 0.4	1.2
Iceland	0.2	0.5	2.0	– 2.3	2.1	0.3
Ireland	1.0	2.0	– 1.0	1.1	– 1.3	0.5
New Zealand	1.2	3.8	0.0	– 2.0	0.0	0.7
Luxembourg	1.7	6.7	– 0.3	– 0.2	– 1.2	1.3
Norway	1.4	0.6	– 2.1	– 2.1	– 3.3	0.5
Portugal	1.0	8.1	– 5.0	1.3	– 3.3	0.4
Spain	1.5	1.3	0.3	– 2.0	– 1.7	0.4
Sweden	1.4	– 0.3	1.1	– 1.8	0.5	0.5
Turkey	– 1.8	2.3	3.1	– 7.5	– 1.9	– 1.4
OECD average	**0.8**	**2.3**	**0.0**	**– 0.7**	**– 0.5**	**0.5**

Notes: Australia 2 is wage share in non-farm GDP at factor cost
All others refer to wage share in GDP at factor cost
Source: OECD National Accounts 1960–86 and DX Database

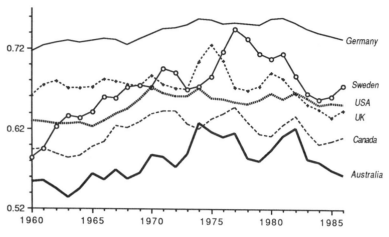

Figure 7.7 Wage shares 1960–86: six countries

only exceptions were North America and Sweden. Many countries had a larger redistribution, and the Australian experience was very close to average (slightly smaller or larger depending on which measure of Australian factor shares is used). The 1975–79 decline in labour share was somewhat greater than the OECD average, but by no means exceptional. Australia's 1979–83 record of minimal growth in labour share reflects the experience of most of the larger OECD economies, and the post 1983 decline represents a move in the same direction as almost all of the other countries, albeit of greater magnitude than most. Figure 7.7 illustrates the common movements in factor shares for Australia and a selection of other OECD countries.

Some of the common movement in wage shares is probably due to simultaneous fluctuations in world output and unemployment. To the extent that some labour is of a fixed or overhead nature in the production process, we expect employment to fluctuate less than output and wage share to fall in boom periods and rise in recessions. Indeed the Australian wage share measures do exhibit some anti-cyclical movement, but the correlation with the unemployment is small ($r = 0.35$ for the GDP measure, 0.19 for the non-farm measure). In other words, most of the variation in Australian wage share is not a direct result of cyclical fluctuations. (An exception to this is the upsurge in wage share which occurred during the resources boom of the early 1980s.) It follows that most of the common movements in factor shares across the OECD are unlikely to be explained as a purely cyclical phenomenon. It seems, rather, that there was a secular experience shared by most European countries and Oceania of a strong and unprecedented redistribution of income from capital to labour in the early 1970s. This redistribution was generally reversed over the following decade.

CONCLUSIONS

Seen in the light of the experience of the rest of the advanced capitalist economies, Australia's experience over the last two decades of dramatic shifts in rates of wage growth and in the distribution of income between labour and capital appears to be largely a reflection of a worldwide phenomenon. The impact of domestic policies appears to have been to slightly amplify the redistribution of income towards labour in the early 1970s and towards capital in the mid 1980s, but Australian governments have for the most part been leaning with, rather than into, the wind of worldwide trends.

Just what lies behind these international trends is an issue far too big and complex to be analysed here in any detail. We may speculate that the long boom period of the 1950s and 1960s with sustained low unemployment and high growth in both productivity and wages led to strong trade union organisation and expectations of continuing growth in living standards. The slowdown in productivity growth which affected nearly all of the advanced capitalist economies in the late 1960s and early 1970s set capital and labour on a collision course over income shares; the cake was not growing fast enough, so the division of the cake became a contentious issue with severe inflationary consequences. In the short term labour appeared to have the advantage in securing an unprecedented high share of income at the expense of a sharp slump in profit shares and rates of return on capital. The reaction in the late 1970s and the 1980s took diverse forms, from sharply rising unemployment and strong anti-trade union measures in some countries to 'corporatist' cooperation between business, labour and government in others. The result has been to redistribute income back to capital.

An important implication of this analysis is that the unique features of Australian labour market policy and institutional structure have not produced wage outcomes which differ very markedly from worldwide trends. That is not to say, however, that these policies and institutions are ineffectual; rather, their effects may have been more noticeable in other areas such as combating unemployment.

ENDNOTES

[1] Much of the evidence presented here on the actions and policies of the Whitlam government is taken from Nieuwenhuysen and Sloan, 1978.

[2] Unless otherwise specified, wage and profit shares are measured as a proportion of GDP *at factor cost*, that is after the deduction of indirect taxes, less subsidies, from the value of GDP *as valued at market prices*. Factor shares can also be evaluated in relation to *net domestic income*, that is GDP less the depreciation costs of capital equipment. In practice, all three wage share measures tend to move in similar directions. The correlation coefficients between the factor cost definition and the market price or net income definitions are 0.97 and 0.95 respectively for the period 1960–86. Note that 'wages' include salaries and supplements.

[3] I follow Covick (1984) in preferring the non-farm definition since national accounting methods are unable to separate out the proprietor's own wage element from the profit element of farm incomes. Covick also discusses and measures the problems in measuring wages and profits in non-market sectors of the economy. His measures of market sector wage share are highly correlated with the aggregate measures used here.

[4] Formally, we should also take account of changes in Australia's terms of trade, the ratio of the price of exports to the price of imports, in explaining the relationship between real wages and wage share. In fact the terms of trade collapsed from a peak in 1973 as OPEC oil prices soared and Australia's export prices fell in response to the downturn in world economic activity. So if factor shares had been to stay constant, real wage growth should have lagged behind productivity growth.

[5] Simple correlation analysis between unemployment and wage share indicates that current values are not significantly correlated ($r = 0.13$); unemployment is strongly correlated with wage share lagged two years ($r = 0.61$) and wage share is negatively correlated with unemployment lagged two years ($r = -0.17$).

[6] The correlation coefficient between the UK series and Australian factor share in non-farm GDP (total GDP) is 0.59 (0.44).

[7] These series are the best comparable indicators the OECD can compile on wage movements in its member countries. Unfortunately, however, the definitions are not identical for all countries, so some of the differences in wage growth may simply reflect definitional differences.

ACKNOWLEDGEMENT

Owen Covick and participants at a seminar at the Australian National University provided useful comments and criticisms, though they still may not agree with the conclusions I have drawn.

REFERENCES

Covick, Owen (1983) 'Relative wage shares in Australia' in Hancock, Keith et al., eds *Japanese and Australian labour markets: a comparative study*, pp. 372–417 Canberra: Australia–Japan Research Centre

Kalecki, M. (1971) *Selected Essays on the Dynamics of the Capitalist Economy* London: Cambridge University Press

Niewenhuysen, J.P. and Sloan, J. (1978) 'Wages policy' in F.H. Gruen ed. *Surveys of Australian Economics*, pp. 91–132 Hornsby: Allen & Unwin

Phelps Brown, E.H. (1969) 'Balancing External Payments by Adjusting Domestic Income' in *Australian Economic Papers*

8 Is the privatisation of Australian schooling inevitable?

DON ANDERSON

This chapter examines the causes of the decline of public schooling in Australia since the 1970s and its probable continued decline during the 1990s. It points out that one of the consequences of privatisation may be a decline in the overall quality of the nation's education because, in the matter of schooling, the aggregation of a host of individual decisions seems unlikely to lead to the greatest good for the greatest number. In the case of education it is the back of Adam Smith's invisible hand that is at work.

The loss of children from Australian public schools is in contrast to most other countries that we would care to be compared with where public schooling is, if not robust, at least stable. Behind the Australian decline is the changing relation between the public and private sectors of schooling, and the different regulatory environments in which each operates.[1] The private option has always been available, but for twenty years or so it has been purchasable at highly subsidised prices. As a consequence the flow to private is accelerating.

This chapter has the following structure. First, there is an examination of some preliminaries, including the historical background of church–state relations and their impact on Australian schooling, the definition of the concept of privatisation, and a classification of schools which develops a more useful typology than the commonly used public, Catholic and other private. Secondly, there is a discussion entitled 'Australia compared' which looks at trends in the public and private sectors of a number of countries and asks why Australia is different. Finally, under the heading of 'The continued privatisation of Australian schools', the dynamics of the decline of public education are discussed and some evidence on performance is reviewed. It is suggested that the availability of a private choice can lead to an overall lowering of the quality of education in a country.

PRELIMINARY CONSIDERATIONS

In order to compare the Australian schooling system with that of other nations, some brief consideration of the impact of historical factors and definition of major terms is necessary.

Historical factors

An adequate appreciation of the present structure of school systems requires some understanding of the impact on schooling of church–state relations in the nineteenth century and the effect of political forces which saw the re-introduction of public funding for private schools in the mid-twentieth century. For our present purposes it is helpful to be aware of four elements in the historical development of Australian schools.

First the dual system of Australian schools emerged from a conflict between church and state, or rather, denominations and state. With the first fleets of Europeans to occupy Australia came spiritual authority in the form of the Church of England. The Church assumed responsibility for the morals and manners as well as the religious welfare of the new residents and, among other things, became involved in schooling for the young. Before too many decades had passed this monopoly over faith was challenged by representatives of the Churches of Rome and of Scotland, who claimed responsibility for the not inconsiderable numbers of Irish and Scots whose transgressions had led them to NSW. Years of denominational squabbling and educational neglect of big sections of the population eventually stimulated intervention by civil authority, first in curriculum, eventually in the establishment of colonial-wide school systems.

Secondly the Catholic system was established in the latter part of the nineteenth century, at enormous cost, by a Church which felt itself to be a beleaguered minority in an intolerant Protestant dominated society. The Church was encouraged by pronouncements from Rome which also influenced the development of Catholic school systems in other countries, but none of these were as successful as in Australia, where about half the children of Catholic parents attend Catholic schools (Anderson, 1988a). The traumas, as well as the successes of a hundred years ago, are still felt by Catholic education authorities.

Thirdly the Protestant schools, which had to charge substantial tuition fees because they did not have the services of teaching priests and nuns, soon became schools of social class. In the early twentieth century these schools, or more particularly, their sponsoring churches, were disinclined to pressure governments for state aid, as that would have advantaged the better organised Catholics. More recently Protestant schools have advanced in the slip stream of Catholic initiatives on state aid.

The fourth point of historical noteworthiness is that, compared with America, the development of schooling in Australia was influenced by an English colonial aristocratic legacy, undisturbed by a revolution; and by the English dual system accentuated by convict colony origins.

Privatisation

Privatisation has a variety of meanings and uses, some of them pejorative. In its most general usage privatisation means rolling back the activities of the state; more restricted meanings include 'fee for service' and businesses run for profit. The non-government schools of Australia would embrace the first of these with alacrity but the second with considerable circumspection; like the sturdy private enterprise Australian farmers who capitalise their gains but socialise their losses. There are no longer any schools worth speaking of offering general education which are run to make a profit for their owners. The last of these disappeared in the 1930s; they were common in the nineteenth century. They are still found, indeed comprise a flourishing little industry, in specialised and vocational areas, and as supplementary crammers to regular schools. There are, however, economists who believe that, for reasons of efficiency, all schools should be private ventures. For example in a paper prepared for the Economic Planning Advisory Council, George Fane (1984: 25) has recommended that 'existing government schools, TAFEs, CAEs and universities be privatised: i.e. that they be sold off to the highest bidder, even if these bidders propose not to use them as educational institutions'. Even Milton Friedman, not known as a supporter of government intervention when individual choice is at stake, draws the line at such complete abdication of collective responsibility. He is on record that governments have a duty to 'require each child to receive a minimum amount of schooling of a specified kind' (1962: 86).

Proposals from within the Reagan administration for the privatisation of schools included greater parental choice with policy and administrative authority located at school level. It was envisaged the system would be driven by a market—a market of schools. The income from parents, paid either out of their own pockets or from vouchers given to them by the state would determine whether a school will flourish or go to the wall. Some economists believe that this mechanism is more efficient than a community school funded from tax revenue. Milton Friedman, who is credited with the idea of publicly financed educational vouchers, says:

> Parents could express their views about schools directly, by withdrawing their children from one school and sending them to another, to a much

greater extent than is now possible. In general they can now take this step only by changing their place of residence. For the rest they can only express their ideas through cumbrous political channels (1962: 91).

Varieties of schools

Private schools in Australia are schools which are not owned by the state, which employ their own teachers on a contract basis, which are not administered and regulated by government authority, and which charge tuition fees. They used to be self supporting, or at least free from state subsidy, but none are now. A few are accumulating capital in preparation for a future where state funding is foregone in preference to greater accountability. Private schools comprise a market of sorts. Parents can shop around, but schools may decline clients on grounds additional to inability to pay, because of their religion, or because of the child's behaviour or intellectual ability.

Government schools in Australia are schools which are owned by the state, staffed by teachers who are employed by the state in a state-wide service, subject to administration and regulation by state authorities, and resourced from the state's coffers.

In case you are tempted to think that any one of these criteria—ownership, administration, fee for service—is sufficient to distinguish public and private consider these exceptions: in New Zealand all Catholic schools are in the public sector but the Church owns the property; in England the Thatcher government's provisions for schools to 'opt out' means that they may leave the publicly administered system although they are still owned by it; and in many parts of the world public education is not free. In the Australian case ownership continues to distinguish government and non-government schools, although in the ACT Catholic authorities have been given special purpose leasehold land on which to build their schools. Private school teachers are not state employees, and, until recently, they eschewed industrial action which has earned public teachers some notoriety.

Private schools are exempt from planning directives (for example: catchment areas, closures and consolidations, school and class size, pupil teacher ratios, and curriculum) which may be visited on public schools. However, as recipients of substantial state subsidies, they are being required to give some account of their public finances. (There is widespread anxiety among private school authorities that accountability will be extended to their educational activities.) Catholic systemic schools in Australia are centrally administered by state and territorial Education Offices which may exercise more central authority than the government systems, and allow parents less opportunity to express their ideas. The amount of fees, but not their existence, distinguishes public and private. Secondary schools in Australia used to charge fees, and there is something very close to a compulsory levy returning to secondary education. Public preschool and higher education is not free.

Despite these blurrings at the boundaries I am using privatisation of education to mean the shift of responsibility, for educating the mainstream of Australian children, from schools owned and regulated by government agencies to individual schools owned, partly subsidised and regulated by non-profit corporations, or to schools which are part of non-government systems.

The private sector is of course not homogeneous. It is common to distinguish between Catholic and other non public schools. For administrative purposes governments also distinguish between systemic and non systemic schools. In the former case funds are handed over to the system office for distribution, for example to the Catholic or Seventh Day Adventist authorities. Part of the funding is available for the maintenance of these offices.

For analytic purposes these classifications are doubly inadequate. They conceal the great diversity of purposes and functions which may be found in both the public and private sectors, and they imply that there are distinct and autonomous sectors which neither overlap nor interact. For the purposes of sociological analysis a more useful typology of schools can be made according to their social function.

Six types can be distinguished, each belonging mainly, but not exclusively, to either the conventional private or public sectors. The first of these comprises elite schools which help reproduce the ruling strata of a society, socialising the young in values of leadership and conservative citizenship (Anderson, 1988b; Sherington et al., 1987; Persell and Cookson, 1985). Since access to the university professions is dependent on high scholastic performance there is an overlap of the social and intellectual elite functions of schooling. Whereas social elite schools are all private there are a few academically selective secondary schools in the public sector which assist the upwards social mobility of bright students from modest social backgrounds.

The second type refers to schools of sub-cultural maintenance which help to maintain religious or ethnic sub-cultures, nurturing the young in their traditions and beliefs. Leaders of some such cultural groups, especially some religious denominations, maintain that separate schooling is a necessary condition for transmission of the faith from one generation to the next. There is evidence which casts some doubt on the effectiveness of church schools in transmitting the faith (Anderson and Western, 1972; Greeley and Rossi, 1966). Sub-cultural maintenance is not necessarily out of bounds for public schools—they may teach about values and beliefs. In fact it is a delusion to think that any education, public or private, is value free. There is a good deal of teaching about religion in public schools, and many make arrangements for instruction in a faith for those who wish it.

Thirdly there are reform or alternative schools which have always comprised a small component of the private sector. Usually they are associated with particular values about community or human development. Examples are Montessori and Steiner schools, and the many so-called community or reform schools which practice a more child-centred education than is common in conventional schools. These schools differ from schools of sub-cultural maintenance in that there is no organised sub-culture which sponsors them. Alternative schools are now found in both the public and private sectors. Parents subscribe to common philosophical or pedagogical views but otherwise come to the school from diverse positions on the religious and cultural maps.

The fourth category is the largest. Community schools, designed to accept all children in a particular community or locality, function as agencies of social cohesion. They are almost always public schools and acquit the responsibilities which governments have assumed to provide universal educational opportunity. The values implicit in community schooling are necessarily broad: tolerance, understanding others, and democratic rights and responsibilities (Connors, 1988). From a perspective within the Catholic community the parochial schools would be regarded as community schools serving the Catholic families of a neighbourhood.

A fifth class of school, private venture schools run by their owners for a profit, have all but disappeared in Australia, except perhaps in the mind of the odd free market economist. Those that remain are for vocational training, supplementary coaching or specialised aspects of a curriculum such as English for foreign students.

The final type are charity schools, once common in the private sector, especially in the USA. Sponsored by religious or altruistic organisations, they educated socially disadvantaged children. These too disappeared after universal public systems were established in the nineteenth century. The closest relatives of these schools today are special schools for handicapped children, almost all of them in the public sector. Should privatisation continue and community schools disappear, charity schools for the poor may reappear in Australia.

In the following discussion the terms public, Catholic and private will be used when referring respectively to government owned, Catholic owned and independently owned schools. When the social functions of different sorts of schools are being discussed, reference will be made to elite, sub-cultural maintenance or community schools. These latter categories are pure types and few particular schools would correspond exactly with any one. Nor is any one category entirely in the publicly or privately administered system although most elite and sub-cultural maintenance schools are non-government and most community schools are public.

AUSTRALIA COMPARED

The public–private division is the first thing about Australia's school system, apart perhaps from the School of the Air, that catches the attention of visitors. Initially it is the size of the private sector that surprises; later the outside observer is likely to remark on the contrast of the myth of an egalitarian society with the role of elite private schools in promoting snobbery and in getting students into universities and the professions.

Of the 3.02 million Australian school children in 1989 72.7 per cent were in public schools, 19.6 per cent in Catholic schools and 7.7 per cent in other private schools. This is the smallest proportion in public schools in the hundred years for which statistics are available and con-

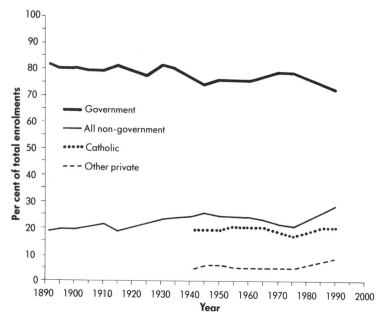

Figure 8.1 Government and non-government school enrolments, Australia 1891–1991

Note: Figures not available prior to 1941.
Source: Australian Bureau of Statistics Commonwealth Year Books 1901 to 1989.

tinues a downward trend from 1975 when the public proportion peaked at nearly 79 per cent (see figure 8.1). Of all western industrialised countries only Spain has a private sector as large as Australia's or as influential in the political realm. Furthermore, while the private sector has been growing in Australia, in most other countries it has generally been static or declining. Of OECD countries in the decade since 1975, Australia is the only case where the proportion of children in private schools increased by more than 2 percentage points at both primary and secondary levels. In fact, according to UNESCO statistics, the only other countries in the world where the private share expanded by any more than a point or two at both primary and secondary levels were Chile, Dominican Republic, Haiti, United Arab Emirates and Zimbabwe (UNESCO, 1989).

It is not, however, the intention in this chapter to compare Australia with developing countries. The most informative comparisons are those among countries which are not dissimilar, economically or politically.

Table 8.1 Percentage of pupils in the private sector

	Primary		Secondary	
	% 1986	Change 1975–1986 % points ±	% 1986	Change 1975–1986 % points ±
Australia	24	+ 4	29	+ 5
Austria	4	+ 1	7	+ 2
Canada	3	+ 1	7	+ 2
Denmark	9		14	
France	15	+ 1	22	+ 2
Germany (FDR)	2	+ 1	7	+ 2
Greece	6		4	− 5
Japan	1	0	13	− 1
New Zealand	2	− 7	5	− 9
Norway	1	0	3	0
Spain	35		35	− 11
Sweden	1		1	
Switzerland	2		5	
Turkey	1		2	
United Kingdom	5		8	0
United States	11	− 1	8	0

Note: OECD countries not included in the table are those for which information is not available or where the distinction between the public and private sector is not very meaningful as in Belgium and The Netherlands. The OECD/UNESCO survey used to collect the information defined private schools as those not managed within the government sector. No entry in the Change column means that this information was not available.

Sources: 1: Education in OECD Countries 1986–87, OECD, Paris, 1989
2: Development of Private Enrolment First and Second Level Education 1975–1985, Division of Statistics on Education, Paris, 1989

In the present case useful comparisons may be made with other Anglo–American countries—United Kingdom, USA, Canada and New Zealand—which share language and other cultural inheritances; and with the three Scandinavian countries where standards of living and levels of industrial development are not unlike Australia's.

Compared with any one of these seven countries Australia has more than double the proportion of children in private education. Before searching for social or educational conditions which might contribute to this difference, it is worth seeing just who it is in the population that is leaving public for private.

Who is leaving public education?

The shift from public to private in Australia is by no means an even migration across the social landscape. For 150 years elite private schools have been patronised by the wealthier and the more influential classes. In the last couple of decades they have been joined by upwardly mobile families at a rate which has caused these schools to double their share of the market. This is illustrated by the censuses of 1976 and 1986 which show that the new clients are concentrated in the gentrified suburbs of the capital cities. In some regions the proportion of resident children attending non-government schools has trebled. A map of Sydney and Melbourne, shaded according to the intensity of residents' participation in private schools, coincides closely with another showing the social standing of the suburbs (Anderson, 1990).

In figure 8.2 information from the 1986 census has been used to plot the social standing of the suburban regions of Melbourne against the proportion of population in each of those regions attending non-Catholic private schools. As may be seen the higher the suburban rating (based on averages of household income, educational levels and property values) the more likely it is that the children will be attending an elite school. If we marked the location of elite schools on a map they would be found in either the older more affluent regions or in central areas. In the newer suburbs of higher status private schools have not yet had time to become established. This does not mean that all the children therefore attend public schools; many travel across the city to the school of their (or their parents') choice, aided by state subsidised school buses or other public transport.

The sociologists' holy trinity of status indicators—occupational status, level of education and income—is linked with parents' choices of the sort of school for their children. For example the 1976 census reveals that whereas family incomes over $20 000 were 'enjoyed' by only around 9 per cent of public school children, and 15 per cent of Catholic school children, some 50 per cent of private school families were in this

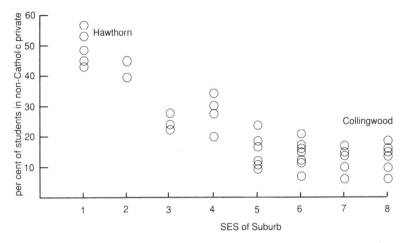

Figure 8.2 SES of residential location × percentage of students at private schools

Source: 1986 Census

bracket. The association would be sharper if the census man had asked about family wealth rather than just income.

While the social profile of Catholic schools approximates much more closely to that of public schools than to other-private, there are elite schools within the Catholic sector. If these could be taken out of the Catholic category the remaining, mainly parochial, Catholic schools would possess a social profile closer to, but still 'above', that of public schools. The Catholic school sector has increased by about 17 per cent since 1975 and constitutes the second large growth area in the non public sector. This contrasts with the trend in USA where the proportion of children in Catholic schools has declined. Most of the newcomers in Australia are recruited from the approximately 50 per cent of Catholic children in public schools, although there is also some demand from non-Catholic children. Since 1976 the census has only asked whether schooling was government or non-government, not whether it was Catholic, so it is not possible to be precise about denominational dimensions of the shift to private. The censuses do show, however, that the suburban regions where growth of participation in Catholic schooling is taking place are of intermediate social standing. This suggests that Catholic school authorities are having difficulty keeping up in the newer western suburbs of Sydney and Melbourne; and maybe that even the modest tuition fees are something of a deterrent in working class suburbs.

Not all of the clients of non-Catholic private schools are well off. Some of the poorest schools in Australia have been set up by alternative lifestylers living in northern NSW and elsewhere. And the schools recently set up by groups with a strong commitment to ethnic or sect type cultures cater in the main for families of average or below average means,

In both Australia and the USA schools sponsored by fundamentalist Christian religions comprise the fastest growing private group. They are relative newcomers to the private sector and include some evangelicals whose predecessors supported public schooling as an expression of common citizenship. Seventh Day Adventists who, along with the Catholic church, have been the most successful in getting members to send their children to their own schools, are also expanding in Australia. We may also find, when the data are analysed, that migrants, or rather the children of migrants, are prominent in the shift from public to private. A small proportion of these will be found in ethnic schools; by far the greater number will, it seems, shift from public to regular elite private schools.

Some idea of the extent of the shift from public to private from one generation to the next is revealed in a national longitudinal study of individuals who commenced full-time university studies in the mid 1960s (Anderson and Western, 1967). In a follow-up in the 1980s these former students were asked where their children went to school, or, if there were no children yet of school age, what sort of school they had in mind for them.

Not unexpectedly, since the sample is of a university educated population, a disproportionate number had attended private schools themselves—some 25 per cent, which is more than three times the fraction in all secondary schools at the time (see figure 8.3). Of the others 53 per cent had attended public schools and 22 per cent Catholic schools. There is a massive exit from public when these graduates choose a school for their own children. Catholic also loses to private, suggesting that for these upwardly mobile families class position is more important than religion when it comes to schooling. Only 37 per cent of the graduates' children would attend public schools, and only 15 per cent Catholic. Forty-eight per cent, almost double the parent generation, would attend private (see figure 8.4). In a front page story on these results the *Sydney Morning Herald* (15/10/88) ran a headline: 'Public school OK for me, not for my children'.

The higher status professions of medicine and law recruit disproportionately from private schools. Furthermore graduates from these professions who happened to have attended public schools themselves are more likely than other graduates to send their children to private schools. The professions with the largest representation in private

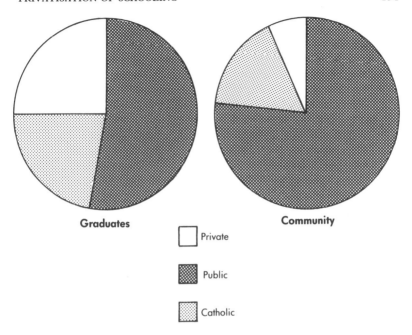

Graduates   **Community**

☐ Private

▓ Public

░ Catholic

Figure 8.3 Where graduates and the general community went to school (circa 1966)

schools are medicine (36 per cent of parents and 69 per cent of children) and law (56 per cent of parents and 35 per cent of children). Forty per cent of the engineers attended private school and 16 per cent of their children will attend; for teachers the proportions are 31 per cent and 17 per cent respectively. Teaching is the only profession with a majority of both parents and children in public schools: 65 and 52 per cent respectively. That might be considered a score for public schools in the public–private debate since teachers would clearly be the best informed of the three professions on conditions in schools. On the other hand the fact that almost half of those teaching in public schools were thinking of sending their own children elsewhere is scarcely an overwhelming vote of confidence in public education.

The academic selective function of private schools is illustrated in figure 8.5 where the rate of participation in university for persons who have attended public, Catholic or private schools is plotted against their age. For example the proportion of graduates among persons born in the period 1926 to 1940 (who, if they attended university, would in the main have done so in the decade immediately after World War II) is

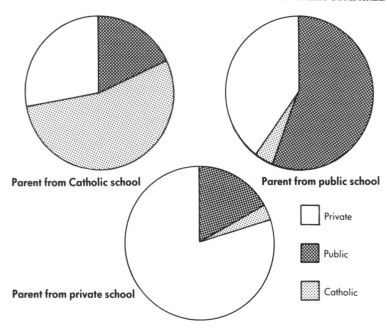

Figure 8.4 Where graduates intend sending their children

23 per cent for those whose schooling was private, 8 per cent for Catholic and 5 per cent for public. The overall rate of participation in university has almost doubled for the next generation (born 1941 to 1954), the greater share of the advance being absorbed by Catholic and private. There was some catching up by those of the 1955 to 1960 generation who had been to public and Catholic schools. By this stage it is also clear that participation in university from Catholic schools has stabilised in a position clearly ahead of public. The dip in the proportions of graduates from both Catholic and public for the post 1960 generation is due to delayed entry to university. Private school students are most likely to move on to full-time university without a break; others, especially public school students, are more likely to have a period in the labour force before starting their university studies, often part-time. Later surveys will pick up many of these as 'mature age' graduates.

Why is Australia different?

On the face of things the reason for the recent expansion of the private sector in Australia seems obvious. As Ross Williams (1984) points out,

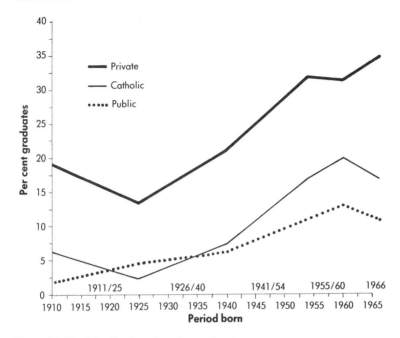

Figure 8.5 Participation in university × school type

Source: National Science (Sample) Survey of the Australian Population, ANU

governments are subsidising it to the extent that 'private schools now rely much more heavily on government funds than did universities prior to 1950'. He estimated that around 1980 each $100 increase in government per capita grants to private schools raised the proportion of their students by around 1.5 percentage points.

Money is by no means the whole story. State aid for private schools is a recent event in the history of universal schooling in Australia. After the creation of 'free, compulsory and secular' public education systems starting in the 1870s, colonial governments cut off funding for private schools. Despite having to rely almost entirely on private funding the Catholic school system grew, and, in the mid 1950s, was educating 18 per cent of all children (and approximately 55 per cent of all Catholic children). At the same time non-Catholic private schools educated more than 5 per cent. This proportion of children in non-government schools in Australia in the period immediately before state aid is much larger than in any Anglo–American or Scandinavian country, then or now. The 'no state aid' policies lasted until the mid 1950s and gained support from most sectors of society with the understandable exception of the

Roman Catholic church. Even the Protestant churches' support for their schools did not match their dislike for Rome and they were generally opposed to state aid, willing to cut off their educational noses to spite their sectarian faces. All that began to change in the mid 1950s when, after the cosmic split in the Australian Labor Party, the conservative Menzies government saw advantage in giving grants to private schools. It was realised that Catholic voters, many of them formerly traditional Labor supporters, might be enticed to switch allegiance with promises to fund their schools. Tax concessions on tuition fees had been introduced by the Menzies government in 1954. This was followed during the next decade by grants for science laboratories, grants for libraries, interest subsidies on bank loans for capital expansion, and per capita grants.

Labor, which was on the federal opposition benches for all this period, had had an egalitarian commitment to public schools and implacable opposition to state aid. But eventually Labor accepted that it must change if it was ever to regain government. There was also genuine concern in the Party at the appalling conditions and standards in many Catholic schools. In the community more generally sectarian rivalries had abated and, with respect to schooling, there was a feeling that Catholic schools, which had such a large burden of responsibility, should get a 'fair go'. By the 1970s an astonishing transformation was complete with bi-partisan political support for public funding to help refurbish and run private schools.

Gough Whitlam, the Labor leader who was responsible for getting Labor to accept a policy of funding private schools—all schools, public and private, were to get federal money according to their needs—claimed that the highly divisive state aid issue was buried for all time. Helped largely by his policies for improving education, Whitlam led Labor into government in 1972. But additional aid did not reduce political leverage, and, before long, following application of judicious pressure, most non-government schools were getting over 80 per cent of their running expenses from governments, federal and state. Even the wealthiest private schools get 40 per cent of their costs from state and federal government. When forty-one elite schools—most of them in Sydney and Melbourne—were threatened by Education Minister Susan Ryan in 1983 with a reduction to their subsidy their cries were heard in Canberra. The *Sydney Morning Herald* reported that:

> Suddenly the business consultants, stockbrokers, pharmacists and academics of Sydney—those who live comfortably but not necessarily extravagantly, who vote conservatively and lead quiet, upright lives—have been stung into action (quoted by Macintyre, 1985: 116).

As Stuart Macintyre observes, the clients of the poorer schools who stood to gain from the reallocation, had neither the means nor the expertise to match the elite lobby—'In any case the Hawke Government regarded them as captive voters who had nowhere else to take their discontent' (1985: 116). The decline of the political fortunes of Susan Ryan dates from that incident.

Generally it is the Catholic lobby which nudges or clouts the government if funding for private schools seems threatened, whichever strategy is appropriate at the time. (A word to the Prime Minister can secure a site for a new senior high school in Canberra; or closure of parochial schools can cause havoc in the local state system, as happened at Goulburn in July 1962.) Even in the case of the forty-one elite schools, none of them Catholic, it was the Catholic bishops who intervened with Mr Hawke. Although they are defending very different education and social values the Catholic authorities see strategic advantage in maintaining solidarity with advocates of privilege. Perhaps it is also believed that association with an establishment lobby reduces the danger of renewed sectarian attacks.

Many hoped that the undignified squabble for funds would end with the establishment of the Schools Commission by the Whitlam Labor government in 1973. The Commission was required to fund schools according to their needs, and to respect the liberty of parents to choose the sort of school they wanted for their children. The latter meant that private and Catholic schools had to be brought to what was deemed to be the standard resource level for a public school. For a dozen years the Commission struggled to reconcile these two objectives. In its first two or three years funds were plentiful and it was possible for the Commission to pursue a policy of equality by giving the greatest resources to those whose needs were greatest, and, at the same time, to facilitate choice by funding private schools.

The day of reckoning came when, with declining resources, the Commission had to be efficient as well as egalitarian and liberal. The conflict, always inherent in the Commission's charter, caused its members to split along interest lines. A minority report by public school representatives, protesting at a majority decision in which equality came second to freedom of choice, gave the Hawke Labor government (never greatly enamoured with participatory decision making) the opportunity to abolish the Commission. Decisions about implementing funding policies are now made in the protective obscurity of the bureaucracy.

The original intention of Labor's reforms was to bring existing schools up to an acceptable standard but education pressure groups were successful in diverting funds to new schools. Indeed, according to the Schools Commission, by using money for expansion rather than raising standards, some private authorities were able to keep the 'needs' of existing schools low enough to attract the maximum subsidy and at the same time build new schools. State and federal subsidies for the establishment, capital expansion and running of non-government schools contributed to the growth of Australia's private school sector. But this is not a sufficient explanation of why Australia is different. Denmark pays even more than Australia towards the running costs of its private schools, and, whereas this has helped a substantial private sector (especially compared with Norway and Sweden which have been reluctant to help non-government schools) it is neither as large nor expanding at the same rate as Australia's.

Why is it that some governments pay only for their public schools? In the USA the constitutional provision that the government shall not aid religions, has been interpreted to mean that private schools, at least the religious ones, and most are, shall not be funded directly from taxes. In Australia a similar constitutional limitation, one consciously patterned on the American model, has been interpreted by the High Court as not being an impediment to state aid for religious schools. This was determined in the celebrated DOGS (Defenders of Government Schools) case when, in 1981, the Court in a majority decision ruled that, so long as government moneys are distributed even handedly, and not for the purpose of creating one state-sponsored religion, there is no breach of the Australian Constitution. William Lowe Boyd, a visiting American professor of politics, was moved to write an article comparing the USA and Australian systems after his 'mistake' (according to academic colleagues at Deakin University) of sending his children to government schools in Geelong. Of the High Court decision he wrote:

> This ruling, along with the breadth, minimal regulations, and apparent social acceptance of federal aid to private schools in Australia, has made it a favorite example for American proponents of educational choice, tuition tax credits, and educational voucher plans (1987: 184).

There is no constitutional limitation in the United Kingdom, New Zealand, Sweden or Norway, yet they do not offer subsidies across the board as Australia does. Why? The cultural heterogeneity of Australia is an important force towards pluralistic structures and the growth of well organised, politically effective religious, ethnic and linguistic pressure groups. But for the enormous efforts of the Catholic Church—sustained for more than a century—and its political leverage at crucial times, the private school sector in Australia, non-Catholic as well as Catholic, would be more like that in the other Anglo–American countries. Such pressure groups, not concentrated in one area but dispersed through all regions, are virtually absent in the Scandinavian countries. In Sweden the largest ethnic minority are the Laps, concentrated in the remote north. Their special educational needs are met with what is virtually a separate regional school system within the public sector. Similarly in Denmark the public schools have been able to adapt to the needs of the German minority in the south. In Canada too, the chief linguistic and religious minority, the French Canadians, is geographically separate in its own province with its own school system.

Lack of diversity in the public education sector, particularly the absence of academically selective high schools, is a third condition contributing to pressures for private schools. In Britain the development of a three tier public secondary sector following the 1944 education act—grammar, secondary modern, and technical—largely survived attempts at comprehensive reform. It has absorbed pressure that otherwise would have inflated the private sector. A nation-wide scholastic examination regulated admission to grammar schools which compete successfully with private schools in getting students into university. Sweden's much vaunted comprehensive system ends with stage one secondary. Stage two is selective. No such selective option exists in Australia; the closest are the handful of prestige schools like Melbourne High or Fort Street in Sydney. Elsewhere public secondary education is comprehensive, high schools taking all comers but having an academic stream for those heading for higher education.

In this respect Australia and America are similar—in the tension between egalitarianism and academic elitism, the balance in public schooling in both countries is weighted strongly towards egalitarianism. Admirable as this may be, ambitious parents are likely to choose an academic private school if one is readily accessible as is generally the case in Australia, or otherwise make sure that they reside in a salubrious neighbourhood as happens in the USA and elsewhere.

The extent of centralised control over public schools is a fourth condition influencing the perceptions and choices made by parents. The classroom is where education happens but the locus of authority over curriculum and the teaching service may lie with the school, or with the local district or with the state. When control is exercised by a centralised state department the public school system can readily be used as an instrument for government purposes; when authority is devolved parents can have a greater say in the management of their own school. The Australian highly centralised educational bureaucracies were designed in the late nineteenth century for what seemed to be very good reasons to policy makers at the time—because there was no tradition of strong local government and because the determined religious secularists of the day didn't trust the local authorities to keep meddling clerics out of the schools.

With administrative structures inherited from that time, state governments can now readily intervene in anything from curriculum for national economic survival to prescribing a loyalty oath. When I was Chairman of the ACT Schools Authority (now replaced by a minister and public service bureaucracy) there were frequent approaches from interest groups which saw public schooling as a means for imple-

menting their particular reforms. Among other things we were pres-
sured about patriotic ceremonies, spelling reform, sex role socialisation,
drug education, economic achievement motivation, corporal punishment (for and against), the work ethic and 'getting to know the police'.
Whatever our response was to the substance of such requests I always
asked the proponents if they had also approached private schools,
pointing out that one third of Canberra's schools were private. In no
instance had a similar approach been made, although some replied that
they would now. I formed the impression that, in matters of social
control—like patriotism or the work ethic or drug education—
reformers viewed public school students as those being in greatest need
of salvation. This vulnerability of Australian public schools to such interventions and the remote centralised bureaucracies provide additional
inducements for concerned parents to exit. As consumers they can, to
quote Friedman again, only 'express their views through cumbrous
political channels'. The other Anglo–American and the Scandinavian
countries have substantial buffers between school and central government: local education authorities in Britain, local school boards in the
USA and Canada, authority devolved to the regions and individual
schools in New Zealand and Canada. Denmark is perhaps the epitome
of a devolved system. There the touch of government is so light that it
refrains even from collecting good educational statistics, for which
shortcoming it has been gently chided in an OECD country review. A
senior bureaucrat in Copenhagen was appalled when I once asked if
there was research comparing the performance of public and private
schools, 'We wouldn't even compare public schools' he said.

Australia's comparative position on these four attributes—the legal-
ity and availability of state aid, cultural heterogeneity, limited choice
within the public sector, and centralisation of authority—may be
roughly summarised with the aid of a score chart. The chart represents
the position over the last fifty years or so, not just the current state of
affairs. If only the contemporary state of play were to be counted some

Table 8.2 Conditions favouring a private education sector

	State Funding Legal	Culturally Mixed Society	Comprehensive Public Education	Centrally Managed Public System
Australia	+	+	+	+
Denmark	+	o	+	−
New Zealand	+	o	+	o
Norway	+	−	+	−
Sweden	+	−	o	−
United Kingdom	+	o	−	−
United States	−	+	+	−

reduction of centralisation and greater choice might have had to be noted in Australia. By the 1980s, however, strong private school structures were well in place and the recent devolution of authority in some states has had no perceptible effect on the flow from public. All countries score on at least two of the attributes favouring privatisation. But Australia is the only instance with a row of unambiguous pluses (see table 8.2).

THE CONTINUED PRIVATISATION OF AUSTRALIAN SCHOOLS?

Obviously the complete privatisation of Australian schools is not inevitable; it is not even likely. But the process will continue for some time yet because of the unstable public–private political balance. Additional aid does not reduce political leverage and pressure groups can pursue their advantage at strategic times. Private school authorities are, however, becoming nervous at the extent of their dependence on government funding. At the same time they are under some pressure from their clients (and potential clients in public schools) to expand and to reduce costs; and from teachers for better salaries. Failure to manage these pressures led to the recent near financial collapse of the Catholic system in Canberra. Some of the wealthiest private schools are using the era of generous public subsidy to so arrange their finances that, come the day when accountability requirements are too irksome, full independence will be possible.

Hoping for a solution to the public–private conflict, the Schools Commission and other agencies have published discussion papers canvassing ideas which would retain parity of esteem between public and private, and which would guarantee equality of access to excellent schooling.[2] Some proposals envisage a convergence of the public and private sectors into a fully funded, uniformly planned system with minimum state and maximum local control where diverse sorts of schools could exist in harmony. Such proposals were strenuously resisted by all private school lobbies and governments rapidly distanced themselves from the ideas.

If the public system continues to decline its function is likely to change from community schooling to a modern equivalent of charity schooling. It will have a residual role, caring for those children left over after the private interests have staked their territories—for the poor, for those in isolated areas and for the handicapped. Alternatively governments may eventually be forced by public opinion to recognise the implications of a dual system that is out of control. Something like the New Zealand system may emerge. There all Catholic schools have joined the public system with guarantees about securing their special identity. Socially elite private schools remain but they pay their own way.

The dynamics of decline

The different obligations and regulatory environments of public and private schools lead to unequal transactions across their common boundary. In this section we examine the movement of students, parents and teachers between public and private. The public sector is obliged to educate all children and generally local schools must accept all applicants in their community whatever their ability, motivation, special needs or parents' circumstances. As was noted earlier the public school functions as an agency for social cohesion. Students from families of diverse beliefs and social origins constitute part of the curriculum. On the other hand elite private schools represent more the values of the market. They can advertise for students and select those whom they think will do well. Those who are troublesome or who perform poorly can be encouraged to transfer to the public sector. In the days of Commonwealth Secondary Scholarships (a national examination introduced in the 1960s by the Menzies government) some elite private schools advertised in the press inviting parents of state school winners in for a chat. The scholarship rewarded winners with a grant. There was no means test, but a bigger grant went to those who were at private schools since they had to pay fees. With the additional grant, plus perhaps the offer of a special reduction on tuition fees, the elite private system attracted some of the public's abler students.

More recently in England the Thatcher government has introduced something similar: an 'assisted places scheme' which pays for poor but able children to attend private schools (Edwards et al., 1989). One effect of this is to induce feelings of guilt among the not-so-poor parents of public school children. They feel that perhaps they should be putting aside money so their children too may have what the government obviously thinks is a superior education. In Australia the massive subsidies to private schools carries a similar implied message—if the government is willing to spend so much helping people to pay the fees, or to bus children past the local public school, perhaps it really thinks that private is better.

In Australia the means accompanies the messages. The subsidy is far larger than in Britain and it is given to the school, not the student, for running costs and capital expansion. The effect is more than a net transfer from public to private and a decline in average ability and home background; there is a qualitative change in environment and function. Bereft of their high fliers public schools lose the contribution these make to lifting the average performance of all students. And as the number of highly able students declines it becomes increasingly difficult to resource more specialised academic studies.

If it were not for the private option the public school system would contain many more influential and articulate parents who would give voice to shortcomings and press for reform. Among the clients of private schools are most of the important decision makers and more powerful citizens, including, I suspect, increasing numbers of Labor politicians, many of whom were uncharacteristically reticent, when asked in pre-election surveys, where they sent their own children to school. Less restrained are some conservative politicians, one of whom recently applauded the greater commitment of parents with children in private schools; or a representative of business and industry who saw public schools as 'intellectual deserts' and their graduates as ill-equipped for service to the labour market, without the work ethic or useful skills. Such outbursts are not common; but the public–private divide remains a source for unobtrusive prejudice and discrimination. Boyd reported of his experience at Geelong, where parents at his public school 'lamented that local employers would hire the graduates of local private schools who had failed the Higher School Certificate exam in preference to graduates of even middle-class state schools who had passed the same important, culminating exam' (Boyd, 1987: 187).

The decisions of teachers in the public sector are the litmus test of educational privatisation in Australia. There is no doubt about the commitment of public school teacher organisations to the values of public education. There are, however, many teachers in public schools whose personal ambitions for their own children transcend their commitment to community values. Teacher unions are not unexpectedly reluctant to collect the information, but, if the longitudinal survey sample (see above) is representative of secondary teachers in the public sector, about half do not send their own children to public schools—one third use private schools and one sixth Catholic. In this respect, too, Australia is different from all other Anglo–American and Scandinavian countries. Elsewhere those who run public education have a personal stake in it. In Australia many of the top officials and teachers do not. This should not be read as a moral condemnation of individuals. They work in a structure which forces a conflict of private values with public interest. But the aggregation of these individual decisions lowers morale among those who remain and increases pressure to defect.

The third unequal exchange, or rather it is a one way migration, across the public–private boundary is of teachers themselves. Until recently private schools did not have to worry much about unions or offer a career structure. They could pick able teachers from the public sector with attractive individual packages; public schools of course are bound to work within a structure of industrial agreements and a state wide teaching service. In the last few years private sector teachers have become unionised. Whereas previously private school teachers got a free ride (without the odium attaching to industrial action) from the flow-on of public union gains, now they are collaborating with public unions for improved salaries and conditions. Under the Hawke government's policy for amalgamating unions it is possible that some form of federation of all teacher unions will emerge.

Government policy can have a much more direct impact on public schools than on private. The most recent and pervasive use of public schools as an instrument of policy has been to defer the entry of teenagers to the labour market by parking them at school. A spectacular turnaround has been achieved in less than a decade: in the 1970s it was the exception to remain at school after year ten, now almost two-thirds do. The large majority of these often reluctant stayers are in public secondary schools. There they are causing enormous strains and creating yet another incentive for the conventionally ambitious parents to exit.

The degenerative process fuels its own momentum. As the capacity of a school to provide a good academic education declines more parents become anxious and exit to the private sector. Teachers' morale declines as the stimulus of more able students is lost and the burden of teaching more difficult students increases. Difficulties in public schools lead to criticism from employers, from governments and from opposition. Thirty-six years after Menzies gave tax remission for school fees, and eighteen years after Whitlam won government for Labor with his needs based funding, votes are still to be had in promoting the private sector.

In the lead up to the 1990 federal election the opposition shadow minister for employment, education and training announced that a coalition (conservative) government would increase private school funding and abolish the 'educational impact reviews', which are now required when new schools apply for funding. The reason given was that the reviews were an unwarranted government intervention impeding growth of the private sector and freedom of choice. The policy statement also implied that private schools would have been exempt from the proposed national standards monitoring programme had the conservatives won government. The message is that private schools can be trusted.

Because my purpose in this chapter has been to tease out some of the collective consequences of individual decisions I have not discussed arguments advanced by some economists for choice. Briefly these are that parents are more likely to support their children's learning in a school which they have chosen and paid for, and that the children will work better in a school which matches their needs. And schools, because they are competing for clients and income, will get the best out of their teachers. This formula comprising a mix of involved parents, motivated students and committed teachers will, so the argument goes, generate better results.

Supporters of schools of sub-cultural maintenance and alternative schools use arguments based on the rights of parents in a free society to choose the sort of schools they want for their children. The UN Declaration of Human Rights speaks of 'the prior right of parents to choose . . .' There isn't much dispute over the right as such so long as it does not limit the rights of others (that is what the educational impact statements are about) or of children, though these are rarely considered. There is, however, deep division in Australia over whether the exercise of these rights should be subsidised with public funds when separate schools are demanded.

Academic results of public and private

Empirical inquiry can't do much to inform the argument over support for schools of sub-cultural maintenance. However the assertion that private schools get better academic results has been the subject of extensive statistical investigation; for example by Williams and Carpenter (1990) in Australia, by van Laarhoven et al. (1987) in The Netherlands and by Coleman et al. (1982) in the USA. The conclusions are pretty consistent and favour non-government schools—sometimes Catholic, sometimes private, due allowance having been made for differences of family background and so on. But there has been an enormous dispute, mainly in America, over what the results mean and what are the policy implications. The three lines of attack have been:

1 that 'other things are never equal' and that the regression equations never capture and control all of the influences in a real life situation;
2 that the effects are not long lasting and, in this respect, two Australian studies (Dunn, 1982; West, 1985) show a reversal of performance once the students get to university;
3 that a significant statistical association will not necessarily survive when it becomes the basis of changed practice.

Richard Murnane (1986), one of Coleman's most effective critics, pointed to the evidence that the social mix of a class or school influences scholastic performance. Thus one public school boy or girl may benefit from switching to private, but if they all go no-one benefits because they take their social environment with them. To test this Murnane re-analysed the Coleman data putting an additional control variable for school social class into the equation. He found that the effect of type of school was no longer significantly associated with results. This control was not used in the Australian analysis. Largely ignored in the argument over whether public or private is better is the fact that the average differences, while significant, are small and that variation in performance within sectors—public, private or Catholic—is far greater than the variation between them. Given this the research question should be to find the characteristics of successful schools, the policy strategy should be to encourage such schools, and parents should be advised to forget about whether a school is public or private and assess each on its merits.

The form to date does not indicate any horse—public, Catholic or private—as a clear winner in the Australian scholastic stakes. A small statistically significant difference puts private in front by a short head in the last race. The handicapping was uneven however, and if the runners had been weighted for compositional effect a different result would have been posted. Other experts say that on a longer course public is odds on as the best stayer. The bookies are set to make a killing from the economic tipsters who backed free market as a certain winner.

One can only speculate what the outcome will be as the public schools continue to lose their more able students. The market analogy 'those schools that succeed will send clear market signals as to the style of education most favoured' does not help because the quality of the product is crucially dependent on the nature of the customers. The quality of food in a restaurant, or of the goods in a store, or of the service in a hairdressers are independent of the quality of the clients; but the quality of education is very largely dependent on the quality of the pupils. Teachers and facilities do make a difference, but they are minor compared to that of the intake. Cream off the able pupils and they will continue to do well, but, after a critical mass is lost, those who remain will decline.

The next round of studies may well show private schools ahead in the Australian scholastic stakes. If so it will be because mix of students has changed. The parent deciding for private may then be deciding rationally; and in advising newcomers where to send their children my honest answer may have to be 'choose elite'. But rational choices for individuals do not provide the basis for a rational national policy. This is because in the longer run the aggregation of all such decisions will result in a system of schools no better, probably worse, than we have now.

It is not possible to specify the particular point of the unstable public–private system when scholastic performance in the public sector will decline precipitously. In Canberra, which has the lowest proportion of students in the public sector, public students are not yet behind in the competition for university entry. Partly this is due to Canberra's superb secondary colleges which are responsible for one of the few reverse flows in Australia from private and Catholic to public; and partly it is because it is the Catholic system rather than the elite component of the private which is strong. The first signs of a qualitative change due to the composition effect will, however, not be from city-wide statistics, but from local areas. There are already reports of public school decline in particular regions within Canberra and other cities where less than two thirds attend public schools.

As top students are removed the decline will be geometric, not linear. Envisage a model constructed on the assumption that the significant influence on pupil performance in different schools is the presence or absence of a group of pace-setters—intellectually able students endowed with high levels of aspiration from their middle class families. The model assumes that this is the distinguishing factor—other influences like high quality teachers or good resources are assumed to be evenly distributed. Short of an empirical investigation it is not unrealistic to guess that after a critical point, each one per cent loss of 'top' students leads to a measurable decline in average performance in public school. At the same time the average performance in elite schools, already endowed with ample pace-setters, remains constant despite the cream from public schools. The immediate net result once this critical point is reached will be a national decline in the average scholastic performance.

The policy dilemma posed for education by the private option is not unlike the game of prisoners' dilemma. In the game two villains apprehended by the law may join in a collaborative strategy, each refusing to give evidence against the other. This guarantees that both avoid the maximum sentence. Or one may defect, secretly giving evidence against his companion in crime, for the (more remote) chance that he will get off scot free while the other earns the maximum sentence. It can be shown that in the long run the collaborative strategy always comes out in front (Axelrod, 1984).

If all parents returned to the public system the standard would improve (not just because of the composition factor discussed in the imaginary model, but also because of the stake-holder effect). 'Defections' to the private sector carry the possibility of individual gain in the short run, but at the certain expense of collective decline in the longer term.

When announcing the historic shift of the Labor Party policy from outright opposition to state aid for private schools to funding all schools according to their needs, Gough Whitlam claimed to have buried the divisive issue of state aid. But he didn't dig deep; the ghost will rise from a shallow grave to haunt future governments.

ENDNOTES

[1] A forthcoming paper *The decline of a public school system* which includes some material from this chapter, develops more formally the idea of public–private schooling as an unstable system.

[2] For example: 'A Search for Common Ground: Government and Non-Government Schools in the ACT', Australian College of Education, Canberra, August, 1985: 'Some Aspects of School Finance in Australia', Schools Commission, October, 1978; 'An Integrated Public Education System', Schools Com-

mission, September, 1982. (See also the Schools Commission 1975 Report for a discussion of 'Supported Schools'.)

These reports and public/private school systems in some other countries are reviewed in *Schools for the ACT: How Public? How Private?*, AGPS, Canberra, 1983.

REFERENCES

Anderson, Don (1988a) 'Denomination and Type of School Attended: The Transmission of an Error' *Journal of Australian Studies*, 22, pp. 33–9

Anderson, D.S. (1988b) 'Values, Religion, Social Class and Choice of Private School in Australia' *International Journal of Educational Research* 12(4), pp. 351–73

—— (1990) *An Australian Educational Atlas* Working Papers in Sociology RSSS ANU

Anderson, D.S. and Western, J.S. (1967) 'Notes on a Study of Professional Socialization' *Australian and New Zealand Journal of Sociology* 3, pp. 67–71

—— (1972) 'Denominational Schooling and Religious Behaviour' *Australian and New Zealand Journal of Sociology* 8, pp. 19–31

Axelrod, Robert (1984) *The Evolution of Cooperation* New York: Basic Books

Boyd, William Lowe (1987) 'Balancing Public and Private Schools: The Australian Experience and American Implications' *Educational Evaluation and Policy Analysis* 9(3), pp. 183–97

Coleman, J.S., Hoffer, T. and Kilgore, S. (1982) *High School Achievement* New York: Basic Books

Connors, Lyndsay 'A National Framework for Public Schooling', Address to Public Schools Night, Canberra, November 1988

Dunn, T. (1982) 'Bias in Higher School Certificate Examination Results' *The Australian Journal of Education* 26, pp. 190–203

Edwards, Tony, Fitz, John and Whitty, Geoff (1989) *The State and Private Education: An Evaluation of the Assisted Places Scheme* Hampshire: The Falmer Press

Fane, George (1984) 'Education Policy in Australia' Office of Economic Planning Advisory Council Discussion Papers 84/08

Friedman, Milton (1962) *Capitalism and Freedom* Chicago: University of Chicago Press, p. 86

Greeley, Andrew M. and Rossi, Peter H. (1966) 'The Education of Catholic Americans' Chicago: Aldine Publishing Company

Macintyre, Stuart (1985) *Winners and Losers* Sydney: Allen & Unwin Australia Pty Ltd

Murnane, Richard J. (1986) 'Comparisons of Private and Public Schools: What Can We Learn?' in Daniel C. Levy, ed. *Private Education* Oxford: Oxford University Press, pp. 153–69

OECD (1989) 'Education in OECD Countries 1986-87' Paris: OECD

Persell, Caroline Hodges and Cookson, Peter W. Jr (1985) 'Chartering and Bartering: Elite Education and Social Reproduction' *Social Problems* 33(2), pp. 114–29

Sherington, Geoffrey, Petersen, R.C. and Brice, Ian (1987) *Learning to Lead* Sydney: Allen & Unwin Australia Pty Ltd

UNESCO (1989) 'Development of Private Enrolment First and Second Level Education 1975–1985' Paris: UNESCO

van Laarhoven, Peter, Bakker, Bart Dronkers, Jaap and Schijf, Hubert (1987) 'Achievement in Public and Private Secondary Education in the Netherlands' *Zeitschrift für internationale erziehungs- und social-wissenschaftliche Forschung* 2, pp. 335–65

West, L.H.T. (1985) 'Differential Prediction of First Year University Performance for Students from Different Social Backgrounds' *The Australian Journal of Education* 29, pp. 175–87

Williams, Ross A. (1984) 'The Economic Determinants of Private Schooling in Australia' mimeo

Williams, Trevor and Carpenter, Peter G. (1990) 'Private Schooling and Public Achievement' *Australian Journal of Education* 34(1), pp. 3–24

9 Comparing income transfer systems: is Australia the poor relation?

DEBORAH MITCHELL

Throughout the 1970s and 80s Australia has been consistently character-ised as the 'poor relation' among the OECD countries when it comes to welfare spending. As Castles (1987: 2) notes: 'Virtually all international comparisons of welfare state spending of Australia and other advanced western societies have shown Australia to be a welfare laggard.' While comparisons of aggregate expenditure—often referred to as 'welfare effort'—provide a useful guide to the relative generosity of welfare states and by implication the welfare of their citizens, such analyses have two major limitations. First, there is an implicit assumption that 'more is better', in other words, that higher levels of expenditure neces-sarily reflect a greater commitment to social well-being. Esping-Andersen (1989: 19) rejects this equation and argues that:

> By scoring welfare states on spending we assume that all spending counts equally. But, some welfare states, the Austrian for example, spend a large share on benefits to privileged civil servants . . . Some nations spend enormous sums on fiscal welfare in the form of tax privileges . . . that mainly benefit the middle classes. In Britain, total social expenditure has grown during the Thatcher period; yet, this is almost exclusively a function of very high unemployment. Low expenditures on some programs may signify a welfare state more seriously committed to full employment.

Secondly, such measures cannot account for the impact of taxes, the efficiency of program delivery nor the incidence of welfare benefits and services. Commenting on these problems, Gilbert and Moon (1988: 339) argue that the theoretical equation of welfare effort with the actual out-comes of these expenditures may not hold empirically:

> The measure of welfare effort should not be confused with that of welfare outcome. Theoretically we would expect higher welfare efforts . . . to result in higher welfare outcome (e.g. reduction of poverty and improvement of other social conditions.) But that remains an empirical question, which

168

among other things depends upon the actual distribution of welfare benefits, how efficiently they are delivered, and their unanticipated consequences for the well being of recipients.

I confine my analysis to a major component of welfare expenditures, namely income transfers. There are two aims of this chapter: one is to examine the extent to which Australia's image as a welfare 'laggard' is justified in terms of the outcomes from its transfer system; the other is to compare the general level of economic well-being of families in ten OECD countries from the perspectives of poverty and income inequality. While most studies of income transfers concentrate exclusively on direct transfers through the social security system, this study takes a comprehensive view of transfer policies by using microdata to examine the incidence and impact of both social security transfers and income taxes.

USING MICRODATA TO COMPARE THE IMPACT OF INCOME TRANSFERS

The type of data which is required to examine the distribution of benefits, the impact of taxes and the efficiency of transfers is collected in most OECD countries in the form of income, expenditure (consumption) or tax file surveys. This data is referred to as microdata and in Australia, the Australian Bureau of Statistics conducts such surveys for example, the 1985–86 Income and Housing Survey. Until recently, the comparability of the individual microdata sets for each country has been extremely low and could not be used with any confidence to make cross-national comparisons of the incidence of income transfers. This study uses a new data set which has been constructed from the survey data of a number of countries and is referred to as the Luxembourg Income Study (LIS).

The outstanding feature of the LIS data is that a number of income and demographic variables have been drawn from reliable, usually government sponsored, survey sources in participating countries and re-coded to form a common framework. The LIS database is comprised of microdata collected in sixteen countries[1] over two time periods: 1979–82 and 1985–87. Through extensive consultation with country coordinators, around sixty income and demographic variables have been made comparable across the data sets.[2]

In the analysis below, I have selected nine countries from the LIS database for comparison with Australia: Canada, France, Germany, The Netherlands, Norway, Sweden, Switzerland, UK, USA. These countries represent a wide range of transfer systems in terms of the balance between direct and indirect transfers; types of transfer programs, that is selective versus universal programs; and diverse levels of government expenditures.

It is important to stress here that the analysis presented below draws on the first wave of the LIS data (circa 1980). At the time of writing, the coverage of countries in the second wave of data (circa 1985) was considerably smaller. Therefore, income transfer policies in many of these countries may have undergone considerable transformation in the intervening period and the outcomes observed, may well be radically different today. Despite this, the analysis presented here maintains its relevance at the general level in terms of tracing the relationship between expenditure and outcomes. In this chapter (because of space limitations) I will not be discussing the comparative institutional arrangements of these countries in detail. For a detailed account of the institutional arrangements, readers may refer to Flora (1986) and Dixon and Scheurell (1989).

WHO ARE THE 'LEADERS' AND 'LAGGARDS' IN THE INCOME TRANSFER FIELD?

The analysis of aggregate expenditures presented here differs from conventional welfare effort measures in two respects: it is confined to expenditures on social security payments, that is it does not include expenditures on 'social welfare' in general which is the measure most frequently used in such comparisons; it takes account of what are termed tax expenditures.[3] The rationale for including tax expenditures is as follows: two countries may make allowance for the cost of raising children, but in country A such allowances may be paid in the form of a direct child benefit; while in country B a tax deduction/concession/rebate may serve exactly the same purpose. Thus, to exclude these tax expenditures is to underestimate the true level of support country B gives to the raising of children.

Table 9.1 sets out the transfer expenditures described above. Column 1 is social security program expenditures, that is the amount of expenditure which goes directly on benefits and does not include administrative costs. Tax expenditures are shown in columns 2 and 3. I have separated non-superannuation expenditures (column 2) for two reasons: where superannuation deductions or concessions are available they are generally the largest single item of tax expenditure; and secondly because their distribution is generally regressive, it may be argued that it is inappropriate to include these expenditures alongside of social security transfers. In this analysis, I include superannuation expenditures as part of social security effort because of its close connection with income maintenance provision for the aged, however readers may wish to compare this material separately.

	1 Social security expenditure	2 Tax expenditure non-super	3 Tax expenditure super	4 Net transfer expenditure (=1+2+3)
Australia	9478	926	1226	11 630
Canada	22 727	3626	3140	29 493
France	470 580	7198	1240	479 018
Germany	242 210	2720	3996	248 926
Netherlands	64 050	3914	9717	77 681
Norway	31 334	*	*	31 334
Sweden	85 090	11 037	11 832	107 959
Switzerland	15 260	*	*	15 260
UK	21 361	2623	1644	25 628
USA	218 796	19 869	36 745	275 410

	5 Social Security/GDP %	6 Social Security per capita 1980 $US**	7 Net transfers/ GDP %	8 Net transfers/ per capita 1980 $US**
Australia	6.9	624	8.5	765
Canada	7.4	838	9.6	1087
France	16.8	1597	17.1	1625
Germany	16.4	1638	16.8	1684
Netherlands	19.0	1836	23.1	2226
Norway	11.0	1136	*	*
Sweden	16.2	1926	20.6	2443
Switzerland	9.0	984	*	*
UK	9.3	771	10.3	897
USA	8.1	906	10.2	1140

Notes: * Data not available
** Converted to 1980 $US using purchasing power parities
Social security transfers: millions of currency unit
Tax expenditures non-super: millions of currency unit
Tax expenditures super: millions of currency unit
Net transfer expenditure: millions of currency unit
Social security transfers as a percentage of GDP

Social security transfers per capita in 1980 $US
Net transfer expenditure as a percentage of GDP
Net transfer expenditure per capita in 1980 $US

Sources: Social security transfers—Varley, R. (1986)
Tax expenditures—OECD (1984); McDaniel, P. and Surrey, S. (1985)
GDP—OECD National Accounts (1986)
Purchasing Power Parities—OECD National Accounts (1986)

Non-superannuation expenditures cover a wide range; for example, the exemption of social security benefits from tax, child deductions, dependents rebates, additional exemption allowances for the aged, blind or disabled, rent concessions and so on.[4] Column 3 shows all expenditures on superannuation-related deductions. Column 4 is the net expenditure on both direct and indirect transfers.

Column 5 shows the percentage of GDP expended on social security transfers. Two distinct groupings emerge—those which spent less than 10 per cent of GDP: the UK, Switzerland, USA, Canada and Australia; and those which spent greater than 10 per cent: Norway, Sweden, Germany, France and The Netherlands.

Country rank on SS/GDP

Netherlands	1	
France	2	
Germany	3	> **10%**
Sweden	4	
Norway	5	
UK	6	
Switzerland	7	
USA	8	< **10%**
Canada	9	
Australia	10	

Country rank on SS/per capita

Sweden	1	
Netherlands	2	
Germany	3	> **$US1000**
France	4	
Norway	5	
Switzerland	6	
USA	7	
Canada	8	< **$US1000**
UK	9	
Australia	10	

Converting to an expenditure per capita basis (column 6), changes the rankings considerably, notably Sweden moves from fourth to first and the UK drops from sixth to ninth. Moreover, the differences between the two groups becomes more marked with, for example, Sweden spending more than three times per capita than Australia.

The addition of tax expenditures (column 7) provides us with measures of Net Transfers Expenditure as a percentage of GDP (NTE/GDP) and per capita (NTE/PC) and results in an even more marked gap emerging between the welfare leaders and laggards: Australia and Canada remained the only countries spending less than 10 per cent of

Country rank on NTE/GDP

Netherlands	1	
Sweden	2	> **20%**
France	3	
Germany	4	
UK	5	**10–20%**
USA	6	
Canada	7	
Australia	8	< **10%**

Country rank on NTE per capita

Sweden	1	
Netherlands	2	> **$US2000**
Germany	3	
France	4	
USA	5	
Canada	6	
UK	7	
Australia	8	< **$US1000**

Table 9.2 Relative composition of transfer expenditure, 1980

	Social security (%)	Tax expenditure non super (%)	Tax expenditure super (%)	Total (%)
Australia	81.5	8.0	10.5	100
Canada	77.1	12.3	10.6	100
France	98.2	1.5	0.3	100
Germany	97.3	1.1	1.6	100
Netherlands	82.5	5.0	12.5	100
Norway	100.0	*	*	100
Sweden	78.8	10.2	11.0	100
Switzerland	100.0	*	*	100
UK	83.4	10.2	6.4	100
USA	79.4	7.2	13.3	100

GDP on income transfers (with the USA and the UK just marginally above).[5] The leaders on the other hand, spent more than 20 per cent of GDP on transfers. On a per capita basis (column 8) Australia's net transfer expenditure falls even further behind with the nearest country (UK) spending nearly 20 per cent more per capita.

Table 9.2 shows the composition of transfer expenditure for each country. Two patterns emerge: in France and Germany almost all transfers are directed through the social security system, with the remaining countries spending around 80 per cent on direct transfers. Within this second group, the bulk of tax expenditures in The Netherlands and the USA are directed toward superannuation concessions, while in Australia, Canada, Sweden and the UK tax expenditures are evenly split.

Even allowing for demographically generated differences in spending patterns (for example age composition), Australia is, indeed, quite distinctive in its social policy expenditure pattern in lagging a long way behind this group of countries in transfer expenditure, whether measured as a percentage of GDP or on a per capita basis. The inclusion of expenditures through the tax system, serves to separate Australia even further from those countries to which it is compared.

Moreover, the Australian social security system stands out in its institutional arrangements because of its reliance on category-based, means-tested programs as the vehicle for distributing social security expenditure. At the other extreme, the Scandinavian countries rely exclusively on universal policy instruments. As the analysis above shows, these extremes in institutional arrangements also correspond with extremes in the volume of expenditure. What then has been the impact of these levels of expenditure on poverty and income inequality and how effectively have these apparently diverse systems distributed this expenditure?

THE IMPACT OF INCOME TRANSFERS ON POVERTY

An enduring feature of the Australian social security system is its emphasis on 'targeting assistance to those most in need' as the most efficient means of alleviating poverty. How do the outcomes of this policy approach compare with other approaches? In a later section I examine whether efficiency considerations play a significant role in these outcomes.

The measurement of poverty, particularly on a cross-national basis, is a thorny issue: all measures are subjective and open to criticism on a variety of grounds. The best that can be claimed for the approach adopted here is that the poverty benchmark—50 per cent of adjusted median income—has been conventionally accepted in cross-national studies and that the equivalence scale used to adjust family income is that recommended by the OECD and which is also becoming a conventional measure.[6] Poverty estimates are frequently presented in the form of a head-count measure, that is, the proportion of the population below a given poverty line. The count itself may be based on persons, families or households. While the head-count is a useful presentational measure, by virtue of its simplicity, it does have a number of drawbacks which have been widely discussed in the poverty measurement literature—see for example, Sen (1979) and Foster's survey (1984). Of these, there are two which most concern this analysis, first, the sensitivity of the head-count to where the poverty line is drawn; second, head-counts may be misleading in comparing the degree of poverty cross-nationally.

One way of overcoming such problems is to use the poverty gap measure. The poverty gap refers to the difference between household or family income and the poverty line. This difference may be expressed in actual monetary terms, for example $X required to bring the family up to the poverty line income either expressed as a percentage of the poverty line rather than in monetary units or aggregated across the population and expressed as a percentage of GDP. The two latter approaches are frequently adopted in cross-national comparisons to standardise comparisons. Both the head-count and poverty gap measures have been calculated for these countries and are analysed below.

Using the poverty line described above, table 9.3 sets out the poverty rates for families pre- and post-transfer for this group of countries. The poverty rates prior to transfer are generally highest in the larger welfare states and these ranks change considerably after social security transfers, with the five largest spenders reducing their poverty rates quite dramatically. It is interesting to note that although Australia is the welfare laggard in this group, its post-transfer poverty rate is lower than the USA, Canada and Switzerland using this particular poverty line. This indicates that the targeting aspect of the Australian system may well have some virtues.

Table 9.3 Comparison of poverty measures

| | Pre- and post-transfer poverty measures | | | | | |
| | Percentage of families in poverty | | | Poverty gap as % of GDP | | |
Country	Pre-	Post-	Red'n	Pre-	Post-	Red'n
Australia	28.0	10.3	63	4.5	0.9	79
Canada	24.9	12.5	50	4.2	1.3	70
France	36.4	7.9	78	6.7	1.0	85
Germany	31.0	6.8	78	6.4	0.6	91
Netherlands	32.5	7.0	78	6.5	1.4	79
Norway	30.6	5.3	83	4.6	0.5	90
Sweden	36.5	5.6	85	4.1	0.4	91
Switzerland	24.3	11.0	55	4.9	1.2	75
United Kingdom	30.0	8.2	73	3.3	0.2	93
United States	27.1	17.0	37	5.6	2.3	60

I noted earlier that the head-count approach gives a very crude picture of poverty. Two further aspects need to be examined: the size of the poverty gap remaining after transfers and the composition of the poor in each country.

On the right hand side of table 9.3, I have estimated the aggregate poverty gap (as a percentage of GDP) for those defined as poor pre- and post-transfer on the left hand side of the table. This measure gives a different view of the outcomes of the transfer process. Again the larger welfare states are prominent in the amount of reduction of the poverty gap achieved by their transfer systems. On the other hand, Australia and particularly the UK, which are considered as welfare laggards on the aggregate measures have transfer systems which are also effective in closing the poverty gap. Combining the information from both sides of table 9.3 helps to balance out some of the sensitivity problems associated with head-count measures and gives a clearer view of the impact of the transfer systems. For example, if we consider the UK we see that while the number of families who are poor post-transfer is the sixth highest in this group, it has the smallest aggregate poverty gap, indicating that although there is a substantial number of families below the poverty line, these families fall short of the poverty line by only a small amount of income. Conversely, in The Netherlands the poverty gap for those below the poverty line is much larger.

Tables 9.4 and 9.5 show the percentage of different family types in poverty pre- and post-transfer. What is interesting about the breakdown of the poverty populations in these countries is that, while the rates of poverty vary quite widely, the make up of the poor populations both before and after transfers are fairly similar, that is the various systems tend to treat the same groups badly and conversely, especially in respect of the aged, tend to do well by the same groups.

Table 9.4 Percentage of family types defined as poor pre-transfer

	Aged (S)	Aged (C)	Single (NC)	Couple (NC)	Lone Parent	Couple (CH)	Other
Australia	82.1	70.2	26.6	12.1	59.3	11.6	25.5
Canada	71.5	55.2	23.5	8.0	50.4	13.5	26.3
France	87.5	77.7	23.2	17.9	39.4	21.5	34.1
Germany	85.8	70.6	24.8	11.5	22.8	4.5	25.1
Netherlands	72.9	64.0	45.2	18.6	73.0	13.5	41.5
Norway	82.7	61.8	26.7	8.1	35.7	4.4	*
Sweden	92.0	81.1	28.2	9.3	33.0	6.4	*
Switzerland	72.8	59.9	18.7	5.2	23.8	3.1	*
UK	86.2	70.1	27.9	6.1	54.3	8.5	29.8
USA	72.6	57.4	21.6	7.9	53.3	11.5	35.0

Notes: * Countries in which data is coded into substantive categories only
(S) = Single; (C) = Couple; (NC) = No Children; (CH) = Children

Table 9.5 Percentage of family types defined as poor post-transfer

	Aged (S)	Aged (C)	Single (NC)	Couple (NC)	Lone Parent	Couple (CH)	Other
Australia	3.8	6.9	13.9	3.8	39.5	10.2	5.1
Canada	11.3	8.7	17.3	5.2	38.7	10.6	13.3
France	1.4	3.4	10.8	7.5	19.4	9.3	12.6
Germany	10.4	8.8	8.2	3.4	9.4	4.7	12.9
Netherlands	4.9	3.0	14.6	5.5	6.0	6.8	11.2
Norway	7.0	2.6	9.1	2.8	9.5	3.2	*
Sweden	0.0	0.0	8.5	1.0	5.4	1.6	*
Switzerland	18.6	11.9	14.2	2.3	17.1	5.8	*
UK	15.6	17.8	9.4	2.4	18.8	4.8	3.4
USA	31.9	16.4	17.3	5.3	45.7	11.7	18.4

First, some general points of similarity—in all countries the aged form the dominant pre-transfer poor group, followed by lone parents and single people without children. Post-transfer (with the exception of Sweden and The Netherlands) lone parents generally have the highest poverty rates of all these family types. Poverty amongst lone parents is most prominent in the USA, Australia and Canada where around 40 per cent of these families remain in poverty after transfers. The implications of this are important when we consider the third of the future scenarios discussed in Geoff McNicoll's essay (chapter 4), that is if Sweden is the pacesetter of family trends and lone parent households continue to rise at a rapid rate, the social security systems in these countries will need radically to transform their mechanisms of support for lone parents. The evidence from this data suggests that many of these countries have been unable to come to grips with existing trends. The next group most likely to be in poverty in all these countries are single persons without children. This group is predominantly comprised of the young unemployed and students.

These results are consistent with the trends discerned in a recent OECD survey (1988: 6) of social security programs which noted that poverty amongst the aged has declined dramatically in the OECD countries in the period since 1945:

> The available evidence indicates that the relative income position of the elderly has improved significantly in most countries; in some countries their average level of economic welfare equals or even slightly exceeds that of the non-elderly population.

The survey goes on to point out that among the OECD countries a number of new groups requiring income support have emerged over the past decade (for example sole parents, the young and long-term unemployed). Unlike the aged these groups do not attract the same level of popular support and these groups have increasingly come to dominate the poor population:

> In those OECD countries which have measures of poverty or low income, the general trend in recent years has been of a static or declining number of elderly poor, with the non-elderly increasingly to be found in the lower parts of the income distribution.

On this basis, we see that countries such as Sweden, Norway and The Netherlands achieve greater balance in poverty alleviation than the other countries—this is an important outcome to be considered in relation to expenditures.

THE IMPACT OF TRANSFERS ON INCOME INEQUALITY

A second enduring characterisation of Australia is that it has a highly egalitarian income distribution: a belief founded on the influential studies of Lydall (1968) and Sawyer (1976).[7] The conclusions of both these studies from an Australian perspective have been questioned (Stark, 1977; Ingles, 1981). As Saunders (1989: 7) comments:

> although the statistical evidence to support this is surprisingly slim, the view has persisted throughout much of this century. It has also contributed to an unwarranted complacency in social policy . . . as well as an undeserved egalitarian respect from others.

Using the LIS database, I examine the extent of income inequality in the LIS countries from two perspectives. The first uses the Gini coefficient, which summarises the degree of income inequality across the

178   AUSTRALIA COMPARED

Table 9.6 Ranks based on Gini coefficients pre- and post-transfer

Rank	Pre-transfer Gini		Post-social security Gini		Post-tax Gini	
1	Norway	.385	Sweden	.241	Sweden	.197
2	Canada	.387	Germany	.280	Norway	.234
3	UK	.393	Norway	.285	Germany	.252
4	Germany	.407	UK	.293	UK	.264
5	Switzerland	.414	Canada	.325	Australia	.287
6	Australia	.414	Netherlands	.329	Canada	.293
7	Sweden	.417	Australia	.336	Netherlands	.293
8	US	.425	France	.344	France	.307
9	Netherlands	.467	Switzerland	.357	US	.317
10	France	.471	US	.369	Switzerland	.336
	range	.086		.128		.139
	coefficient of variation	7.2%		12.6%		14.9%

population.[8] The second distinguishes separately the redistributive effects of the social security and taxation systems.

Table 9.6 shows the Gini coefficient for each of these income measures, based on adjusted family income.[9] Starting with column 1 we see that Norway, Canada, the UK and Germany produce the most equal distribution of incomes in the market place. Switzerland, Australia and Sweden produce virtually identical outcomes and are ranked in the middle of this group. At the bottom end of the table is the USA and there is a considerable gap to the last two countries, The Netherlands and France, which, as table 9.1 shows, are two of the largest spenders on social security as a percentage of GDP. After social security transfers considerable re-ranking takes place. As would be expected from the welfare effort table, the larger welfare states achieve redistributions of upwards of 25 per cent (Sweden 42 per cent), placing most of these countries in the top half of the table. It is interesting to note that, although Australia lags considerably behind countries such as France and Germany on social security expenditure, it achieves comparable rates of redistribution and maintains its position around the centre of this group. Again the explanation for this may lie with the extensive means testing of Australian social security transfers. The relegation of Switzerland and the USA to the bottom of the table may be similarly explained by poor targeting of expenditure.

After taxes, Australia and the USA move up the table partly due to greater progressivity in these tax systems. It should be noted however, that this apparent reduction in the Gini coefficient may also be explained by the disproportionate effect which transfers around the modal income class have on the Gini measure. Thus, tax expenditures accruing to middle income earners (for example superannuation deductions) may overstate the true level of redistribution accruing to taxes.

Examining each country individually, at each stage of the transfer process, we see that Norway, Germany and the UK maintain a fairly constant position at the top of the table. Australia also holds its position around the middle of the table. Sweden jumps five ranks after transfers and maintains its position at the top of the table after taxes. Switzerland, on the other hand, is relegated to the bottom end of the table after transfers for the reasons discussed above. After transfers France rises to seventh position which it maintains after taxes. The Netherlands achieves considerable redistribution through the social security system, however the level of redistribution achieved by the taxation system is lower than that achieved by a number of the 'low spenders' on direct transfers, and so The Netherlands falls in the rankings. While Canada and to a lesser extent the USA begin with a better outcome from the market distribution of income as compared with France and The Netherlands, they achieve low levels of net redistribution (less than 25 per cent), so that these countries are passed by the larger welfare states after income transfers.

It is also interesting to examine here whether the LIS countries diverge or converge in the distribution of income during the transfer process. At the market income stage, the range of the Gini coefficients between the top country (Norway) and the bottom (France) is 0.08. After social security transfers, the range increases to 0.13 and post-tax it increases slightly to 0.14. This indicates that while social security and taxation systems do reduce the level of inequality within each country, the amount of reduction achieved varies considerably across countries and has the effect of increasing the inter-country differences in inequality.

Another question of interest is whether it is the social security or the taxation system which has the greatest impact in reducing inequality. In principle, social security and taxation are alternative (or complementary) instruments for lowering inequality. For example I noted earlier that support to low income parents can be achieved either through child benefit payments or through child tax allowances.

In table 9.7 the net redistribution effected by the total transfer system is shown in the first column (net R). The second column shows the redistribution which occurs between market and gross incomes, that is the redistributive effect of the social security system (R post-ss). The final column shows the redistribution which occurs between pre-tax income and disposable income, that is the redistributive effect of taxation (R post-tax). Note that the second and third columns do not sum to equal the first because they have different denominators.

While social security transfers have the greatest impact on inequality,

Table 9.7 Redistributive effects of social security and taxation systems (per cent)

Net R		R post-SS		R post-tax	
Sweden	53	Sweden	42	Sweden	18
Norway	39	Germany	31	Norway	17
Germany	38	Netherlands	30	Australia	14
Netherlands	37	France	27	US	13
France	35	Norway	26	France	11
UK	33	UK	25	Netherlands	11
Australia	31	Australia	19	Germany	9
US	25	Canada	16	Canada	9
Canada	24	Switzerland	14	UK	8
Switzerland	19	US	13	Switzerland	5

there are several countries whose taxation systems generate a significant amount of the overall redistribution, most notably, the USA, Australia, Canada and Norway. In table 9.7 the net redistribution is broken down into the proportions carried out by the social security and taxation instruments. The social security share of net redistribution (R to SS) is calculated as [(R post SS)/net R] and the taxation share (R to taxes) is calculated as [1 − (R to SS)]. In all countries except the USA social security transfers account for more than 60 per cent of the net redistribution. In Germany, The Netherlands and Sweden the social security system is responsible for over 80 per cent of the net redistribution.

In general, it is the countries which achieve the largest amount of redistribution through social security transfers which are the most successful in reducing income inequality. There is a positive correlation between net R and R to SS, the simple correlation coefficient is $r = 0.54$. An important exception to this relationship is Norway which is ranked second both in terms of amount of redistribution achieved and post-tax inequality. Unlike the other countries which are most effective in reducing inequality, Norway achieves sizeable redistribution through its tax instruments.

It appears, therefore, that, although social security is the principal instrument for reducing inequality, taxation can play an important and independent role.

EXPENDITURES AND OUTCOMES

In the preceding analysis I have pointed out several instances where expected outcomes, based on expenditure levels, are not observed. In this section, I examine the relationship between aggregate expenditures on social security and outcomes more closely. I do not use the net trans-

Table 9.8 Comparing expenditures and outcomes

Rank on SS/per capita	Rank on post-transfer head-count	Rank on post-transfer poverty gap	Rank on post-transfer Gini coefficient
1 Sweden	2	2	1
2 Netherlands	4	9	7
3 Germany	3	4	3
4 France	5	6	8
5 Norway	1	3	2
6 Switzerland	8	7	10
7 USA	10	10	9
8 Canada	9	8	6
9 UK	6	1	4
10 Australia	7	5	5

fer expenditure measure because this will exclude Norway and Switzerland from the comparisons. A comparison of the ranks of countries on the expenditure and outcome measures is shown in table 9.8.

A first point to note is that apart from Sweden, Germany and to a lesser extent Canada, using aggregate expenditures to predict outcomes would be highly misleading. Several countries—the UK, Norway and Australia—do considerably better than their aggregate expenditures would predict; while France, The Netherlands, Switzerland and the USA all have a lower level of outcome than countries with lower expenditures. Part of the explanation for the variance between expenditures and outcomes may be attributed to the role of taxation. As the analysis above shows, Norway and Australia achieve substantial redistribution through their taxation systems, while France and The Netherlands do relatively less well in this respect. In the following section I consider whether the targeting (selectivity) of social security transfers plays a role in the outcomes observed in these measures.

SELECTIVITY: VICE OR VIRTUE?

In earlier sections, I have noted that some of the larger welfare states appear not to do as well as we might expect in redistribution/poverty alleviation given the size of their expenditures. Part of the explanation for this may lie with the fact that these countries start from a lower base: either very unequal income distributions and/or high poverty rates. Alternatively, the distribution of these expenditures may be 'inefficient' in the sense that a considerable proportion of this expenditure may accrue to the non-poor. Ringen (1987: 13) for example, argues that:

The large and/or universal welfare state may be seen as wasteful and as giving benefits to people who do not need them, at the cost of unnecessarily high taxes, and the small welfare state as more effective because selective and targeted policies give more bang for the buck.

Limited support for this view has already been presented in this analysis, where it appears that Australia, as the undeniable laggard in this group, does better than expected. Views on the efficacy of targeting in Australia are mixed, as Travers (1989: 1) points out:

> Australia is notable for the degree of selectivity in its social security programs.
> This is seen by some as a virtue because of the efficiency with which
> benefits are targeted. Others point out . . . that the redistributive impact of
> Australian income maintenance programs is low by international standards.

So which view is correct? To test the impact of program efficiency on poverty alleviation, I use an approach to efficiency developed by Beckerman (1979) whose measures attempt to provide answers to the following questions: what percentage of social security expenditure accrues to the pre-transfer poor (targeting efficiency)? How much poverty does each unit of social security expenditure alleviate (poverty reduction efficiency)?[10] To make clear the ensuing analysis it is necessary to introduce Beckerman's methodology, the essential elements of which are summarised in figure 9.1.

Families classified as poor, prior to transfers, are found in the range 0 to P^0, the size of their poverty gaps being the distance from the line Y^0Z to the poverty line. Thus the areas marked A and D represent the total sum of the pre-transfer poverty gap. After transfers, the poor are found in the range 0 to P^1, the size of their poverty gaps being the distance between Y^1Z and the poverty line. Thus the area D represents the sum of the post-transfer poverty gap. Pre-transfer poor families who are raised above the poverty line, are those in the range P^1 to P^0; and their distance above the poverty line is the distance between Y^1Z and the poverty line. The area B then represents the total amount by which transfers have raised these families above the poverty line. Beckerman argues that if we were to assume that the most efficient way of directing expenditures was to take families to the poverty line but not beyond, the area B represents some level of inefficiency, that is where expenditures 'spillover'. There are a number of problems with this interpretation and these will be raised below. For the present, it may be that spillover is an indication of efficiency. A more telling measure of targeting efficiency, however, is the size of the area C which represents the sum of the transfers which accrue to the non-poor.

Using these concepts, Beckerman defines three efficiency measures: vertical expenditure efficiency (VEE) or the proportion of transfers accruing to those who were poor prior to transfer; spillover (S); and

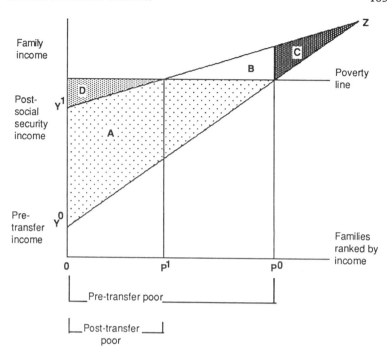

Figure 9.1 Beckerman's efficiency model

poverty reduction efficiency (PRE) which combines the VEE and spill-over measures. To summarise, the areas defined in figure 9.1 correspond to the following magnitudes:

$$A + B + C = \text{total social security transfer expenditure}$$

$$A + B = \text{total transfers received by the pre-transfer poor}$$

$$A + D = \text{pre-transfer poverty gap}$$

$$D = \text{post-transfer poverty gap}$$

Beckerman's efficiency measures are given by:

$$\text{VEE} = (A + B)/(A + B + C)$$

$$S = B/(A + B)$$

$$\text{PRE} = A/(A + B + C) = (1 - S) \times \text{VEE}$$

Table 9.9 Targeting efficiency measures

	Vertical expenditure efficiency %	Spillover %	Poverty reduction efficiency %
Australia	68.4	24.1	51.8
Canada	51.7	25.2	38.7
France	69.4	50.6	34.3
Germany	65.1	44.4	36.2
Netherlands	64.0	57.3	27.3
Norway	67.0	44.8	37.0
Sweden	61.5	61.2	23.9
Switzerland	63.2	35.3	40.9
UK	44.3	27.6	32.1
USA	59.8	30.7	41.4

These measures have been calculated for each country and are shown in table 9.9. Beginning with the spillover measures we see that those countries with elements of means-testing in their systems: Australia, Canada, the UK and USA have significantly lower levels of spillover. On the other hand, the universal systems of Sweden and The Netherlands have much larger levels of spillover.

There are two ways of interpreting these results, on the face of it we might wish to conclude that means-testing does result in much greater expenditure efficiency than universal systems. A second, and equally plausible, explanation is that lower levels of spillover reflect lower levels of expenditure, that is the less funding you put into a system the less likely that it will spillover. As Beckerman himself notes (1979: 54): 'the easiest way to reduce spillover to zero, for example, is to spend nothing'.

In my view, a stronger measure of efficiency is the second measure, vertical expenditure efficiency. Essentially this measure captures the overall level of targeting, that is the level of expenditures which go to the pre-transfer poor. On this measure Australia and the larger welfare states succeed in directing 60 per cent to 70 per cent of their transfers to the poor. On the other hand, the UK, Canada and the USA do not do as well as the larger welfare states.

The last measure, poverty reduction efficiency, is a composite of the two previous measures: it captures the extent to which transfers go to the poor and the extent to which these transfers take families up to the poverty line without spilling over. Given Australia's high degree of efficiency in both these areas it is not surprising that it is significantly ahead of all these countries, while Sweden with a much higher spillover and a moderate vertical expenditure efficiency ranks last.

These results suggest that efficiency may be a contributing factor to outcomes. For example, Australia's low level of expenditures appears to be efficiently directed to the poor—while the net redistribution of income is around 30 per cent, the poverty gap is reduced by 80 per cent and the number of families in poverty is reduced by just over 60 per cent. This also partly applies to Norway which is the fifth largest spender but which arguably produces a welfare outcome second only to Sweden. On the evidence presented here, Norway's better than expected outcome would appear to be due to a combination of a high level of vertical expenditure efficiency (that is the percentage of transfers accruing to the poor, 67 per cent) and the redistributive impact of its tax system.

These measures are also useful in explaining why it is, for instance, that France and The Netherlands, which are both large spenders on social security, do not achieve outcomes consistent with these expenditures. For example, The Netherlands which is the second largest spender in per capita terms is ranked ninth in terms of poverty reduction efficiency. This is consistent with its post-transfer poverty gap and Gini coefficient ranks. On the other hand, the post-transfer head-count measure puts The Netherlands in the top half of the table. One explanation for this seemingly contradictory evidence can be gleaned from the spill-over result in table 9.9. The Netherlands has the second highest level of spillover indicating that transfers lift recipients a long way above the poverty line and that perhaps, this may be to the cost of those who remain poor post-transfer. A similar but slightly weaker effect is observed for France.

CONCLUSIONS

These findings present us with three sets of observations. First, there is clear evidence (from the income transfer aspect) to support the doubts raised by a number of writers concerning the relevance of aggregate expenditures as a means of comparing welfare states. For this reason, judgments concerning welfare leaders and laggards based on expenditure measures should be tempered by other considerations such as the outcomes of welfare programs. Australia is a foremost example here. Whilst in the expenditure related terms of columns 7 and 8 of table 9.1, Australia stands out as a conspicuous laggard, in terms of both post-transfers poverty gap (table 9.3) and the post-tax gini measure of inequality (table 9.6), Australia is very clearly in the middle of the distribution of this group of nations. In these latter terms, it is not perhaps in quite the same league as Sweden and Norway, but manifests an appreciably lower poverty gap than the USA, The Netherlands or Canada and substantially greater equality than Switzerland, the USA and France.

Secondly, the poverty analysis shows that while there is a considerable variance in poverty rates, there is a great deal of similarity between the countries in terms of the groups most/least likely to be in poverty. However an important issue which deserves further consideration, is that of the effectiveness of these countries (and indeed welfare states generally) in addressing poverty across a range of demographic groups. As Gruen (1989: 23) has argued, aggregate measures disguise the extent of equitable treatment between different sub-groups in the poor population.

Thirdly, which country is Australia most like among this group? Policy analysts here traditionally look to the English speaking world for comparison. It is true that this group of countries share many characteristics in terms of institutional arrangements, levels of spending, the size and composition of their poor populations. However, on this analysis the UK and Australia are clearly separated from Canada and the USA because of their substantially better outcomes from the transfer process, despite the earlier evidence that they spend less in per capita terms than any other of the LIS nations; while the UK uniformly provides better outcomes for the poor than any of this group of Anglo-Saxon countries.

ENDNOTES

[1] Australia, Belgium, Canada, France, Germany, Hungary, Italy, Israel, Luxembourg, The Netherlands, Norway, Poland, Sweden, Switzerland, UK, USA.
[2] A fuller description of the LIS database can be found in Buhmann et al. (1988).
[3] Tax expenditures are so-called since they represent the taxation revenue foregone by governments through the operation of deductions, concessions and rebates and are thus retained in household disposable income in much the same way as a direct benefit.
[4] A full description of these may be found in OECD (1984) and McDaniel and Surrey (1985).
[5] Taxation expenditure data not available for Norway and Switzerland.
[6] See Mitchell (1990: 14) for a fuller discussion of the poverty line used here.
[7] Sawyer (1976: 16) notes that Australia, Sweden and Japan record the lowest degree of inequality in the post-tax distribution.
[8] A discussion of the Gini coefficient can be found in Cowell (1977). The critical point to note here is that the lower the size of the Gini coefficient, the lower the level of income inequality within the population.
[9] The unit of analysis is the family, incomes have been adjusted by using the OECD equivalence scale: 1st adult = 1; second and subsequent adults = 0.7; children = 0.5. The use of equivalence scales in this type of analysis is not unproblematic, for further discussion see Buhmann et al. (1988).
[10] Beckerman's study was one of the first serious attempts to make cross-

national comparisons of the impact of income maintenance programs on poverty. For a more detailed account of the methodology readers are referred to Beckerman (1979).

REFERENCES

Beckerman, W. (1979) *Poverty and the Impact of Income Maintenance Programmes in Four Developed Countries* International Labour Office Geneva

Buhmann, B. et al. (1988) 'Equivalence Scales, Well-Being, Inequality and Poverty: Sensitivity Estimates Across Ten Countries Using the Luxembourg Income Study Database' in *International Review of Income and Wealth*, 34, pp. 115–42

Castles, F. (1987) 'Trapped in an Historical Cul-de-sac: The Prospects for Welfare Reform in Australia' in Saunders, P. and Jamrozik, A. eds *Social Welfare in the Late 1980s: Reform, Progress or Retreat?* Social Welfare Research Centre: University of New South Wales

Cowell, F. (1977) *Measuring Inequality* Deddington, Phillip Allen

Dixon, J. and Scheurell, P. eds (1989) *Social Welfare in Developed Market Countries* London: Routledge

Esping-Andersen, G. (1989) 'The Three Political Economies of the Welfare State' in *Canadian Review of Sociology and Anthropology* 26(1), pp. 10–36

Flora, P. ed. (1986a) *Growth to Limits: The Western European Welfare States since World War II*, vol 1, Berlin: de Gruyter

———— ed. (1986b) *Growth to Limits: The Western European Welfare States since World War II*, vol 2, Berlin: de Gruyter

Foster, J. (1984) 'On economic poverty: a survey of aggregate measures' in *Advances in Econometrics*, 3, pp. 215–51

Gilbert, N. & Moon, A. (1988) 'Analyzing Welfare Effort: An Appraisal of Comparative Methods' in *Journal of Policy Analysis and Management* 7(2), pp. 328–32

Gruen, F. (1989) 'Australia's Welfare State—Rearguard or Avant Garde?' *Centre for Economic Policy Research Discussion Papers* Australian National University

Ingles, D. (1981) Statistics on the Distribution of Income and Wealth in Australia, research paper 14, Canberra: Development Division Department of Social Security

International Labour Office (1967; 1975; 1978; 1981) *The Cost of Social Security*, International Labour Office: Geneva

Lydall, H. (1968) *The Structure of Earnings* Oxford: Oxford University Press

Mcdaniel, P. and Surrey, S. (1985) *International Aspects of Tax Expenditures: A Comparative Study* Netherlands: Kluwer

Mitchell, D. (1990) 'Targeting Efficiency of Social Security Programs' in *Australian Journal of Public Administration* 49(1), pp. 12–16

OECD (1984) *Tax Expenditures: A Review of the Issues and Country Practices* Paris: OECD

———— (1987) *Revenue Statistics of OECD Member Countries 1965–1985* Paris: OECD

———— (1988) *The Future of Social Protection: The General Debate*, paper distributed to the meeting of the Manpower and Social Affairs Committee, 6–7 July 1988 Paris: OECD

Ringen, S. (1987) *The Possibility of Politics* Oxford: Clarendon

Saunders, P. et al. (1989) 'Income Inequality in Australia and New Zealand: International Comparisons and Recent Trends' *Social Welfare Research Centre* discussion paper No: 15

Sawyer, M. (1976) 'Income Distribution in OECD Countries' in *OECD Economic Outlook—Occasional Studies* Paris: OECD

Sen, A. (1979) 'Issues in the measurement of poverty' in *Scandinavian Journal of Economics*, 81, pp. 285–307

Stark, T. (1977) 'The Distribution of Income in Eight Countries', background paper 4, *Royal Commission on the Distribution of Income and Wealth* London: HMSO

Travers, P. (1989) 'Salami Tactics and the Australian Welfare State' paper presented to International Seminar on the Sociology of Social Security, Edinburgh

PART III POLITICS

10 Interest group politics: corporatism without business?

TREVOR MATTHEWS

WHY FOCUS ON INTEREST GROUPS?

This chapter is about the political preconditions of economic performance. It may not be entirely self-evident why, in wishing to account for
the success or failure of a nation's economic management, we should
emphasise its interest groups. Far more important, some would argue,
is the state's capacity to anticipate evolving economic problems, to
design appropriate policies, and to coordinate the effective implementation of those policies. Others would emphasise the international
economic context: how vulnerable a country is to the vicissitudes of
the international economy; how dependent it is on foreign capital and
imported raw materials—particularly energy. Others again would choose
to emphasise the influence of cultural factors on economic outcomes:
whether business, for example, is internationally-oriented; whether
there is a well-entrenched work ethic; or whether labour and capital
exhibit a spirit of social partnership. Yet, in an effort to explain the
marked variation in economic performance among seemingly similar
industrialised market economies during the decade and a half following
the end of the long boom, many political scientists and political economists have argued that interest groups hold the key. Some—such as
Samuel H. Beer and Mancur Olson—have laid the blame for a country's poor economic performance and its 'ungovernability' at the door
of sectional interest groups.

British politics in the 1970s, Beer (1982) has argued, suffered from
'pluralistic stagnation': interest groups were too aggressive, too self-
serving and too numerous. By offering 'subsidies for all' in an effort to
win the consent and cooperation of economic interest groups and by
competitively bidding for votes by offering welfare benefits to a widening circle of groups, the logic of British politics allowed pluralistic
process to triumph over public purpose. Olson (1982, 1984) has similar-

ly ascribed the economic ills of countries such as Britain and Australia to the self-interested and self-defeating pursuit of distributional gains by narrowly-based special-interest groups. So long as most groups are small in relation to the total society, Olson argues, it will be economically rational for them to lobby not for policies that will increase the size of society's 'pie' but for policies that will ensure that their own group gets a bigger slice of that 'pie'. Labelling these groups 'distributional coalitions',[1] Olson posits that the denser they are in a society the more negative will their effect be on economic growth and the efficient allocation of resources. Australia, he claims, fits his theory 'like a pair of gloves' (Olson, 1984: 135). Its unimpressive economic growth and its failure to export more than a small fraction of its manufactured goods stem directly from the high levels of tariff protection secured over seven decades by self-serving distributional coalitions of manufacturers and of urban workers (see also Pincus, 1987).

Other analysts, in contrast, have argued that it is the existence of centralised, cohesive and hierarchically-organised economic interest groups and their integrated participation in policy-making that explains why a number of the smaller open economies in Western Europe have been able to return better economic performances than a number of more 'liberal' and 'statist' market economies (Schott, 1984; Paloheimo, 1984; Martin, 1986). They argue that these so-called corporatist states have been able to avoid destructive distributional conflict and to adjust effectively to the vicissitudes of the international economy (Katzenstein, 1984, 1985). In addition, these countries have been less prone to ungovernability and to an overload of group demands than countries that lack corporatist forms of 'interest intermediation'. Schmitter (1981: 315) purports to show statistically that governability is associated less with the magnitude of the economic and social problems a country faces and more with the way its interest groups are structured.

A link between these two sets of judgments about the impact of interest groups on a country's economic and political performance is to be found in Olson's notion of 'encompassing organisations'. These are interest groups whose size and comprehensive coverage make it economically rational for them to consider the effect their demands have on society as a whole. They possess the outlook and authority to engage in the collaborative positive-sum bargaining with the state and with other peak interest groups said to be characteristic of corporatism. Olson (1986) notes a high degree of overlap between corporatist countries—such as Austria, Sweden, and Norway—and those with encompassing interest organisations. He also notes 'that none of the English-speaking countries has anything approximating neo-corporatist arrangements and none of them has any encompassing interest groups either' (Olson, 1986: 179). And none of them, he adds, have performed well economically.

Australia in the 1980s would appear to disprove Olson's sweeping generalisation that the English-speaking market economies lack encompassing organisations. In fact, two high-ranking Australian bureaucrats have used Olson's analysis to explain the successful reorientation of economic policy during the first six years of the Hawke Labor government (Keating and Dixon, 1989). They argue that the emergence and growing influence of more encompassing peak organisations of business and labour in the 1980s, combined with their involvement in the Labor government's consensus-based economic policy making, has made possible the 'bargained consensus' on which the new policy direction was based.

This chapter examines these developments. It asks whether the organisation of Australia's economic interest groups—for labour, business and agriculture—is distinctive. In doing so, it compares and contrasts Australia with:

1   the smaller corporatist states of Western Europe (such as Sweden, Norway and Austria);
2   the larger non-corporatist industrialised states (such as the United States, Britain and France);
3   the smaller English-speaking and commodity-exporting economies (such as Canada and New Zealand).

The chapter argues that Australia's distinctiveness lies in the organisational asymmetry of its producer (that is, economic interest) groups. On the one hand, labour and agriculture each has a single, centralised, comprehensive organisation to represent its interests. On the other, business is characterised by a remarkable degree of organisational rivalry and fragmentation. Among industrialised market economies, Australia alone has this particular pattern. The chapter concludes by examining whether this organisational asymmetry explains what appears to be the Hawke government's strategy of 'corporatism without business'.

TRADE UNIONS

Critics within and outside the trade union movement generally agree that Australia has too many small unions organised on craft and occupational lines. Fully half of Australia's 300 unions claim fewer than 1000 members. Some even boast memberships of less than 200. Many of the small unions only operate in one State. This proliferation of small unions, the critics argue, spreads scarce union resources too thinly, complicates industrial relations at the workplace, prevents workers gaining a broad range of skills, and promotes an unacceptable level of inter-union demarcation disputes.

Alongside these small unions is a significant degree of membership

concentration. The unions with memberships of less than 1000 actually
account for under 2 per cent of all union members in Australia. The
great bulk of the union movement belongs to a few dozen large unions:
80 per cent of all union members are in the forty-five unions with memberships exceeding 20000. While this indicates a considerable degree of
membership concentration, Australia has lagged behind many other
countries (including the United States and Britain) in terms of the proportion of union members who belong to the ten largest unions (see
table 10.1). In Austria and West Germany the figure today is over 90
per cent; in Sweden it is over 80 per cent; but in Australia it is somewhat less than 50 per cent.

Australia's system of compulsory industrial arbitration has, along
with federalism, largely been responsible for the proliferation of small
trade unions. For more than eight decades the Commonwealth's rules
for the registration of trade unions stipulated that registration would
not be given to a trade union if there was already a union in existence to
which workers could 'conveniently belong'. The effect of this rule was
to allow many of the small craft unions established in the early years of
the century (and often confined to one State) to survive. Other rules
made union mergers difficult. The existence of separate industrial tribunals in the States further reinforced the narrow geographical orientation of many small unions.

The proliferation of trade unions in Australia is seen in the number of
unions affiliated to Australia's dominant union confederation, the Australian Council of Trade Unions (ACTU). In 1989 the ACTU reported
having 153 affiliates. Compare this with Austria's central trade union
federation, the ÖGB, which in 1984 had no more than fifteen industry-
based affiliates; West Germany's DGB which had seventeen; Sweden's
LO, twenty-four, and Norway's LO, thirty-five (ACTU/TDC, 1987:
179–80). The ACTU has more affiliated unions than Britain's Trade
Union Congress, the Canadian Labour Congress, and even the American Federation of Labor and Congress of Industrial Organizations
(AFL–CIO). They have around 100 affiliated unions each. A considerable degree of vertical integration has, however, been achieved through
the six State Trades and Labor Councils, to which almost all State-
based unions are affiliated. These Councils constitute the State branches of the ACTU.

Representing over 90 per cent of Australia's trade union members, the Australian Council of Trade Unions can with justification be
described as an encompassing organisation in Olson's sense of the term.
The only union confederation not now under the ACTU umbrella is a
small one representing salaried professional employees. The ACTU's
exceptionally high coverage was attained in the years 1979–1981 when a
confederation of white-collar unions and one of government employees
merged with it. Until then the ACTU's affiliated unions covered
75 per cent of all union members. With those two mergers the Austra-

Table 10.1 International comparisons of trade union density and organisational concentration

Country (density %)[a]	Coverage[b] (%)	Representativeness[c] (%)	Number of affiliates[d]	Concentration (10 largest affiliates)[e] (%)
Australia (58%) ACTU	90	52	156	38.6
Austria (60%) ÖGB	100	60	15	91.5
Canada (31%) CLC	56	21	78	—
Federal Republic of Germany (43%) DGB	80	34	16	90.5
New Zealand (45%) NZCTU	78	35	69	—
Norway (50%) LO	84	42	35	77.2
Sweden (94%) LO TCO	98	90	25	84.7
United Kingdom (54%) TUC	86	46	92	61.7
United States (20%) AFL–CIO	83	18	111	47.4

Notes: [a] Union members as percentage of workforce (1983; for New Zealand late 1980s). *Sources:* Bamber and Lansbury, 1987: 257; Kumar, 1986: 109; Vowles, 1989: 278
[b] Percentage of unionists covered by central confederation (early 1980s). *Sources:* Windmuller, 1981: 47; Banting, 1984: 20; Marin, 1985: 95
[c] Representatives = density × coverage
[d] For the years 1983–86. *Sources:* Bamber and Lansbury 1987, *passim*; ACTU/TDC, 1987: 179; Rawson and Wrightson, 1984; Kumar, 1984: 102; Vowles, 1989: 278
[e] For the years 1977–78 for all countries except Australia (1979). Concentration is a measure of the percentage of the membership in the ma,or central confederation who are members of the 10 largest affiliated unions. *Sources:* Windmuller, 1981: 50; Rawson and Wrightson, 1980

lian union movement was able to eliminate a major structural division between white and blue-collar workers that still divides the union movements in many other countries. In Sweden, Norway and West Germany, for example, the dominant trade union confederation faces smaller confederations variously representing white-collar, technical, professional and governmental employees. In contrast, the ACTU virtually stands alone (Martin, 1989: 189). Nor, it should be added, does it face rival confederations organised along party-political, religious, ideological or linguistic lines as occurs in France, Japan, The Netherlands, Belgium and Canada.

To say, however, that a trade union peak council stands alone is not to say that it effectively exercises authority over its affiliates. The British TUC and the AFL–CIO in the USA are each the single peak organisation in those countries, yet they lack extensive authority to intervene in their affiliates' internal affairs or to determine their affiliates' stand on questions of wages and working conditions. Their autonomy, moreover, is limited by the very small share they receive (around 2 per cent) of total dues income collected by their affiliates.

At the other end of the authority spectrum stands Austria's ÖGB. Covering all trade unionists in Austria (except for a farm workers' union), it receives 80 per cent of all union dues and employs a staff of 2000. Its fifteen member unions are not affiliates in the normal sense but ÖGB sub-divisions. The ÖGB controls their finances, appoints their staff and sets their policies. In the ÖGB, organisational authority is clearly 'where the money is: at the top' (Marin, 1985: 99).

In terms of its authority over the union movement, where does the ACTU stand? Using a peak council's ability to influence the settlement of pay and working conditions as 'the litmus test' of its authority, Martin's comparative study places the Norwegian LO and the Swedish LO closest to the Austrian ÖGB. The ACTU is judged to come some way behind, but to be closer to the ÖGB end of the scale than to the AFL–CIO end (Martin, 1989: 191). The authority the ACTU now enjoys is new. It has largely been gained during the years of the Hawke government. (For earlier assessments see Windmuller, 1975 and Rawson, 1982.) Even so, the ACTU's organisational and financial resources are modest. The ACTU's expenditure in 1985 was only $A1.9 million compared with the Swedish LO's expenditure then of $A102 million (ACTU/TDC, 1987: 191). In that year the ACTU's total full-time staff only numbered forty-two. Windmuller (1985: 93) has advanced the general proposition that 'the larger the confederation's share of total income received by the [union] movement, the stronger and more centralised it is likely to be in relation to its affiliated unions'. Because the ACTU receives a very small share of union income (probably not exceeding 5 per cent), its autonomy *vis-à-vis* its affiliates will remain somewhat circumscribed.

The irony in the ACTU's new-found standing as an authoritative trade union centre is that its standing has been attained as the union movement's density has been declining. For many years, the proportion of the workforce belonging to unions in Australia has been higher than for many other countries. Hovering around 56 per cent for the years 1975–1984, union density in Australia considerably surpassed that in the United States, Japan, France, West Germany and Canada. But in the latter half of the 1980s the proportion has been falling. By 1989, it was 53 per cent. These statistics are based on official union returns to the Australian Bureau of Statistics. Sample surveys of the workforce conducted by the Bureau of Statistics show a more gloomy picture: they indicate that the proportion of the workforce belonging to unions may be considerably less than that shown in the official union returns. According to these surveys, union density has fallen from 49 per cent to 42 per cent in the years 1982–1989. Although this fall is nowhere near what has occurred in the United States, where union density is less than 20 per cent of the workforce, it has taken place across all age groups and in almost all industries.

To stem this erosion in its membership, the ACTU has realised that it must develop effective recruitment campaigns and provide a far better level of services to individual union members. But to do so requires a more efficient use of resources than the proliferation of small unions allows. The ACTU's answer to this problem has been to encourage union amalgamations. It would like to see the number of unions reduced to around two dozen industry-based unions. Changes in 1988 to the Industrial Relations Act were designed to facilitate this process by removing a number of legislative impediments to union mergers. So far, however, progress has been slow.

FARMERS' ORGANISATIONS

The 'predominant characteristic' of Australian farm organisations has long been their commodity-orientation (Campbell, 1968). For many decades, the most influential of the farm groups were those representing the producers of a single commodity. This orientation was reinforced by the commodity-basis of much agricultural policy (not least the various marketing and price support schemes) and by the parallel organisation of Commonwealth and State departments of agriculture along commodity lines.

Complicating the commodity-based pattern of farm organisations has been the simultaneous existence in the states of 'general purpose' organisations representing mainly (but not exclusively) the interests of 'mixed farmers', those who combine wheat growing with wool and meat production. These organisations competed with the State branches of national commodity federations for members and government recognition. So too, until the 1960s, did the State divisions of the Australian Primary Producers' Union, a unitary organisation to which individual farmers could belong. The result for many years was a tangled web of associational affiliations at the State and national levels which hindered the creation of a single comprehensive association with the authority and coverage to speak for all Australian farmers. Until 1969, two groups competed for this role. Even when they amalgamated, the authority of the new confederation was limited. The reluctance of many national commodity federations to cede to it any of their powers weakened its authority, as did the refusal of one large wealthy and politically influential federation, the Australian Woolgrowers and Graziers' Council, to affiliate.

During the twenty-three years of Liberal–Country party government from 1949 to 1972, various ministers—including the leader of the Country Party, Sir John McEwen—called on the farmers to speak with a more united voice. McEwen warned them that organisational competition spelt weakness not strength. Ironically it was the intimate relationship between the farm sector and the Country Party that blunted the urgency of these warnings. In the 1970s, however, three developments brought home to farm leaders the need for a single well-funded, professionally-staffed national organisation. First, the election of a Labor government in 1972 taught them that effective lobbying had to rely on simply more than 'twisting the arms of our friends in the Country Party'. Many farm groups found themselves stumbling in the dark. Shortly after the election of the Whitlam government, a farmers' newsletter wrote:

> That knocking noise one hears so frequently these days is the tapping of the white sticks of Australia's farm leaders, groping their way blindly through the uncharted and unlit hazards created by the new Federal Government (cited in Richmond, 1980).

Secondly, the establishment of the Industries Assistance Commission—charged with advising the government on the economic efficiency of assistance to rural as well as to secondary industry—required farm organisations to develop their economic expertise if they were to produce submissions that would be taken seriously. No longer was it possible to justify assistance on the grounds that the farm sector was 'the backbone of the nation'. Thirdly, the economic difficulties of rural industries in the latter half of the 1970s caused financial difficulties for farm organisations. This occurred at the very time that they were being pressed to augment the professional expertise of their staff. A number of groups realised that they could no longer afford the luxury of organisational duplication. Indeed, mergers and amalgamations between wheat and woolgrowers' organisations, first in New South Wales and later nationally, led to the decision of the Woolgrowers and Graziers' Council to abandon its stand-alone strategy and to join the about-to-be formed National Farmers' Federation (NFF).

Launched in 1979, the NFF brought together twelve federally-organised national commodity councils and ten general purpose State-based organisations. Its coverage is broad—no major commodity group is outside its fold—and its membership density is high. Representing over 80 per cent of Australia's 170 000 farms, the NFF can rightfully claim an organisational monopoly in representing Australian farmers. (One hesitates to apply Olson's term 'encompassing organisation' to a group whose constituents account for only 5 per cent of Australia's Gross Domestic Product.) Although based on autonomous commodity groups, the NFF has created a remarkably centralised, hierarchical and integrated system of representation for Australia's farmers. If, as Coleman (1988: 105) has argued, a high level of group differentiation and a high level of group integration are the signs of a 'developed' system of interest representation, Australian agriculture is more 'developed' than labour or business. With a single voice and a membership density exceeding 80 per cent, the system of farmers' representation in Australia is comparable to that in the United Kingdom, West Germany and Italy—three countries where agriculture is highly organised and indeed highly 'corporatised' (Keeler, 1987: 255–85). In each country agriculture is represented by a single organisation covering at least 75 per cent of the country's farmers.

In a comparison of agricultural groups in France, Britain, West Germany, Italy and the United States, Keeler (1987: 264) demonstrates that in each country the membership density of the largest farmers' organisation is significantly higher than that of all trade unions; in fact, it is almost twice as high. With trade union density in Australia now around 45 per cent, the membership of the NFF closely fits the pattern Keeler depicts. But the high level of membership density in the NFF still needs to be explained. This is because the NFF and its affiliates have not been able to rely on the array of selective incentives that the British, West German and Italian peak organisations have had at their disposal. The National Farmers' Federation in Britain, for example, has long relied on cut-rate insurance to attract members; the Coltivatori Diretti in Italy controls a private insurance firm which offers special terms to its members; while in Germany the Deutschen Bauern Verband's recruitment has been assisted by its close links to the German Federation of Cooperatives on which German farmers depend for a wide range of goods and services, including the marketing of their products. Nor has the NFF (or its affiliates) been able to maintain a dense network of specialists in rural areas to provide technical, legal and business advice to members—as have the British, West German and Italian

groups. Nor again—except in Queensland[2]—has the NFF or its affiliates been helped by compulsory membership as has, for example, the
Austrian Chamber of Agriculture.

There are a number of reasons why high membership densities have
for many years been a characteristic of Australian farm organisations.
The first is a heightened sense of separate identity amongst farmers.
Once known as 'country-mindedness', this outlook was expressed as a
distrust of the cities and an antipathy towards the trades union movement. In recent years, the realisation that agriculture is a rapidly declining sector in the economy has reinforced the value of solidarity and
encouraged a siege mentality among some farmers. The second is the
pressures on a farmer from others in the locality to join the region's
dominant farm group. The fact that most farmers in the region produce the same commodity (or narrow range of commodities) augments
their sense of solidarity. The third reason has been the exceptionally
low subscriptions charged by all but a few farm groups. This has helped
overcome the free-rider problem. Lastly, the close clientele relationship
between commodity groups and departments of agriculture in Australia
has been used by these groups as a potent reason why individual
farmers could ill afford not to join. Just as corporatist involvement
in national policy-making helps account for the high density of membership in peak agricultural organisations in Britain, France, West Germany and Italy (Keeler, 1987), so these clientelistic group-government
links in part account for the success of Australian farm groups in enroll-
ing a high proportion of their potential constituents.

Despite its organisational achievements, the NFF faces an uncertain
future. Since the 1950s, the importance of agriculture to the economy
has been declining. Its contribution to Gross Domestic Product has
fallen from around 24 per cent (in 1949–50) to 5 per cent today; and its
contribution to export earnings has fallen from 80 per cent to less than
40 per cent over the same period. Its pool of eligible members is also
diminishing: since the mid-1960s, farmers have been leaving the land at
the rate of 2 per cent a year, a rate that agricultural economists predict
will continue as farmers face an increasingly severe cost-price squeeze.
The NFF will also have to manage the conflicting interests of two sets
of members—traditional farmers operating small family farms and the
new 'agribusinesses' upon whom farmers are increasingly dependent
for inputs (machinery, seeds, fertiliser) and for the processing and distribution of their output.

Developments in Canada and Britain also suggest that the internal
unity of large encompassing farm organisations is often quite fragile.
The Canadian Federation of Agriculture (whose commodity and territorial structure closely resembles that of the NFF) suffered debilitat-
ing secessions in 1980 when it failed to integrate the conflicting interests
among and between grain growers and grain handlers. The unity of the

National Farmers' Federation in Britain has been weakened by a growing conflict between livestock and cereal producers (Grant, 1987: 161). Its standing has also been damaged by the formation in the 1980s of two rival organisations representing tenant farmers and small farmers. In Australia, the NFF's unity came under threat in 1990 when four commodity councils announced they were reviewing their affiliation because of their dissatisfaction with the NFF's commitment to the removal of all tariffs.

BUSINESS AND EMPLOYERS' ASSOCIATIONS

Diversity, disarray and disunity have been the hallmarks of business and employer representation in Australia. Many thought that the formation of the Confederation of Australian Industry in 1977 would change all that. They were mistaken. But disarray and disunity do not in themselves make Australian business associations distinctive. For organisational overlap and competition, along with weak vertical integration, have been features of business representation in the other industrialised English-speaking democracies—the United States, Canada, New Zealand and, to a lesser degree, the United Kingdom. The stark contrast is with the pattern of business interest representation in the democratic corporatist countries of Western Europe, particularly Austria and Sweden, as well as in West Germany.

Austria presents, as it does with trade union centralisation, the extreme case of a highly integrated and cohesive system of business representation. One body, the Federal Economic Chamber, holds an officially-sanctioned monopoly to speak for business, and all firms—public and private, industrial and financial—are required to belong. The Chamber organises its members by sector (into 130 industry and trade groups) and by region (one for each of Austria's nine regions). With an immense budget and a staff of more than 4000 the Federal Economic Chamber has the resources for sophisticated policy analysis and for offering a wide range of services to its members. While the Federation of Austrian Industrialists, a group which represents large private corporations, sometimes publicly differs with it on particular issues, the Chamber's standing and authority are unquestioned.

Neither Sweden nor West Germany possesses a single or dominant business association: in each country a number of comprehensive groups are active. But in each country, cooperation between the groups, combined with a clear and well-established division of labour between them, has ensured a high level of business cohesion. In West Germany, for example, the German Employers' Association (BDA) concentrates on industrial relations; the Federation of German Industry (BDI) on broad economic and industry policy; the Chamber of Commerce and Industry on foreign trade, transport and communications; and the Chamber of Artisans on vocational training. In addition, cohesion is reinforced by a clear hierarchy of sectoral and geographical representation within each of the peak groups: the most specialised industry associations belong to broader sectoral associations, which in turn are affiliated to one of the general peak associations. The BDI for example only has thirty-nine member associations but they in turn represent 500 more specialised groups (Coleman, 1989: 20).

Contrast Australia. No single association enjoys a dominant and unchallenged position as the voice of business as does Austria's Federal Economic Chamber. Nor does any single association even enjoy a preeminent position. No clearly-established division of labour pertains between the national business groups. Nor does any arrangement ensure that the scores of regional and industry groups are integrated vertically and horizontally into a cohesive national system.

In Australia, at least four groups compete to speak on behalf of business. They are the Confederation of Australian Industry, the Business Council of Australia, the Australian Chamber of Commerce, and the Australian Chamber of Manufactures. The Confederation of Australian Industry, formed in 1977 with the merger of the Australian Council of Employers' Federations and the Associated Chambers of Manufactures of Australia, was intended to be an encompassing organisation along the lines of the Confederation of British Industry. By 1979, the CAI had enrolled more than forty national employers' and industry associations representing a wide cross-section of the economy. Among its affiliates were groups as diverse as the Australian Bankers Association, the Metal Trades Industry Association, the Australian Woolgrowers and Graziers Council, and the Australian Council of Local Government Associations.

The CAI encountered organisational problems from the very start. First, it was never fully representative. Absent from its membership were not only many of the large public sector employers but also a number of important industry groups such as the Australian Mining Industry Council, the Australian Finance Council, the Federal Chamber of Automotive Industries, and the Australian Chamber of Commerce. Secondly, unlike the Confederation of British Industry, it did not allow large corporations to be members in their own right. With this rule, it in effect shut the door on the active involvement in its affairs by the chief executives of many of the country's major corporations. (Some large monopolistic companies, however, got around the bar on individual company membership by establishing industry associations in which they were the dominant members: CSR, the Australian Sugar Refiners' Industry Association; BHP, the Iron and Steel Industry Association.) In general, however, large corporations came to see the CAI as oriented too much to the interests of small business. Thirdly, its division into two secretariats—one in Melbourne handling industrial relations and one in Canberra handling trade, tariff and industry matters—created tensions. Some rural sector affiliates (such as the NFF) resented having to pay for the upkeep of the Canberra secretariat, which they saw as a manufacturers' lobby; they also objected to the CAI's lingering commitment to protectionism. Other affiliates who competed with the CAI in representing the interests of manufacturing industry (such as the Metal Trades Industry Association) wanted the CAI to confine itself to industrial relations. Others again criticised the CAI for supporting the centralised wages system. Fourthly, the CAI ran into financial difficulties. Dissatisfaction with the Confederation's policy and with hefty hikes in affiliation fees led to many resignations. Among the powerful associations that chose to leave were the National Farmers' Federation, the Australian Retailers' Association, the Metal Trades Industry Association and the Insurance Council of Australia.

To meet some of the discontent and to rationalise its operations, the CAI in 1989 decided to close its Canberra secretariat and to move to Melbourne, where it would devote itself to its industrial relations role. But it was dealt a severe blow at the end of the year with the resignation of the Australian Chamber of Manufactures—formerly the Victorian and NSW Chambers of Manufactures. That departure deprived the CAI of a quarter of its income. Whether the CAI can retain its status as the major comprehensive employers' organisation is uncertain. Its authority as the voice of employers has been challenged by resignations; by a number of 'new right' groups claiming to speak for small employers; by independent appearances at national wage cases by, among others, the National Farmers' Federation, the Australian Chamber of Commerce, and the Metal Trades Industry Association; and, most importantly, by the growing stature and influence of the Business Council of Australia (BCA). Under the Hawke government, the BCA has largely eclipsed the CAI as the generator of broad business strategy on questions of public policy.

The catalyst for the formation of the Business Council in September 1983 was the damaging lack of cohesion among business representatives at the National Economic Summit Conference held earlier that year. The business contingent at the conference consisted of five from the CAI; another group representing fourteen business groups; and eighteen 'independents', all of whom were the chief executives or chairmen of the largest corporations. The contingent lacked leadership and a consistent position on the central issues on the conference agenda: the *Australian Financial Review* described it as a rabble. This experience convinced the 'independents' of the need for a forum, backed by a sophisticated research capacity, through which big business could articulate a 'first best' position on issues concerning the future direction of the Australian economy.[3]

Modelled on the Business Roundtable in the United States, the BCA (like its Canadian and New Zealand counterparts) consists of an invited group of chief executive officers from the largest corporations in the country, public as well as private. Membership now numbers around eighty. These corporations (in 1989) earned more than $216 billion in sales revenue, gave work to over one million employees, and possessed assets in excess of $500 billion. If we rank corporate enterprises, governmental as well as private, in terms of their 1989 sales revenue, twenty-three of the top thirty were members of the BCA. The BCA's members also included twenty-three out of the thirty biggest corporate employers and seventeen out of the thirty corporations with the largest asset holdings. Along with such corporate giants as BHP, Elders IXL, Coles Myer, BTR Nylex, Adelaide Steamship, and Pacific Dunlop, the BCA's membership list includes the CEOs of four banks (ANZ, Commonwealth, NAB and Westpac), three life insurance companies (AMP, Colonial Mutual, and National Mutual), five oil companies (BP, Caltex, Esso, Mobil, and Shell), five automobile manufacturers (Ford, GMH, Mitsubishi, Nissan, and Toyota), three government trading enterprises (OTC, Telecom and Qantas), and seven mining companies (Alcoa, CRA, MIM, North Broken Hill Peko, Renison Goldfields, Santos, and Woodside Petroleum).[4] If productive capacity can be taken as an index of whether or not an organisation is 'encompassing', there is little doubt in the case of the BCA: the collective gross revenue of its eighty members in 1989 amounted to no less than 64 per cent of Australia's GDP.

WHAT EXPLAINS THE ORGANISATIONAL DISUNITY OF AUSTRALIAN BUSINESS?

The failure of Australian business to create a viable comprehensive organisation is puzzling. Why should business be characterised by this quite extraordinary pattern of rivalry among its leading associations whereas the Australian trade union movement and the farm sector each has been able to weld together a single comprehensive organisation to advance and protect its interests?

It might be argued that competition and disunity among business associations presents no puzzle. Some scholars, for example, claim that business has a lesser need than labour or farmers for collective action. For one thing, business is already organised in the form of the corporation; and corporations, for reasons of competition, prefer to respond individually rather than collectively to market constraints and opportunities (Offe and Wiesenthal, 1979). For another, the collective interests of business are effectively articulated by the 'inner circle' of the capitalist class—the set of interlocking directors of the country's largest companies (Useem, 1984). In addition, the interests of business are privileged because the state, operating within the constraints imposed by the economic requirements of capital, must necessarily attend to the long-term needs of business (Lindblom, 1977). Others claim that conflicts of interest within business, not to mention competition between firms and industries, are formidable obstacles to business unity. Among these conflicts are those based on size, on nationality of company ownership, on market orientation (whether domestic or export), and on stages in the product cycle (whether an industry faces declining or expanding markets). The executive director of the Business Council of Australia has argued that 'a single common voice' is inappropriate for Australia's 'diverse and competitive' business sector. Instead of 'agglomeration' (with its tendency to lowest common denominator decision-making) he advocates co-ordination (McLaughlin, 1990: 10–11).

Despite these arguments, the fact remains that business in a number of industrialised market economies *is* comprehensively organised into a cohesive and integrated set of business interest groups (see Coleman and Grant, 1988). To explain the national variations in business mobilisation, it is necessary to examine the institutional context in which business operates. A rigorous statement of this approach is advanced by Schmitter and Streeck (1981). Their starting point is that business associations are intermediaries between firms on the one hand and the state and the trade union movement on the other. Collective action by business is a response to two separate but interrelated imperatives: the need to attract and retain the support of members ('the logic of membership'); and the need to exercise adequate influence over governments and trade unions ('the logic of influence').

Particularly significant is shaping the structure of nationwide business organisation in Australia have been the following institutional factors.

Dual economy

Australia has long been economically divided between a commodity sector dependent on export markets and a manufacturing sector dependent on a protected home market (Schedvin, 1987). The interests of the two sectors have often diverged strongly on such matters as tariff protection, exchange rates, foreign investment, and wages policy. The sectors have also differed in their strategy towards the trade union movement. They have also had their own organisations. The dual economy distinguishes Australia from the smaller corporatist economies of Western Europe, where manufacturers have been export-oriented and have sat side by side in the same organisations with the domestic suppliers of their raw materials.

Federal system of government

The division of economic powers between the Commonwealth government and the States has resulted in a system of business interest groups
shaped by federalism. The vast majority of business groups in Australia
are State-based; and most nationally-organised groups possess a federal
(or more accurately a confederal) structure. Not only has federalism
promoted a proliferation of business groups, it has also created problems of cohesion and integration. Jealous of their powers and preroga-
tives and concerned to preserve their autonomy, the State branches of
national groups have often weakened the cohesion of federal groups. So
too, on occasion, have internal policy conflicts between the State
branches over proposals to increase the constitutional powers of the
Commonwealth government (see Matthews, 1990).

Policy instruments

Australia's distinctive policy instruments for determining wages and
allocating tariff protection have helped to fragment organised business.
By creating a market for specialist services, the procedures of the industrial tribunals and the Tariff Board offered competing umbrella
groups in the States the opportunity to use selective incentives in the
struggle for organisational survival and growth.

In the case of industrial arbitration, the demand for services derived
from the legalism of the system and the complexity of its industrial
awards. Competing for members, employers' federations and chambers
of manufactures in New South Wales, Victoria and South Australia, in
the years 1910–20, sought to tap this market by appointing industrial
officers to inform and advise members about industrial awards and to
represent them before the tribunals. Thus was entrenched a rivalry between the employers' federations and the chambers of manufactures in
these three States that has continued to this day.

Following the creation of the Tariff Board in 1921, the Chambers of
Manufactures in Victoria and New South Wales set up their own tariff
departments to advise their members on the intricacies of the tariff and
to help them present effective submissions for tariff protection to the
Board. Tariff services were an important impetus in the organisational
growth of the chambers: they strengthened the appeal of the chambers
over the employers' federations in the eyes of manufacturers. For this
reason the Victorian and New South Wales chambers were never willing to surrender that function to their national organisation, the Associated Chambers of Manufactures.

The arbitration and tariff systems underwrote the organisational
competition between the two State-based umbrella associations in yet
another way. The occupation and craft-based system of industrial awards,
which reflected the structure of the union movement, encouraged a

proliferation of employers' organisations. The tariff likewise spawned a host of small and ill-funded industry associations, all dependent on tariff protection. These groups were courted by the local employers' federations and chambers of manufactures, who discovered that an effective way to augment their own membership was to undertake the secretarial work of these industry associations in return for requiring them to become affiliates. This competition among umbrella groups in each State has resulted in complex networks of affiliations among business groups that vary markedly from State to State. It is responsible for the lack of any clear and consistent pattern of vertical and horizontal integration among Australia's regional and national business groups.

Labour movement

Australia is not alone in having a fragmented and disunited business sector. So too do Canada and the United States. In accounting for the absence of encompassing business associations in those two countries, observers have stressed the weakness of organised labour (Coleman, 1988: 220; Wilson, 1982: 232). How relevant is trade union organisation in explaining the fragmentation and competition among peak business groups in Australia? Plowman (1989) rejects the applicability of the 'countervailing power thesis' as an explanation for employer organisation in Australia. He argues that employers in Australia have never mobilised to check and balance the industrial powers of trade unions. The reason, he suggests, lies in the Australian system of industrial relations. Compulsory arbitration has lessened the significance of sheer union muscle in industrial relations: it has enabled a weak union to create an interstate dispute and bring employers before the tribunal through the simple expedient of serving a log of claims on employers. Consequently, it has been far more important for employers' organisations to be effective in adversarial advocacy before the tribunal than to be in a position to take on the unions in direct industrial confrontation.

This is true. But to argue that countervailing power and organisational parallelism have not been major forces in the development of Australian employers' organisations is to take too narrow a view of the question. By only considering the employers' response to the industrial power of trade unions, Plowman disregards the employers' response to the political power and influence of the labour movement.

In a number of countries, business has mobilised in reaction to what it sees as a direct threat to its hegemony by Social Democratic and Labor parties. In other countries, again Canada and the United States are the prominent examples, the absence of social democracy has removed the incentive for business to create 'strong' peak associations. 'The USA, the country in which the challenge to capitalism has been the weakest, is also,' writes Wilson (1985: 130), 'the country in which employers' organisations have been the most fragmented.'

In Australia, reaction to the Labor Party has prompted business mobilisation. On four distinct occasions when Labor governments (or Labor Party influence) was seen as particularly threatening, business responded by taking steps to mobilise more cohesively. The first occurred during the first decade of Federation when presence in the national Parliament of three parties enabled Labor to trade its parliamentary support for legislative concessions. It was to counter this early and unexpected legislative influence of the Labor Party—not simply to 'counter the activities of the state' (Plowman, 1989: 109)—that led employers both to organise and to campaign prominently in electoral politics under the 'anti-socialist' banner (see Rickard, 1968). The second took place when Labor first helf office in its own right (1910–13). The third occurred in reaction to the centralist policies of the Curtin and Chifley governments (1942–49), particularly the Chifley government's attempt to nationalise the banks. The Whitlam government's three years in office (1972–75) witnessed the fourth period of business mobilisation. The inability of business to influence the Whitlam government or to match the effectiveness of the ACTU was a major spur to the merger negotiations that eventuated in the formation of the CAI. In that sense, the CAI must be interpreted as a response by business to the political power if not the industrial strength of the labour movement.

Why, though, has the Labor challenge not been sufficient to induce business to create an effective encompassing organisation? One reason is that Labor governments in Australia have been relatively infrequent. Periods of heightened concern have been followed by lengthy periods of non-Labor rule. Following the Chifley government's defeat in 1949, the two decades of conservative Liberal–Country Party government removed the need for business to be strongly and cohesively organised. A second reason is that not all Labor governments have challenged business. The big business orientation of the Hawke Labor government has meant that organisational unity has lost its urgency, as the CAI found to its cost. A third reason is the absence of a corporatist tradition in Australian politics. Unlike social democratic governments in Scandinavia, Austria and West Germany, Australian Labor governments have not relied on tripartite corporatist arrangements for making and implementing economic policy. As a consequence, Australian business has not been faced with the imperative, as has business in those Western European countries, to organise cohesively and comprehensively in order to bargain effectively with its corporatist 'partners'—the state and organised labour. But given, however, the Hawke government's allegedly corporatist-style of decision making, it is necessary to explore whether that development has had an integrative effect on business representation. It is also necessary to examine the converse, whether the organisational asymmetry of Australia's producer groups has determined the form that those supposedly corporatist approaches have taken.

AUSTRALIA: CORPORATISM WITHOUT BUSINESS?

The term corporatism entered the Australian political vocabulary during the years of the Hawke government. To many observers, the government's pursuit of 'consensus politics', its early enthusiasm for summoning labour, business and government leaders to national summit conferences, its decision to create a number of tripartite consultative and planning bodies, and, above all, its prices and incomes Accord with the ACTU were all evidence of a decisive shift towards corporatist policy making (Stewart, 1985; Gerritsen, 1986; Stilwell, 1986). Some commentators even went so far as to speak of the Hawke government's corporatist 'revolution' (West, 1984).

These developments raise the question whether Australia's distinctively asymmetrical pattern of producer group representation (see table 10.2) has resulted in an uneven incorporation of producer groups into the policy process? If the organisational weakness of labour in Japan has led to a system of 'corporatism without labour' (Pempel and Tsunekawa, 1978), has the fragmentation of organised business in Australia been responsible for the Hawke government's apparent strategy of 'corporatism without business'?

Table 10.2 Capacity of sectoral interests to act as 'encompassing organisation'

Country	Labour sector	Agricultural sector	Business sector
Australia	High	High	Low
Austria	High	High	High
Canada	Low	Medium	Low
France	Low	High	Medium
Germany	High	High	High
Italy	Low	High	High
Japan	Low	High	High
New Zealand	Medium/High	High	Medium
Norway	High	High	High
Sweden	High	High	High
United Kingdom	Medium	High	High
United States	Low	Low	Low

Note: Capacity is an assessment of the degree of organisational monopoly, centralised authority and membership density. The assessment recognises that effective coordination between a number of groups in a sector can be a functional equivalent to organisational monopoly and centralisation (see Regini, 1984).

As mentioned earlier, Keating and Dixon (1989) have drawn on Olson's concept of encompassing organisations to argue that the Hawke government's successful reorientation of economic policy between 1983 and 1988 was made possible by the new-found organisational capacity of peak interest groups to pursue a collective gain strategy, to engage in policy trade-offs 'to protect their primary goals', and to sell the outcomes 'to the disadvantaged sectors of their constituents'. This account overlooks the organisational disunity of business. In addition, by explaining encompassing behaviour in organisational terms, this account (like Olson's) fails to consider the political conditions that permit an organisation to adopt an encompassing strategy. For example, a strong trade union confederation is unlikely to pursue a collective-gain strategy unless it has some guarantee that workers will benefit from their industrial restraint. One form this assurance may take is a commitment by the government to use the 'social wage' to compensate workers for their wage restraint. Since such assurances are far more likely when a Social Democratic or Labor party government is in office, many analysts now argue that corporatism is contingent on the coexistence of a strong centralised trade union confederation with a social democratic governance (Maier, 1984; Cameron, 1984; Lange and Garrett, 1985; Panitch, 1986). The commitment of Social Democratic parties both to full employment and the welfare state and to trade union participation in policy formation has been the context in which 'trade union leaders (and members) were prepared to turn their long-standing attachment to social democratic parties into the offer and practice of wage restraint for social democratic governments facing economic or electoral difficulties' (Panitch, 1986: 45).

This approach is central to an understanding of the Accord. In its origins, purpose and implementation, the Accord has been embedded in Labor politics. The Accord began life as an agreement between the ACTU and the Australian Labor Party. It was part of the ALP's strategy to wrest office from the Coalition at the 1983 elections. Electorally the party needed a credible commitment from the trade unions that they would act 'responsibly' under a Labor government. It was crucial that the party be able to demonstrate to voters that a new Labor government would not be blighted by a wages scramble as had occurred in the mid-1970s when Labor last held office. For their part the unions, chafing under the Fraser government's policy of wage cuts and anxious about rising unemployment, were determined to see the Labor Party elected to office. They were willing to offer wage restraint to a Labor government in return for a reciprocal commitment to full wage-indexation, employment-creation, and welfare policies to benefit low wage-earners. Even though the Hawke Labor government made the Accord the centrepiece of its economic strategy, it continued to be an arrangement between the industrial and political wings of the labour movement 'for the achievement of their disparate but related political, economic and social objectives' (Singleton, 1990: 192).

> The Accord is Australian labourism dressed in contemporary clothing. It is a strategy for the achievement of traditional union objectives and principles through the political process. It is a strategy for Labor in government to manage the Australian capitalist economy in combination with the trade union movement to secure the electoral and social justice objectives of the ALP (ibid.: 198).

The bilateral character of the Accord distinguishes it from the tripartite forms of corporatist policy-making found in Western Europe, which typically involve direct concertation between the 'social partners'— business and labour (Lehmbruch, 1984; Katzenstein, 1984 and 1985; Panitch, 1986). At best business has been consulted by the Accord partners. Even then, in the words of a spokesman for the Business Council of Australia, 'we usually find the die is cast' (*Australian Financial Review*, 30 December 1985). Business has been fully aware of its peripheral role. For example, far from viewing the 1983 National Economic Summit as an exercise in tripartite policy making, business felt, to quote Sir Peter Abeles, 'as though we have been invited to play singles tennis against a championship doubles combination' (NESC, 1983: 194). But Abeles did not speak for other business leaders when he challenged the government to convert the Accord from a bilateral into a trilateral agreement. In fact, the Business Council later made a strategic decision not to engage in tripartite bargaining, but to concentrate instead on advancing 'first best' solutions (McLaughlin, 1990). Its leaders also knew that even if it were to negotiate deals with the ACTU, there would be no guarantee these deals would be accepted by other business groups, especially the numerous 'new right' groups speaking for small employers. In periods of severe economic downturn, many small employers see no need for a centralised incomes policy. Faced with an industrially weakened trade union movement, they would prefer to rely on the market rather than on political arrangements to secure wage restraint.

This is not to say that business has been economically injured by its exclusion from the Accord. Business has benefited economically from the unions' strategy of wage restraint, for the Accord has delivered reductions in real wages and in industrial conflict (Chapman and Gruen, 1990). To the extent, then, that corporatism is viewed as essentially 'a system of institutionalised wage restraint in which labour, acting "responsibly", voluntarily participates in and legitimises the transfer of income from labour to capital' (Cameron, 1984: 146), the Accord in a formal sense is indeed 'corporatism without business'.

Despite these economic benefits, however, business has been critical of many of the concessions secured by the trade unions. These include

the extension of superannuation to a greater proportion of the workforce and the union veto on a consumption tax. As Australia's international competitiveness declines, employers are less prepared to bear the
uniform costs associated with a nationally bargained policy. Like employers in Western Europe (Streeck, 1984), they look to decentralised
enterprise bargaining as a means of avoiding these costs.

Business, in any case, has always been politically suspicious of the
Accord. It is disturbed by the privileged influence the ACTU has exercised under the Hawke government; it has been wary about being
coopted into tripartite arrangements that could be used to benefit the
Labor Party electorally; and it has been annoyed that political deals
between the industrial and political wings of the labour movement have
slowed the pace and perhaps the commitment to labour market, coastal
shipping and waterfront reforms (McEachern, 1986; McLaughlin,
1990). In addition, important elements in the business world and in the
non-Labor parties have become increasingly critical of a fundamental
tenet of the Accord—the centralised system of wage-fixing.

To be a beneficiary of the Accord process, in other words, does not
imply being a partner to it (contrast Stewart, 1985). Party politics pre-
clude this. It is the partisan nature of the Accord, not the organisational
fragmentation of business, that explains why business has never been a
party to the Accord negotiations. The Accord has been, as Singleton
(1990: 192) argues, 'an alliance or partnership in government between
the Australian trade union movement and the Australian Labor Party'.
Business, by definition, cannot be a full partner. Moreover, the fact
that the Liberal and National Parties are politically opposed to the
Accord and to the Labor Party's stand on wages policy prevents any
significant business group from negotiating a wages agreement with the
labour movement. Bargaining between organised business and the
ACTU to forge a consensual national incomes policy is simply not a
political option. Australia, in this sense, reinforces Lehmbruch's
observation (1984: 74–8), based on the experience of 'corporatist concertation' in Western Europe, that stable corporatist relationships between labour and capital are not compatible with polarised party
politics.

CONCLUSIONS

The 1980s saw a transformation in the organisation and objectives of
Australia's economic interest groups. The Australian Council of Trade
Unions and the National Farmers' Federation attained an organisational monopoly in their sectors; the Business Council of Australia, while
not a 'peak' organisation, rapidly gained in authority; all three made use
of research-based advocacy; and, by espousing collective gain solutions

to Australia's economic problems, all three acted as encompassing organisations.

The decade also saw a fundamental transformation in the terms of
economic debate in Australia and in the direction of economic policy.
The once widespread acceptance of protection-all-round gave way to a
growing consensus in favour of economic deregulation, trade liberalisation, micro-economic reform and real wage restraint. The major economic interest groups reflected and helped shape this consensus. Some
observers go further:

> In sum, it has been the increased authority of encompassing groups and their
> capacity to adjust their position to protect primary goals in the light of the
> turbulent events of this period, and to sell the changes to disadvantaged
> sections of their constituents, which provided the basis for the major
> redirections of policy (Keating and Dixon, 1989: 70).

To explain this development largely in terms of the organisational
capacity of interest groups is to tell only half the story. By adopting
Olson's idea of encompassing organisations, Keating and Dixon commit Olson's error of assuming that it is possible to infer a group's objectives and behaviour from its organisational attributes, without regard to
the objectives themselves or to the political context in which the group
operates. A group's readiness to engage in 'consensual bargaining' and
other sorts of 'encompassing' behaviour depends on two other conditions:

1 its expectations of how others will behave;
2 its calculations of the relative costs and benefits to it of participating
  in such bargaining.

This chapter has argued that these expectations and calculations are
shaped in important ways by party politics. It contends that the Accord
cannot be understood outside the context of the union movement's
commitment to 'labourism'. The ACTU believed that a Labor government would ensure that workers would share in the economic benefits
expected to flow from sustained wage restraint. The Business Council's
reluctance to take part in tripartite negotiations must similarly be
understood in terms of party politics: its disquiet at what it saw as the
Labor government's disposition to exploit the Accord for its own electoral advantage.

Is the Accord, Australia's distinctive form of 'corporatism without
business', likely to continue? The answer, like corporatism itself, is
contingent on party politics. Being a product of Labor politics, its future depends on the Labor Party remaining in office and on the ACTU
leadership and its affiliated unions remaining satisfied that the costs of
wage restraint are outweighed by the benefits. As a form of centralised
incomes policy based on a union–government bargain, the arrangement

will not survive a change of government. An incoming Liberal–National Party government, committed to a dismantling of the centralised system of wage fixation (on which the Accord was built), is not about to enter a bargained wages agreement with the trade union movement embodying significant non-wage (not to mention political) concessions to the unions. It would seek to weaken, not strengthen, the power of the union movement. It would look to the market to achieve wage restraint. Such a political program leaves little room for corporatist-style consensual bargaining. It leaves none at all for 'corporatism without business'.

ENDNOTES

[1] Some commentators have interpreted the term 'distributional coalition' to mean a collaborative coalition between sectional interest groups (e.g. a coalition between manufacturers and trade unions in favour of tariff protection). In Olson's usage, however, the term simply refers to any narrow special-interest group.

[2] In Queensland the Primary Producers Organisation and Marketing Act of 1926 required primary producers to belong to commodity boards. (Wool and meat producers were exempt.) These statutory boards are presently centralised under the umbrella of the Queensland Council of Agriculture.

[3] The BCA in effect was a merger of two groups that had been attempting to perform this role: the Australian Industries Development Association and the Business Roundtable.

[4] Missing from its membership are the three media giants (News Corporation, Consolidated Press and Fairfax); the two New Zealand-based heavyweights (Fletcher Challenge and Brierley Investments); the two Japanese trading companies with extensive Australian operations (Mitsui and C. Itoh); all the State banks and State superannuation funds; and most government-operated utilities, even though they are among Australia's largest employers (for example, Australia Post, the Victorian SEC and Queensland Rail).

REFERENCES

ACTU (1987) 'Future Strategies for the Trade Union Movement', paper prepared for the 1987 ACTU Congress

ACTU/TDC (1987) *Australia Reconstructed: ACTU/TDC Mission to Western Europe* Canberra: Australian Government Publishing Service

Bamber, Greg and Lansbury, R.D. eds (1987) *International and Comparative Industrial Relations* Sydney: Allen & Unwin

Banting, Keith (1986) 'The State and Economic Interests: An Introduction' in Banting, Keith ed. *The State and Economic Interests*, Studies of the Royal Commission on the Economic Union and Development Prospects for Canada, 32 Toronto: Toronto University Press

Beer, Samuel H. (1982) *Britain Against Itself: The Political Contradictions of Collectivism* London: Faber and Faber

Cameron, David R. (1984) 'Social Democracy, Corporatism, Labour Quiescence and the Representation of Economic Interest in Advanced Capitalist Society' in Goldthorpe, John H. ed. *Order and Conflict in Contemporary Capitalism* Oxford: The Clarendon Press

Campbell, Keith O. (1968) 'Australian Farm Organizations and Agricultural Policy' in Hughes, Colin A. ed. *Readings in Australian Government* St Lucia: Queensland University Press

Chapman, Bruce and Gruen, Fred (1990) 'An Analysis of the Australian Consensual Incomes Policy: The Prices and Incomes Accord' *Centre for Economic Policy Research, Discussion Papers*, 221, Canberra: Australian National University

Coleman, William D. (1986) 'Canadian Business and the State' in Banting, Keith ed. *The State and Economic Interests*, Studies of the Royal Commission on the Economic Union and Development Prospects for Canada, 32 Toronto: Toronto University Press

—— (1988) *Business and Politics: A Study of Collective Action* Kingston and Montreal: McGill-Queens University Press

—— (1989) 'State Traditions and Comprehensive Business Associations: A Comparative Structural Analysis' (typescript)

Coleman, William and Grant, Wyn (1988) 'The Organizational Cohesion and Political Access of Business: a Study of Comprehensive Associations' *European Journal of Political Research*, 16, 5, pp. 467–87

Gerritsen, Rolf (1986) 'The Necessity of "Corporatism": The Case of the Hawke Labor Government' *Politics* 21, pp. 45–54

Grant, W. (1987) *Business and Politics in Britain* London: Macmillan Education

Katzenstein, P.J. (1984) *Corporatism and Change: Austria, Switzerland and the Politics of Industry* Ithaca: Cornell University Press

—— (1985) *Small States in World Markets: Industrial Policy in Europe* Ithaca: Cornell University Press

Keating, Michael and Dixon, Geoff (1989) *Making Economic Policy in Australia 1983–1988* Melbourne: Longman Cheshire

Keeler, J.T.S. (1987) *The Politics of Neocorporatism in France: Farmers, the State and Agricultural Policy-making in the Fifth Republic* New York: Oxford University Press

Kumar, Pradeep (1986) 'Union Growth in Canada: Retrospect and Prospect' in Riddell, W. Craig ed., *Canadian Labour Relations* Studies of the Royal Commission on the Economic Union and Development Prospects for Canada, 16 Toronto: Toronto University Press

Kuwahara, Yasuo (1987) 'Japanese Industrial Relations' in Bamber, Greg and Lansbury, R.D. eds *International and Comparative Industrial Relations* Sydney: Allen & Unwin

Lange, Peter and Garrett, Geoffrey (1985) 'The Politics of Growth: Strategic Interaction and Economic Performance in Advanced Industrial Democracies' *Journal of Politics*, 47, 3, pp. 792–827

Lehmbruch, Gerhard (1984) 'Concertation and the Structure of Corporatist Networks' in Goldthorpe, John H. ed. *Order and Conflict in Contemporary Capitalism* Oxford: The Clarendon Press

Lindblom, C.E. (1977) *Politics and Markets* New York: Basic Books

McEachern, Doug (1986) 'Corporatism and Business Responses to the Hawke Government', *Politics*, 21, pp. 19–27

McLaughlin, P.A. (1990) 'How Big Business Relates to the Hawke Government: The Captains of Industry' paper presented to a seminar on How Labor Governs: the Hawke Government and Business, Australian National University, 6 July 1990

Maier, Charles S. (1984) 'Preconditions for Corporatism' in J.H. Goldthorpe ed. *Order and Conflict in Contemporary Capitalism* Oxford: The Clarendon Press

Marin, Bernd (1985) 'Austria: The Paradigm Case of Liberal Corporatism?' in Grant, Wyn ed. *The Political Economy of Corporatism* London: Macmillan

Martin, Andrew (1986) 'The Politics of Employment and Welfare: National Policies and International Interdependence' in Banting, Keith ed. *The State and Economic Interests* Studies of the Royal Commission on the Economic Union and Development Prospects for Canada, 32 Toronto: Toronto University Press

Martin, Ross M. (1989) *Trade Unionism: Purposes and Forms* Oxford: The Clarendon Press

Matthews, Trevor (1990) 'Federalism and Interest Group Cohesion: The Case of Australian Business Groups', *Publius: The Journal of Federalism*, 21, 4

NESC (1983) *National Economic Summit. Documents and Proceedings*, 2, Canberra: Australian Government Publishing Service

Offe, Claus and Wiesenthal, Helmut (1979) 'The Two Logics of Collective Action: Theoretical Notes on Social Class and the Political Form of Interest Organization' in Zeitlin, Maurice ed. *Political Power and Social Theory*, 1, Greenwood, Conn.: JAI Press

Olson, Mancur (1982) *The Rise and Decline of Nations: Economic Growth, Stagflation and Social Rigidities* New Haven and London: Yale University Press

———— (1984) 'Australia in the Perspective of the Rise and Decline of Nations' *Centre for Economic Policy Research, Discussion Papers* 109, Australian National University

Paloheimo, Heikki (1984) 'Distributive Struggle and Economic Development in the 1970s in Developed Capitalist Countries' *European Journal of Political Research* 12, 2, pp. 171–90

Panitch, L. (1986) 'The Tripartite Experience' in K. Banting ed. *The State and Economic Interests* Studies of the Royal Commission on the Economic Union and Development Prospects for Canada, 32, Toronto: Toronto University Press

Pempel, T.J. and Tsunekawa, K. (1979) 'Corporatism Without Labor? The Japanese Anomaly' in Schmitter, Philippe C. and Lehmbruch, Gerhard eds *Trends Toward Corporatist Intermediation* Beverly Hills and London: Sage Publications

Pincus, Jonathan J. (1987) 'Government' in Maddock, Rodney and McLean, Ian W. eds *The Australian Economy in the Long Run* Cambridge: Cambridge University Press

Plowman, David H. (1989) 'Countervailing Power, Organizational Parallelism and Australian Employer Associations', *Australian Journal of Management*, 1, pp. 97–113

Rawson, Don (1982) 'The ACTU: Growth Yes, Power No' in Cole, Kathryn ed. *Power, Conflict and Control in Trade Unions* Ringwood, Vic.; Penguin Books

Rawson, D.W. (1986) *Unions and Unionists in Australia* Sydney: George Allen and Unwin, second edn

Rawson, D.W. and Wrightson, S. (1980) *A Handbook of Australian Trade Unions and Employers' Associations*, Occasional paper 15, Canberra: Department of Political Science, Research School of the Social Sciences, Australian National University

Regini, Marino (1984) 'The Conditions for Political Exchange: How Concertation Emerged and Collapsed in Italy and Great Britain' in Goldthorpe, John H. ed. *Order and Conflict in Contemporary Capitalism* Oxford: The Clarendon Press

Richmond, Keith (1980) 'The Major Rural Producer Groups in New South Wales' in Scott, Roger ed. *Interest Groups and Public Policy: Case Studies from the Australian States* Melbourne: The Macmillan Company of Australia

Rickard, J. (1984) *Class and Politics: New South Wales, Victoria and the Early Commonwealth 1890–1910* Canberra: Australian National University Press

Schedvin, C.B. (1987) 'The Australian Economy on the Hinge of History', *Australian Economic Review* 1, pp. 20–30

Schmidt, Manfred (1982) 'Does Corporatism Matter? Economic Crisis, Politics and Rates of Unemployment in Capitalist Democracies in the 1970s' in Lehmbruch, Gerhard and Schmitter, Philippe eds *Patterns of Corporatist Policy-Making* London and Beverly Hills: Sage Publications

——— (1983) 'The Welfare State and the Economy in Periods of Economic Crisis: A Comparative Study of Twenty-Three OECD Countries' *European Journal of Political Research* 11, 1, pp. 1–26

Schmitter, Philippe C. (1981) 'Interest Intermediation and Regime Governability in Contemporary Western Europe and North America' in Berger, Suzanne ed. *Organizing Interests in Western Europe* Cambridge: Cambridge University Press

Schmitter, Philippe C. and Streeck, Wolfgang (1981) *The Organization of Business Interests: A Research Design* Berlin: Wissenschaftzentrum

Schott, Kerry (1984) *Policy, Power and Order: The Persistence of Economic Problems in Capitalist States* New Haven: Yale University Press

Singleton, Gwynneth (1990) *The Accord and the Australian Labour Movement* Carlton: Melbourne University Press

Stewart, Randal G. (1985) 'The Politics of the Accord: Does Corporatism Explain it?' *Politics* 20, 1, pp. 26–35

Stilwell, Frank (1986) *The Accord and Beyond: The Political Economy of the Labor Government* Sydney and London: Pluto Press

Streeck W. (1984) 'Neo-corporatist Industrial Relations and the Economics Crisis in West Germany' in J.L. Goldthorpe ed. *Order and Conflict in contemporary Capitalism* Oxford: The Clarendon Press

Useem, Michael (1984) *The Inner Circle: Large Corporations and the Rise of Business Political Activity in the USA and the UK* New York: Oxford University Press

Vowles, Jack (1989) 'Business, Unions and the State: Organizing Economic Interests in New Zealand' in Gold, Hyam ed. *New Zealand Politics in Perspective* second edn Auckland: Longman Paul

West, Katharine (1984) *The Revolution in Australian Politics* Ringwood, Vic.: Penguin Books

Wilson, Graham K. (1982) 'Why There Is No Corporatism in the United States' in G. Lehmbruch and P. Schmitter eds *Patterns of Corporatist Policy-making* Beverley Hills: Sage

—— (1985) *Business and Politics: A Comparative Introduction* London: Macmillan

Windmuller, John P. (1975) 'The Authority of National Trade Union Confederations: A Comparative Analysis' in Lipsky, David ed. *Union Power and Public Policy* Ithaca, N.Y.: New York School of Industrial Relations, Cornell University

—— (1981) 'Concentration Trends in Union Structure: An International Comparison' *Industrial and Labor Relations Review* 35, 1, pp. 43–57

11 Has the old politics reached an impasse?

DON RAWSON

My answer to the question posed above by the editor, like the answers to many questions, begins in the form 'It all depends on what you mean by. . . ' Definitions (d) and (e) of 'politics' in the *Shorter Oxford Dictionary* set out the relevant alternative meanings well enough. Definition (d) refers very broadly to 'Political affairs or business; political life', referring back to a definition of 'political' as 'pertaining to the state, its government and policy'. Definition (e) refers more narrowly to 'the political principles, opinions or sympathies of a person or party'. Following from the second definition, 'politics' is often used to refer to conflict between parties, as in 'Don't bring politics into (the affairs of the church, the golf club etc.)'. There is less ambiguity in the other noun in my title. An 'impasse' is 'a road or way having no outlet; a blind alley'.

There are, therefore, two related matters to be considered. The broader question is whether modern political systems, especially the Australian and those comparable with it, provide adequate means for the processing of subjects on which society is divided but on which it should, or must, come to authoritative decisions. The content of these subjects often changes and is certainly changing at the present time. Subjects involving environmental protection, gender and ethnicity (including Aboriginality) are obvious examples. There is no doubt, therefore, that we are faced with 'new politics'. What is questionable is whether existing parties and party systems can adjust sufficiently to changing political demands to survive in recognisably their present forms. I suggest that the party system which we see in Australia, and by extension some similar systems elsewhere, should *not* be considered fundamentally outdated, and therefore at an impasse. As a consequence, I do not see them as facing any imminent threat of radical reconstruction, though they are certainly changing and will continue to

219

change. We may hope that party systems do not survive when they are manifestly incapable of handling what are generally seen as the major political conflicts of the era. Consequently, I shall be suggesting that the 'new' politics, which unquestionably exist, can be processed through 'old' (though not unchanging) party structures.

The durability of many party systems in democratic countries is an old story. To quote a justly famous sentence from Lipset and Rokkan (1967: 50):

> . . . the party systems of the 1960s reflect, with few but significant exceptions, the cleavage structures of the 1920s. This is a crucial characteristic of Western competitive politics in the age of 'high mass consumption'.

This belief that there was a noteworthy stability in party systems was tested, and generally supported, by closer examination of data for the fifteen years or so following World War II (Rose and Urwin, 1970). It has since been argued that in the 1960s and 1970s European party systems showed more signs of change:

> There can be little doubt that the electoral stability that characterised European party systems has recently given way to a situation of greater change and instability . . . it is clear that European party systems cannot now be regarded as inherently stable structures.

The author wisely added:

> We may note . . . that the real world has a rather consistent habit of upsetting the prognostications of social science: and, as we have seen in this paper, the recent electoral patterns in Europe offer a good example of such a process. In other words, we must be wary about forecasting possible future patterns of party politics (Maguire, 1983: 92–3).

If the events of the 1960s and 1970s indicated more rapid change in the party structures of Europe, it may be thought that events of the 1980s have been still more indicative of such change; and that such a conclusion also applies to Australia. In particular, it may seem that events of 1989 and 1990 have strengthened such a view; especially the increased prominence of environmental protection as an issue and of recently established parties which have sought to make this issue their own. And so it may be. But we should bear in mind not only Maguire's general caution but her 'admission' that 'there remains a substantial degree of persistence' in the 'old' party structures. This is not the first time in recent decades that we have been told that fundamental change in the party system is upon us. I shall consider, with reference to Australia but with some glances at other countries, whether such predictions are likely to prove more valid this time than in the past.

PARTIES: OLD, NEW, RE-NAMED, DEFUNCT

Australia provides only a minor exception to Lipset and Rokkan's 1967 proposition that the party systems of the 1960s reflected the 'cleavage structures' of the 1920s. The effective division of Australian politics between the Australian Labor Party on the one hand and either a single non-Labor party or two such parties in close alliance dates from the 'fusion' of the earlier non-Labor parties in 1908; earlier than the 1920s but not by any great margin. And if we choose to date the party system from the separate appearance of the Country (now National) Party, the minor party in such alliances, this brings the date forward to 1919.

Since the federal election of 1910, therefore, the effective choice offered Australian electors, in terms of parties, has not changed fundamentally. I wrote many years ago:

> This type of party system had endured since the fusion of the non-Labor parties in 1908, not fundamentally threatened by the frequent internal troubles which beset the Labor Party and its principal opponent, which began as the Liberal Party and resumed the title, after trying two others, in 1945. It was not threatened even by the establishment of the Country Party which quickly settled down, except in Victorian state politics, as a permanent partner in a non-Labor alliance. It was, however, threatened by the events which led to the formation of the Democratic Labor Party. The 1958 election showed that the threat, contrary to most expectations, was persistent, while suggesting that, after all, it might end merely as a threat (Rawson, 1961: 3).

This now has an old-fashioned sound, in several respects. One is the reference to the Country Party. The change in the party's title from Country to National, which was completed in 1982, implied a change in substance. A move was to be made away from the specifically regional and rural appeal which the party had always sought to make towards a broader, 'national' appeal which would extend to the cities where most of the voters live.

Such a change was not unique to Australia, though in this case Australia lagged behind other countries and the change in Australia seems to have been largely abortive. One of the political developments common to Australia and to some of the Scandinavian countries, and in this case to no other countries, was the establishment in the 1920s of Country (their titles have usually been translated as 'Agrarian') parties. At both ends of the world, such parties drew upon a general feeling of neglect by country dwellers and more specifically on problems facing primary industry. Perhaps because of the far greater measure of geographic isolation in Australia, the Country Party was happy to retain this frankly sectional image until the 1970s, though the increasing proportions of city and near-city residents and electors inevitably worked against it.[1]

In Sweden, Norway and Finland, the growing weakness of parties which depended specifically on a section of the shrinking rural vote became apparent at an earlier stage. Consequently, these Agrarian parties changed their name to 'Centre' during the 1950s and sought city as well as country support. To do this, they had to broaden their policies and have become associated particularly with policies of environmental protection. Despite these significant changes, these Centre parties remained part of what in the present context we may call the 'old' politics. They, as well as the other long-established Scandinavian parties, have recently been seen as under challenge by 'new' parties, such as the Green party of Sweden.

If the reformed Country parties of Scandinavia have not proved a threat to the established party systems, this is even more true of the National Party in Australia. Here the attempt to broaden the basis of the party from rural and provincial areas was seriously attempted only in Queensland. Even in that state, it has shrunk back to its rural origins following heavy defeats in state and federal elections in 1989–90; and in the other states it never looked like moving out of them. To say the least, there is no sign of the National party becoming part of any 'new politics'.

The National Party has at least survived. That was not true of the Democratic Labor Party, the party which was sometimes seen in the 1950s and 1960s as posing a possible challenge to the existing party system. The DLP ceased to have any parliamentary members after 1974, and wound itself up some years later. In retrospect it is easy to dismiss as merely one more breakaway from the ALP, of which there were many between 1916 and 1955, certain either to wither or to find its way back unto the ALP, and therefore as no more than another temporary modification of traditional Australian politics. But this is not the whole truth.

The DLP survived longer and was stronger, as a national grouping, than any previous Labor breakaway. In 1967, having already been represented in the Senate since 1955, it polled 10 per cent of the Senate votes. This was more than has been polled by the Australian Democrats at any election prior to 1990. And even in 1990 the Democrats polled 13 per cent; an impressive figure certainly but not overwhelmingly greater than that secured by the DLP in the 1960s. While the DLP as its name indicates, sought to present itself as a Labor party (and sometimes as the true successor of the undivided ALP of the years prior to 1955) it sometimes sought to appear as a new party, more suited to the economy and society of the later twentieth century. In this sense the very word 'Labor' was a dubious asset; and in presenting the party's policy in 1958 the party's leader actually used the phrase, 'the Democratic Party is here to stay' (Rawson, 1961: 37). This aspect of the DLP is worth remembering because it reflects a common view in the 1950s that parties such as the ALP were essentially outdated and due for replacement. Such a view needs to be recalled forty years later, when this is again suggested, after a period during which the ALP has not only survived but, at times, triumphed. Much the same is true of the Liberal Party and even of the National (nee Country) Party. Past predictions of the obsolescence of the 'old' parties, and especially of the Labor Party, have been falsified by events. Present predictions of the same type should, at least, be examined with care.

Such changes as have taken place in the Australian party system have so far modified it rather than transformed it. Much the same could be said of the party systems in the other developed capitalist countries. What Lipset and Rokkan (1967: 50) referred to as 'the freezing of the major party alternatives' has largely continued. How much longer this 'freezing' will persist depends, of course, on the persistence of the circumstances which produced it. Lipset and Rokkan's passage referred to '. . . the freezing of the major party alternatives in the wake of the extension of the suffrage and the mobilisation of major sections of the new reservoirs of potential supporters.' These were seen as joint necessary conditions for the emergence of the 'modern' party systems. The extension of the suffrage was, we may hope, a once for all, irreversible change. The early achievement of manhood suffrage and then of universal suffrage in Australia may perhaps be relevant to the somewhat earlier 'freezing' of the party system in Australia (Aitkin & Castles, 1989: 216–219). Be that as it may, the other leg of the argument, the 'mobilisation of major sections' of the voters, is more relevant to the future, because different 'major sections' may appear and seek to be represented through the party system. We therefore need to consider what were these 'major sections' which gave rise to the 'old' politics; and whether those sections have changed fundamentally, or are in the process of doing so.

OLD AND NEW 'CLASS POLITICS'

What were these 'major sections', in Australia and elsewhere? In principle, they could have various origins. They could be the inhabitants of different geographic regions or of other physical locations, such as city dwellers and country dwellers. They could be religious denominations or ethnic communities. Or, most pervasively and most problematically, they could be 'classes'. The model which was most commonly found was that the division between parties was between that (or those) supported by 'the working class' and that (or those) supported by other sections of the community, such as 'the middle class'.

Some such model became the principal means of explaining the existence of parties, and the divisions between them, in many countries, including Australia. In Australia, together with Britain, New Zealand, Sweden and Norway, such an explanation was given formal recognition by the formation of labour parties, in the sense of parties to which trade unions belonged, by the process of affiliation. To me it still appears useful, as it did many years ago, to distinguish 'labour' parties, which have affiliated trade unions, from 'social democratic' parties, which do not (Rawson, 1969), but I should say at once that such a distinction is not essential to the argument of this chapter.

The unions, together with the parties, were sometimes referred to as 'the working class movement'. The more valid this description, the more the other party or parties seemed to be, almost of necessity, the parties of some other class.

In the rest of Western Europe, where and when the population had any choice, there were no labour parties; but there were parties, called socialist or social democratic, which also sought or claimed to have the support of 'the working class'. Here too, the more they secured the support of 'the working class', the more other parties seemed to represent another class.

This chapter will focus almost entirely on labour parties and their closest equivalents. It has been the labour and social democratic parties which have most often been regarded as obsolescent and whose supposed decline or fall was thought likely to produce a major change in the party system. Since such changes have in fact been very limited, we need to explain the longevity of labour and social democratic parties. And if we are to postulate future change, we need to establish that the decline of labour and social democratic parties is at last, after so many falsified predictions, truly upon us.

At the time such parties were formed and began to flourish, unionism was very largely confined to manual workers. Even when other workers also became unionised, it was the manual workers' unions which joined the labour parties (where such parties existed) or openly declared their support for social democratic or, occasionally, communist parties. In the late nineteenth and early twentieth centuries, the predominant ideology of unionism could justly be described as class consciousness. That is, it was believed not only that unionists had special interests which should be defended, which is true of interest groups of all kinds, but that they had shared general interests as an unfairly disadvantaged section of society and therefore required the general transformation of that society.

V. Gordon Childe, writing in the early 1920s, drew attention to such assumptions, though he did not necessarily endorse them:

> I have assumed without criticism the hypothesis that the present organisation of society involves some sort of exploitation and enslavement of the workers, and that the object of a Labour Movement as such must be to bring about such an alteration in society as shall end this. This seems to me the essential

presupposition of a Labour Party or Trade Union as distinguished from a
Radical-Liberal Party or a Friendly Society (Childe, 1964 [1923]: xi).

Childe was writing during the brief heyday of radical and quasi-
revolutionary ideas in the Australian labour movement, this being part
of a world-wide trend. But the belief that the labour movement existed
to remedy a general 'exploitation' of workers, an exploitation which
went far beyond their immediate conditions of employment, remained
labour orthodoxy, in Australia as elsewhere. A representative Australian trade union official of the 1950s, later secretary of the Australian
Council of Trade Unions (ACTU), put it like this:

> For the workers, the union is not merely an expression of their dissatisfaction
> with the terms of employment but also a form of protest against their
> disfranchised position in the community as a whole (Souter, 1956: 74).

The labour parties, in Australia and elsewhere, had to speak for the
unions' broader social objectives as well as their more concrete 'industrial', objectives. Since these parties never saw themselves as being only
the political mouthpiece of the unions, there was always the likelihood
of tension between union leaders and party leaders. In Australia this
tension was more common and more destructive than elsewhere. This
was in part because the ALP had the bad luck to be successful many
years before any other labour party and so to hold office at times when it
was particularly difficult to reconcile conflicting demands on the party.
The best time for such a party to take office for the first time was in the
aftermath of the great depression of the 1930s, when there was nowhere
to go but up. The labour parties of Sweden, Norway and New Zealand
had this good fortune.

The Australian Labor Party, coming to office with a parliamentary
majority for the first time in 1910, in less propitious circumstances economically and in time to confront the tensions arising from World War
I, soon encountered public disillusionment and internal disruption.
Nevertheless, if we date the party from the establishment of the Australian Labour Federation in Queensland in 1890, it has survived for a
century and been the largest single Australian party for nearly all that
period. What is equally notable is that its most prolonged period of
electoral success has come at the end of that period, during the 1980s
and (at least) the early 1990s. This record raises questions about
whether, or to what extent, Labor has been a 'class party'. Was it ever
such? Was it so at one time, but later ceased to be such a party? In that
case there is at least a paradox in the fact that it has been most successful when it departed from its original character. Again, 'it all depends
on what you mean by. . .'; in this case, what we mean by class.

In 1963, Robert Alford's *Party and Society: the Anglo-American Democracies* did much to confirm a common assumption that 'the working
class' could be defined operationally as those with manual occupations,

as distinct from the 'middle-class' or white-collar workers (Alford, 1963: 116). Alford's theoretical treatment of class was in fact more sophisticated than this would suggest but nevertheless his operational definition of 'class voting' has remained the predominant interpretation of class for those concerned with the explanation of political attitudes, in Australia and elsewhere. Of the most influential Australian studies, Kemp based his chapter, 'The Class Cleavage' on the manual/non-manual division (Kemp, 1978: 45–91); though Aitkin, to his credit, used the terms 'middle class' and 'working class' to refer to self-identification, using 'occupational grade' to refer to the distinction between manual and non-manual workers (Aitkin, 1977: 118–142). It was quite common to define the working class as manual workers for operational purposes. Thus McKenzie and Silver (1968: 79) combined a quite sophisticated historical analysis of 'Working Class Conservatives in Urban England' with a definition of the working class, for operational purposes, as 'those living in households where the chief wage earner was employed in a manual occupation (or, if retired, had been so employed for most of his working life)'.

The only thing in favour of defining 'class' by whether people follow manual or non-manual occupations is that so often it has seemed to provide the right answers! Nevertheless, it is a distinction which is arbitrary and question-begging (are dentists manual or non-manual?). It has very imperfect associations with what might seem more substantial questions, such as level of income or the exercise of power at the workplace. It has virtually nothing to do with classical Marxist conceptions of class; while attempts at neo-Marxist adjustments may leave confusion worse confounded. Yet the fact remains that it has been difficult to find any 'objective' bivariate association with party identification or with voting behaviour which is stronger than this untidy, dubious characteristic of manual employment (see, for example, McAllister and Ascui, 1988: 230). There may be a stronger association between one's own politics and those of one's parents but this, though interesting, somehow seems less satisfying.

Nevertheless, there are both theoretical and practical complications arising from using manual as distinct from non-manual work to explain political attitudes and activities. It is by no means easy to explain why this distinction should give rise to the crucial political division in societies like our own. It does not have any of the apparent clarity of the classical Marxist distinction between bourgeoisie and proletariat. The only difficulty about that is that it does not correspond at all well with what people actually do. But then, it might be said, it is also the case that the manual/non-manual division has a diminishing association with political behaviour. Manual workers, in Australia as elsewhere, are increasingly likely to vote for non-labour parties; and non-manual workers, in Australia as elsewhere, are increasingly likely to vote for labour parties (Kemp, 1978: 352). In this sense there has been, in Australia as elsewhere, 'a substantial decline in the importance of class as a structural basis for voting behaviour' (Kemp, 1978: 352).

If we assume both this definition of class and that the Australian and related party systems have been class-based, this seems to suggest a certain fragility in the systems and a likelihood that they are becoming vulnerable to major change. In all the relevant countries, the proportion of manual workers has been declining as a proportion of the workforce. It follows that, if one party or party bloc depends solely or predominantly upon the support of manual workers, it is likely to face a secular decline.

And this, of course, is just what has been predicted of the ALP, and of similar parties in other countries, at various times over the last half century. But, obviously, this has not happened. In most countries where labour and social democratic parties were strong fifty years ago— in Britain, Australia, New Zealand, Sweden and Norway (the labour parties); and in France, The Netherlands and Belgium (the social democratic parties)—they are still strong, despite having had some scary times over the years. Where they were weak fifty years ago (Ireland, Canada) they are still weak. In Austria, (West) Germany, Spain and, to a much lesser degree, Italy such parties bounced back, after the Nazi, Franco and Fascist parentheses. Only in Denmark has the Social Democratic Party appeared to suffer a decisive and permanent setback. Where these parties are strong, the history of the last half century is littered with the bodies, sometimes still breathing feebly, of parties which, at one time or another, were thought of as possible replacements for them.

The case of the DLP in Australia has already been mentioned. The rapid rise and then fall of the Social Democratic Party in Britain is a much clearer example of a party which was based on a breakaway from a Labour Party which it saw as outdated, hoped to attract widespread support as a party of the future but then dwindled into insignificance. The Liberal Party in Britain, which prior to the 1920s was a major party, has since had a long history of unfulfilled hopes of regaining such a status. These hopes have been associated with the question, 'Must Labour Lose?'; a question asked in the 1950s (Abrams and Rose, 1960) and again in the 1980s (Zentner, 1981) but which events have answered in the negative.

Why have labour and social democratic parties survived and flourished despite the supposed 'decline of class voting'? If support for them has been sustained while the proportion of manual workers has declined, then these parties must have either mobilised more of the manual workers or more of the non-manual workers, or possibly both. There is quite widespread evidence that such parties have maintained their strength largely by attracting more non-manual workers. Over the long term, this has compensated them for the declining number of manual workers and also for some decline in the proportion of manual workers who support them. Does this really mean that the logic of their existence is diminished? Why should we assume that it is the manual workers who are their necessary and distinctive source of support? Could it not be quite appropriate that this support now comes more evenly from each side of the arbitrary manual/non-manual divide?

We can get some hints in this direction by looking further at what used to be called the 'industrial wing of the labour movement', that is, trade unionism. One very common characteristic of unionism in developed countries since World War II has been its growth among non-manual workers. Because of the declining number of manual workers, the only alternative to such a development would have been a severe decline in union membership, as in fact happened from the mid 1950s in the United States. Elsewhere there was a marked expansion of non-manual union membership which more than compensated for the decline in manual unionism. The 'industrial' wing grew by the same process as enabled the 'political wing' to maintain its position—by mobilising more of the non-manual workers. Both of these trends were to be found in most developed capitalist countries, at least from the mid 1950s to the mid 1970s. Had they not occurred, the labour/social democratic vote, or trade union membership, or both, would have been expected to decline.

The growth of non-manual unionism was sometimes followed, after some time lag, by the entry of most non-manual unions into the principal trade union federation in their respective countries, hitherto composed almost entirely of manual unions. Such developments were particularly clear in Australia where there are now very few unions of any consequence which are not affiliated with the ACTU or with one of its state branches. But much the same tendencies can be seen in Britain and New Zealand, and perhaps elsewhere. Sweden is the only notable exception to the tendency for manual and non-manual unions to move in the direction of greater organisational unity. And it is in Sweden that the 'old-fashioned' connection between being a manual worker and voting labour remains strong. 'In Sweden there is a wider gap between workers and the middle strata than there is elsewhere [in the Nordic countries]' (Esping-Andersen, 1985: 255). And, it might be added, wider than in Australia.

These are developments which do not suggest the decline of class politics, unless class is defined on the dubious basis of manual versus non-manual occupations. We have seen a growth and a unification of trade unions, accompanied by a maintenance of voting support for the political party with which they have traditionally been associated. And as long as such parties can expect to gain something approaching half of the votes, the possibilities for change in the overall party system are, to say the least, limited.

Is there, however, a reduced community of interest between this broader trade union movement and the labour/social democratic parties? If we continue to assume that unions tend to be composed of disadvantaged sections of the community, this might seem likely. But unions, and the 'trade union movement', now contain relatively few who could reasonably be described as 'having a disfranchised position in the community as a whole'. The unionised manual workers, now more secure, and the unionised non-manual workers, now with fewer illusions as to their superior status, have come together in a more or less comfortable middling position. There remain 'disfranchised' people—in Australia's case many Aborigines, exploited 'irregular' migrant and other outworkers, long-term social security recipients—but, unfortunately, such people have little to do with unions or vice versa.

What we have sometimes seen is not a breaking of ties between unionism and labour/social democratic parties but a strengthening of these ties. The period of union consolidation across manual and non-manual occupations, and therefore the increased occupational heterogeneity of the 'trade union movement' may be a period of closer connections between unionism and labour parties. The 'Accord' between the Australian Labor government and the ACTU is a particularly clear example, and so far a successful one, of such an outcome (see Singleton, 1989; Chapman and Gruen, 1989). Such a close connection is compatible with a very wide range of policy options, outside an essential core of policies to regulate the labour market. Among other things, it is compatible with either universalist or selective social welfare policies.

It is, in fact, compatible with almost anything except with socialism, in the sense of the public ownership of at least the major industries. In Australia as in capitalist countries generally, there has been an inverse relationship between the frequency of use of the word 'socialism' and its solid content. When it has a fairly definite meaning, which includes the economic dominance of the public sector, its use has been avoided by the ALP and by similar parties in other countries. When it can be fudged to mean something much vaguer, it becomes somewhat more popular. Humphrey McQueen has said, 'Saying that the ALP is non-socialist is like saying that it is non-Buddhist; the terms of reference are simply irrelevant' (McQueen, 1984: 230). That is true; and it is true of every labour or social democratic party. All are non-socialist and (a related point) all are class-collaborationist, these days proudly so. That is one reason why they survive and, often, succeed. It can be said of all such governments, as has been said of those of Sweden, 'Social Democratic Governments have consistently pursued a pro-business policy' (Hadenius, 1990: 188). They may not always be sufficiently 'pro-business' to satisfy business! And, of course, they pursue other policies too.

All parties, like other institutions, depend for survival on their powers of adaptation. None of the 'old' parties of the 1920s or even of the

1960s could have maintained themselves without constantly modifying
their activities and policies; changes which are often obscured by their
apparently rigid structures. In the case of the ALP and its related organisations, some of these changes have already been mentioned. Not
only has trade unionism gained strength among the non-manual workers but their unions have joined the ACTU and as such have been fully
involved in the unprecedentedly close relations between the ACTU and
the government. The party has adjusted to the changed political attitudes and demands of women so that the long-standing tendency of
women to give it less support than men has been virtually eliminated
(McAllister and Ascui, 1988: 228). The party's relations with movements for environmental protection are more complex, but the party's
victory at the 1990 federal election at least indicates that it has made
some such adjustments, not without success.

For whatever reasons, the 1980s were periods of success for some of
the labour parties of Scandinavia and of Anglo–Australasia. These parties have been in office in Sweden since 1982; in Australia since 1983;
and in New Zealand since 1984. In Norway, Labour has fallen into
major difficulties, though it held office during 1986–89. An even more
obvious exception has been Britain, where Labour has been out of office
throughout this period. But the British story can be illuminating. It was
here that successive electoral failures during the 1950s raised most insis-
tently the possibility that Labour was doomed because of its inability to
adjust to a changing society. 'What is at issue today is the survival of the
Labour Party as we know it' (Abrams and Rose, 1960: 57).

The question 'Must Labour Lose?' was quite soon answered by the
party's electoral victories in 1964, 1966 and 1974, despite its defeat in
1970. But in retrospect it is clear that such adjustments as had been
made were inadequate, especially as regards the role of the trade
unions. '. . . the more intimately involved [Labour] ministers and officials became with the trade unions, the more shocked and exasperated
they grew' (Jackson, 1982: 44). And not only ministers and officials;
more importantly, the same was true of the voters. The eventual outcome was the 'winter of discontent' of 1978–9; the beginning of the
Conservative government under Margaret Thatcher; and the establishment of the Social Democratic Party, as an alternative to Labour, in
1981. During the mid 1980s, the British labour movement appeared to
be in real danger, with not only successive electoral defeats but a sharp
decline in union membership and an unwillingness even by unionists to
support the party. But, as at other times and places, these difficulties do
not seem to have been irreversible. By the end of the decade the Social
Democratic Party had collapsed; the decline in union membership had
been at least checked (Beardwell, 1990: 126) and the public repute of
the unions much improved (Edwards and Bain, 1988; Marsh, 1990);
and Labour was well ahead of the government in opinion polls.

It is at least clear that the Labour Party will again be a serious challenger of the Conservatives for office at the next election; and that it will
continue to be the only serious challenger. The changes which have
taken place in the party and in trade unionism since the mid 1980s are
too complex to set out here; but it is beyond question that the labour
movement in Britain has deliberately set itself to adjust to changing
circumstances and with some apparent success.

As an example of the hazards of analysis at a time of rapid but incon-
sistent change, a recent and impressive account refers to 'the collapse of
Labour's challenge to the Conservatives and revival of centrist voting in
the 1980s . . . ' (Dunleavy, 1989: 286). By the end of the 1980s, the
Labour Party was again looking much more formidable. Nevertheless,
it is true that British Labour has so far failed to produce either 'the kind
of ideological hegemony enjoyed by social democratic ideas in Sweden'
(Dunleavy, 1989: 263); or the successful integration of unionism and a
labour government which has marked the Accord years in Australia.

The types of adjustment which are necessary in current circumstances are not always self-evident. Some distinctly old-fashioned, if not
archaic, aspects of a party can survive for a long time and may have
good or bad consequences. This could be said of the distinguishing
characteristic of labour parties, their affiliated trade unions. A British
writer on the Swedish labour movement has said that 'The great disadvantage of the [British] Trade Union Congress is that less than half of
its members are affiliated to the Labour Party, so that it has to keep at
arm's length from the party, especially at election time; whereas the
[Swedish] LO is far closer to the party than its counterpart, the TUC'
(Linton, 1985: 1–26). Australian experience shows that in the present
era of labour politics affiliation with the party may be of limited consequence. Given an acceptable basis for agreement, a body like the
ACTU (or the TUC) may have closer relations with a labour government than ever in the past, despite the fact that in each case many of its
affiliated unions are not also affiliated with the party. A unified, and
therefore heterogeneous, trade union movement may be more devoted
to Labor success than the overwhelmingly manual union federations of
the past.

Nevertheless, as I have argued elsewhere, a situation in which manual unions are party-affiliated but non-manual unions are not may have
advantages. It means that people associated with the manual unions
make up a significant proportion of Labor members of parliament.
Without them, people with experience of manual occupations (the so-
called working class) would have almost completely disappeared from
the Labor parliamentary parties (Rawson, 1986: 55). It can therefore be
argued that the ALP of the 1980s approaches the epitome of a labour
party in its close relations with a comprehensive trade union movement.
In this respect it is closer to that model than was the party at the time

of, say, the Chifley or Whitlam governments; and closer to it than most such parties in other countries. There are, of course, those who deplore the policies which result (for example Maddox, 1989); but that is another question.

I have concentrated here on the future of the ALP, as the Australian exemplar of a common type of major political party. My argument has been that there is no reason to regard such parties as inevitably outdated. Although I have said very little about other 'old' parties, as represented in Australia by the Liberal and National parties, it can well be argued that, if the Labor party maintains the major status which it has had since at least 1908, the prospects of other fundamental change in the party system are limited. With the appropriate adjustments as to detail, the same proposition applies to other countries where there are labour parties, or something like them.

While I have therefore been concerned to make a case, I am not blind to arguments and evidence on the other side. While these can be better presented by people who are more impressed by them, I should at least indicate that I am aware of some of them and of why I do not regard them as decisive.

DOUBTS AND ALTERNATIVES

There is no doubt that the content of political debate has changed, and will go on changing. What is at issue is the capacity of the established parties, singly or together, to adjust to this new content. In some cases, such as gender issues, they appear to have done so with undoubted success, so far. That is, issues such as women's pay, child care, the representation of women in public office and laws relating to abortion have become much more prominent political issues. New organisations have appeared to express such viewpoints, with varying success. What has not appeared is any tendency for parties based on such questions to appear, let alone to achieve major status. The 'old' parties have added such items to their agenda with relative ease.

Similarly, while there is every indication that immigration and questions related to ethnicity will become increasingly prominent, there seems to be no indication whatever that such matters will bring significant new parties into existence or transform the character of existing parties. Whatever the outcomes, they will not please everybody. But there is nothing new in that!

Religion should be mentioned in this context because this has become an issue which now produces *less* modification of a party system divided between Labor and non-Labor forces than in the past. Whereas for most of this century there was a marked tendency for Catholics to vote Labor, independently of other factors, this has now been greatly reduced. This is one aspect of a more general separation of the churches from most general issues of public debate:

> The character of religion has changed in the 1980s, at least for the mainstream churches. Religion can be characterised as a comfortable private option lived out by those who have the education, money and time to enjoy its traditions. It is concerned with nurturing family but it appears to have disengaged from the major issues of the secular society (McCallum, 1988: 184).

While all such matters have distinctively Australian aspects, they are consistent with what has been happening in the developed capitalist societies of Western Europe and North America, subject to possible modification with respect to the role of religion in the United States. In other respects what is true of Australia seems broadly to be true elsewhere. Scandinavia, for example, continues to have minor religious parties such as the Christian Democrats in Sweden and the Christian People's Party in Norway. They date from the 1920s; they were marginal players then; and they have remained marginal players ever since.

THE ENVIRONMENTALIST EXCEPTION?

The case for an 'impasse' therefore rests very largely on the propositions that policies for protection of the environment have become much more salient and that this will continue; that the 'old' party system is essentially unsuited to dealing with such questions; that we can already see resulting changes in the political systems of Australia and other countries; and that such changes will result in the transformation of these systems.

The Australian Democrats have now contested five successive elections for the Senate (where they have been more successful, in votes as well as in seats, than for the House of Representatives). Their share of the national vote varied between 8 and 11 per cent, before increasing to 13 per cent in 1990. This was the first time, therefore, that their vote had exceeded that won by the now defunct Democratic Labor Party in the 1960s and 1970s. Their greater success in 1990 may be attributed in part to an increased public interest in environmental protection; certainly the Democrats made every effort to attract this vote. Other 'new' parties, much newer than the Democrats, also sought such support and obtained another 2 per cent of the Senate vote. There was thus a considerable minority of voters who gave a high priority to environmental issues and who sought a means outside the 'old' parties to express this. Following the 1990 election the Democrats, like the DLP before them, continue to hold the balance between the 'old' parties in the Senate; although, again like the DLP, they have never won a seat in the House of Representatives.

An even more noteworthy outcome occurred in the 1989 election for the state parliament in Tasmania. Here almost all the environmentalist vote (17 per cent of the total) went to a group calling themselves Green Independents with a further 1 per cent going to Democrats. The Greens, who won five seats, then allied with Labor (thirteen seats) to defeat the Liberal government (seventeen seats) and replace it with a Labor government which had given undertakings to the Greens. It will be noted that the Senate, but not the House of Representatives, is elected by proportional representation; and that the Tasmanian House of Assembly is the only state lower house (which determines the government) which is elected by proportional representation.

Australia has recently seen a significant rise in support for environmentalist parties but one that so far leaves them a long way short of major status; while their political impact has depended on the extent to which the various electoral systems provide barriers against the emergence of new parties. These propositions could be said to apply to a number of other countries.

In Sweden elections are by proportional representation but a minimum national vote of four per cent is required for a party to gain representation in the Riksdag (national parliament). An Ecology Party (now the Green Ecology Party) contested elections in 1982 and 1985 but was unable to reach this minimal level. In 1988, however, it secured 5.5 per cent of the votes and so obtained twenty seats. The Labour government, with its Communist allies, retained an absolute majority of seats and remained in office (Hadenius, 1990: 176–181).

In Norway, a Green Party was formed in 1988 with the aim of contesting the election of 1989, but in fact played no part in this election. The notable change in 1989 was a dramatic rise in support for the right-wing populist Progress Party, which increased its vote from 3.7 per cent to 13.0 per cent. At the other extreme, the Socialist Left Party also increased its vote, from 5.5 per cent to 10.0 per cent. While these results certainly showed voter dissatisfaction with the major parties, including the Labour Party, it is not easy to see them as consistent with broad international trends or with what has been happening in Australia.

In The Netherlands, a coalition of radical parties under the title Green Links gained 4.1 per cent of the votes in the 1989 election. Proportional representation enabled it to obtain six parliamentary seats. The centre-left, under the title Democrats 66, who have something in common with the Australian Democrats in their environmental concerns, won 7.9 per cent of the votes, compared to 6.1 per cent in 1986, and obtained nine seats, an increase of three on 1986. As in Australia, such results certainly show greater concern for the environment and some limited willingness by voters to support a smaller party on these grounds. They hardly suggest, as yet, any transformation of the party system.

West Germany has a longer history of Green party activity than other countries and so may give a better indication of such parties' prospects elsewhere in Europe. In January 1987 the Greens won 8.3 per cent of the votes at the federal election. They have also contested a number of state elections with varying results, sometimes failing to gain the minimum 5 per cent of the vote required to gain representation. In some cities combined Social Democratic and Green administrations have been formed, while in 1989 the Green party resolved in favour of a coalition with the Social Democrats at the federal level, should this be possible after the next federal election. On this and other questions, the West German Greens have already experienced a good deal of disunity and internal disruption.

The European parliamentary election of 1989 was contested by Green parties in most countries of the European Community. The Green Group won thirty of the 518 seats in the parliament, the 'Rainbow Group' winning a further thirteen. Green candidates in several countries polled better in this European election than they were likely to perform in their national elections, examples being a 13.9 per cent Green vote in Belgium and a 10.6 per cent vote in France. In West Germany, the Green vote at 8.4 per cent was almost unchanged from the previous European election in 1984. The most remarkable result was in Britain, where Green candidates polled 15 per cent of the votes but, because of the application of simple majority voting, failed to win a single seat. There is no indication from opinion poll or other sources that they would poll anything like as well at a national election. The Social and Liberal Democratic Party, made up of the old Liberal Party and some of the fragments of the short-lived Social Democratic Party, obtained 6.4 per cent of the votes (the above figures from Keesing, 1989:36737–8 and Europa Yearbook, 1990:1118, 1861, 1966). All of this indicates a real measure of support for new environmentalist parties but little evidence that they are heading for major status.

These are stories which clearly illustrate the importance of voting systems in permitting or discouraging changes to the party system. The presence of minor party or independent members in Australian parliaments has depended almost entirely on whether proportional representation is used (though there are occasional exceptions, such as the election of one independent member to the House of Representatives in 1990). Proportional representation enabled 5.5 per cent of the Swedish voters to elect twenty Green members to the Rikstag in 1988; whereas 11.3 per cent of Australian voters failed to elect a single Democrat member to the House of Representatives in 1990.

Preferential voting, used in all Australian lower house elections except for the Tasmanian state parliament, is somewhat less discouraging for new parties than a simple majority system, in that voters can avoid the risk of 'wasting' their vote by giving their second preferences to one of the major parties. This enables the leaders of minor parties to exer-

cise considerable power by advising their voters to cast these preferences in a particular direction, although the voters may not necessarily
follow such advice. And a major party may largely avoid the consequences of the rise of a small one if it can successfully appeal to the smaller
party's supporters to cast their second preference votes in its direction.
The Australian Labor Party made such an appeal, with apparent success, to Democrat and other environmentalist voters at the 1990
election.

HOW MUCH CHANGE?

All politics are, in one sense, 'new' politics; and the politics of rapidly
changing societies will have many new elements. My concern here has
been to argue that individual parties and party systems in countries like
Australia have adjusted to social change and so have strong prospects of
survival. While it is true that there are new emphases in politics to
which the time-honoured division between Labor and non-Labor is not
entirely suited, especially in relation to environmental politics, the 'old'
parties have adjusted to these changes to some extent and may well
adjust further. If so, it is not impossible that we are already seeing the
maximum extent not of 'green' politics but of 'green' parties, in Australia and elsewhere.

Such an argument depends in part on the continued validity of labour
parties and other parties which base their claims on protecting the
interests of employees. In some countries, including Australia, the
strength of trade unionism is highly relevant to the long term prospects
of these parties. The future of unionism raises questions which are too
large to be disposed of here. However, two points should be noted
which tell against any simple assumption that such parties are in terminal decline. Firstly, there are some countries, such as Sweden,
Austria, Norway and Belgium, in which there is no evidence that
unionism is declining. Secondly, there are countries, such as France,
Italy and The Netherlands, in which unionism is in fact weak and declining but where there is no sign of any drastic reformulation of the
party system, or of the rise of new major parties, as a consequence.

The most persuasive argument for the belief that environmentalism
as an issue is inappropriate to the 'old' party system asserts that parties
which depend on supporters of 'development', whether investors, managers or employees, will be unable to address issues of environmental
protection. In the case of labour parties, this will involve unions, especially those concerned with extractive industries. While this is a valid
argument, it should not be exaggerated, since the numbers directly
involved may be quite small. For example, the Australian Timber
Workers' Union, which has been most immediately concerned with
controversy over the protection of forests, has about 13000 members,

or 0.4 per cent of all Australian unionists. The Australian Teachers' Union, for purposes of comparison, has 173000 members (ACTU, 1989: 91).

It is therefore much too soon to suggest that the 'old' parties, individually and as parts of a system, are doomed to dwindle or to disappear. They are now in the course of adjusting themselves to rapid social change and the appearance and (modest) growth of environmentalist parties in several countries shows that they are confronting difficulties in doing so. But they have confronted difficulties before and overcome them, as illustrated by the rise and fall of the Democratic Labor Party in Australia and the Social Democratic Party in Britain. For better or worse, they may very well do so again.

If, as I am tempted to think, Australia may be a case where the 'old' party system has successfully adapted to the 'new' issues of politics, it should not surprise us that party allegiance in Australia has shown unusual stability, at least in comparison with Britain and the United States (Bean, 1989: 46 and chapter 5). Since that data was collected, the 1990 election result has done something to strengthen the case for saying that more substantial change may be upon us and that by the end of the century the content and the structures of democratic politics will look quite different. For myself, I remain unpersuaded.

ENDNOTE

[1] In view of these similarities between the Australian and Scandinavian Country parties, it should be said that whereas the Australian party was always very definitely on the non-Labor side, except for limited periods in Victorian state politics, the Scandinavian parties were much less hostile to labour; as exhibited particularly by the 'red–green' (Labour–Agrarian) coalition governments of Sweden between 1948 and 1957.

REFERENCES

Abrams, M. and Rose, R. (1960) *Must Labour Lose?* Harmondsworth: Penguin

ACTU (1989) *Executive Report. . . 1989*, Melbourne, ACTU

Aitkin, D. (1977) *Stability and Change in Australian Politics* Canberra: Australian National University Press

Aitkin, D. and Castles, F.G. (1989) 'Democracy untramelled: the Australian political experience since federation' in Hancock, Keith ed., *Australian Society* Sydney: Cambridge University Press

Bean, C. (1989) 'Politics and the Public' in Kelley, J. and Bean, C. eds, *Australian Attitudes* Sydney: Allen & Unwin

Beardwell, I. (1990) 'Annual Review Article 1989', *British Journal of Industrial Relations*, 28, 1

Chapman, B. and Gruen, F. (1989) 'An Analysis of the Australian Consensual Incomes Policy: the Prices and Incomes Accord', CEPR Discussion Paper

221, Canberra, Research School of Social Sciences, Australian National University

Childe, V.G. (1964 [1923]) *How Labour Governs: A Study of Workers' Representation in Australia* Melbourne: Melbourne University Press [first published London, Labour Publishing Company, 1923]

Dunleavy, P. (1989) 'The United Kingdom: Paradoxes of an Ungrounded Statism' in Castles, F. ed., *The Comparative History of Public Policy* Cambridge: Polity Press

Edwards, P. and Bain, G. (1988) 'Why Are Unions Becoming More Popular?', *British Journal of Industrial Relations*, vol. 26

Esping-Andersen G. (1985) *Politics Against Markets: the Social Democratic Road to Power* Princeton: Princeton University Press

Hadenius, S. (1990) *Swedish Politics During the 20th Century* Swedish Institute

Jackson, M. (1982) *Trade Unions* London: Longman

Jaensch, D. (1989) *The Hawke-Keating Hijack: the ALP in transition* Sydney: Allen & Unwin

Kemp, D. (1978) *Society and Electoral Behaviour in Australia* St Lucia: University of Queensland Press

Linton, M. (1985) *The Swedish Road to Socialism* London: Fabian Society

Lipset, S. and Rokkan, S. (1967) *Party Systems and Voter Alignments: Cross-national Perspectives* New York: Free Press

McAllister, I. and Ascui, A. (1988) 'Voting Patterns' in McAllister, I. and Warhurst, J. *Australia Votes* Melbourne: Longman Cheshire

Maddox, G. (1989) *The Hawke Government and Labor Tradition* Ringwood, Vic.: Penguin

Marsh, D. (1990) 'Public Opinion, Trade Unions and Mrs Thatcher', *British Journal of Industrial Relations*, 28

McCallum, J. (1988) 'Belief versus Church; beyond the secularisation debate' in Kelley, J. and Bean, C. eds *Australian Attitudes* Sydney: Allen & Unwin

McKenzie, R. and Silver, A. (1968) *Angels in Marble; Working Class Conservatives in Contemporary England* London: Heinemann

McQueen, H. (1984) *From Gallipoli to Petrov* Sydney: Allen & Unwin

Maguire, M. (1983) 'Is There Still Persistence? Electoral Change in Western Europe, 1948–1979' in Daalder, H. and Mair, P. eds *Western European Party Systems* London: Sage

Rawson, D. (1961) *Australia Votes: the 1958 Federal Election* Melbourne: Melbourne University Press

——— (1986) *Unions and Unionists in Australia*, 2nd edn, Sydney: Allen & Unwin

——— (1969) 'The Life-Span of Labour Parties', *Political Studies*, 17, no. 3

Rose, R. and Urwin, D. (1970) 'Persistence and Change in Western Party Systems since 1945', *Political Studies*, 18, 3

Singleton, G. (1989) *The Accord and the Australian Labour Movement* Melbourne: Melbourne University Press

Souter, H. (1956) 'The Goals of Unions and Management Today: a Trade Union View' in K. Walker ed. *Unions, Management and the Public* Nedlands: University of Western Australia Press

Zentner, P. (1981) *Social Democratic Britain: Must Labour Lose?* London: John Martin

12 Does the new politics have a future?

ELIM PAPADAKIS

THE PROBLEM AND ITS AUSTRALIAN CONTEXT

The label the 'new politics' has been attached to the development and impact of social and political movements since the early 1960s, including the student and civil rights protests and the environment and peace movements. In European countries it has been associated with leftist and radical groups and organisations (Poguntke, 1987). In the United States, it has been opposed to mainstream politics, though, at times (from the 1970s onwards), it found a strong voice in the Democratic Party (Miller and Levitin, 1976). In Australia it could plausibly be associated with the impact of environmental issues on electoral politics. The most recent dramatic illustration of the new politics was in the 1990 Federal election in which the Democrats, with 11 per cent of first preferences for the House of Representatives, secured the largest vote for a party other than the two major parties since Federation. The preferential voting system meant that the Democrats gained no seats in the House of Representatives. However, the Labor Party only succeeded in forming a government because it received the larger portion (approximately two-thirds) of the second preferences of Democrat voters.

The new politics has contributed to the restructuring of governments and societies along more realistic and relevant lines. Although it has not completely displaced the old politics, in so far as the latter reflects a concern with economic issues, the new politics has radically changed perceptions of economic problems.

The new politics is associated with a range of political issues, political constituencies and forms of political organisation in different countries. In Australia the new politics is linked with concern about the environment, women's rights, popular participation in decision-making, social equality and individual freedom. Although some of these concerns are not strictly speaking new, they have made a significant impact on struggles over the programme, the ideologies and the social bases of established parties. This chapter argues that the new politics has contributed to the transformation of party systems in western democracies, including Australia.

The timing of changes, the institutional forms and the types of reform will vary from country to country. A detailed comparative assessment of the new politics would explore its influence on party programmes, on forms of political organisation and on the state. It would examine the potential social bases for support. In several countries the new politics has been associated with the formation of new parties (Poguntke, 1989).

Unlike many other countries, Australia has not produced a new politics party which is represented in the Federal Parliament, although the Australian Democrats have increasingly taken on the mantle of a new politics party and are represented in the Senate. The electoral system, with the exception of the one devised for Tasmanian state elections, makes it particularly difficult for minor parties or independent candidates to be elected to the House of Representatives. The most recent exception to this pattern was the election of the independent candidate Ted Mack in the 1990 Federal election. In terms of his constituency and some of the issues on which he stood, he came close to being a representative of the new politics. Similar electoral obstacles exist in the United Kingdom and the United States. By contrast, in most advanced industrialised democracies in Western Europe, parties which have campaigned on a new politics platform have had some success in gaining representation (Poguntke, 1989).

One way of gaining some leverage on the significance of the new politics in Australia is to examine its impact on established organisations. The other way of assessing the potential support for new politics parties is to examine the spread of 'postmaterialist' values in western democracies (see Poguntke, 1989: 187). According to Inglehart (1971), postmaterialists tend to take economic security for granted and to place greater emphasis on aesthetic and intellectual goals than on the pursuit of economic gain.

There are important differences between countries in the themes taken up by the new politics, in its articulation through established groups and leaderships, in the opportunities afforded by electoral systems and by organisational modes. However, one of the striking aspects of this comparative analysis is the strong similarity in patterns of support for the new politics across western democracies by the young, the well-educated and the relatively affluent. Support for postmaterialist values is strongest among these groups.

The analysis in this chapter will not be confined to values as a measure of the prospects for the new politics. However, in order to be able to compare the new politics in different nations and to gain some understanding of its significance, the controversial notion of value orientations developed by Inglehart (1971) is used. The chapter argues that, rather than accept some of the conclusions of Inglehart about the rise of postmaterialism, his measure of values offers a partial insight into the significance of the new politics both in Australia and other countries over a limited period of time. The context for the development of the new politics is changing all the time. New criteria are needed in order to evaluate their significance.

There are also certain logical problems in any attempt to predict the future of the new politics. If the new politics (as conceptualised by social scientists) does have a future it will, by definition, no longer be regarded as the 'new' politics. In addition, some of the assumptions underlying this notion are as old as the study of politics. To that extent, the new politics has a past, a present and a future.

Another argument developed in this chapter is that the idea of a 'stable party system' that is frequently used in political analysis is of limited use in analysing the new politics. The major parties in Australia have certainly been successful in incorporating challenges to their dominant position throughout this century. However, in doing this, they themselves have been transformed with respect to their programmes, ideology and social bases.

First, as in other countries, this is associated with changes in the occupational structure, in levels of affluence and in levels of education. It is more than a question of the increasing difficulty of predicting voting behaviour on the basis of the crude distinction between manual and non-manual groups. At any rate the problem of predicting elections on the basis of this division does not necessarily imply a reduction in conflicts between groups in society. Factors other than the struggle over economic resources have been just as important in social conflicts. More often than not these conflicts have been articulated by groups that do not consciously see themselves as classes. Secondly, the public is often mobilised around conflicts over particular issues or sets of issues which frequently do not correspond in any obvious ways to the classic divisions of socioeconomic status, religion and geography. Thirdly, there has been an emergence of leadership styles which are based on direct appeals to the electorate rather than to the party faithful. Fourthly, some of the constraints on political action (derived, for example, from educational background and material well-being) have been circumvented by the relative autonomy of ideas (especially those pertaining to the new politics and supported by the growing proportion of the population with much higher levels of education) and the relative autonomy of sections of society from traditional forms of employment (particularly in occupations which are relatively well-paid and appear to offer greater scope for individual decision-making and autonomy).

This chapter can only elaborate on some of these issues. It speculates on the impact of the new politics in Australia by referring to some recent changes in the political agenda and by linking evidence of the significance of postmaterial values in Australia to evidence from other countries. The relationship between postmaterial values and support for issues commonly associated with the new politics is only partial (Papadakis, 1988). However, the analysis of values provides a rough guide to potential support for these issues and to pressures for change in the political agenda.

NEW POLITICS AND THE POLITICAL AGENDA

In the 1980s nearly all established parties in western democracies took up aspects of the new politics. For instance, environmental policies advocated by political and social movements have become less distinguishable from those of the major parties (Commonwealth of Australia, 1989; Papadakis, 1989). Divisions over the new politics have been as strong within as between parties. In Australia, concern about the environment has become a major issue in elections and in debates within the major parties. For example, in response to these pressures, the Australian Labor Party appointed one of its most senior politicians, Senator Richardson, to the environment portfolio after the 1987 election. It introduced measures to ensure greater coordination of policy in this area. It intervened in an unprecedented manner in disputes over the environment. It went to great lengths to attract the support of the conservation lobby (Papadakis, 1990a). This was apparent in the campaigns leading up to the 1983, 1987 and 1990 Federal elections.

Despite the efforts of the Labor Party to attract environmentalists, the major conservation groups advised their supporters during the 1990 federal election to direct their first preferences to the Australian Democrats. However, they recommended that second preferences should be directed to the Labor Party and thereby ensured the re-election of the fourth Hawke ministry. The new politics has posed particular dilemmas for modern parties. The problems for major parties include how to achieve a balance between economic and environmental imperatives. This can be illustrated with reference to conflicts over mining in Kakadu National Park, the mining and export of uranium and the logging of forests. Environmental policy has emerged as a major factor in determining the feasibility and desirability of economic developments (Papadakis, 1990a).

In the words of Mr John Kerin, the Minister for Primary Industries and Energy, 'any government in advanced countries that is not conservation-minded and environmentally aware is crazy'. This observation was combined with a polemical attack on 'greenies':

> If all the opposing arguments are put together into a coherent whole the policy would be to head back to the caves and eat grass seeds. But even here we are told that plants have feelings and corn experiences pain when it is

placed in boiling water . . . The patron saints of the new pantheism and its high priests are formidable media performers for mere ministers, business firms and workers to take on (The *Canberra Times*, 6 November 1989).

The underlying philosophy of the two approaches, in other words of the old politics of economic growth and the new politics of radical environmentalism is, in most respects, incompatible. However, in the messy world of politics, these fundamental differences count for a lot less. In 1989, the Australian Labor Party in Tasmania did what the West German Social Democratic Party had already done in the early 1980s—namely, entered a coalition with the Green Party. This kind of alliance is bound to pose problems for both sides.

For instance, there is a deep concern within the Labor Party that its traditional goals are being undermined and that it will find it difficult to appeal to 'traditional' working class voters and to the 'urban middle classes'. In the words of one commentator:

> . . . the Commonwealth government's enthusiasm for preventing development projects is threatening, if not Australia's economic future, certainly that of a large segment of our population . . . Shutting down the Australian economy to preserve the rustic romanticism of the urban middle classes is going to be paid for by the next generation of taxpayers who will be saddled with the burden of increasing numbers of welfare beneficiaries (Rolf Gerritsen, The [Melbourne] *Herald*, 1989).

The attempt by established parties to absorb the new politics has been crucial to their electoral survival. They will, however, remain under pressure, not only from well-organised interest groups, but from the many parties that have been formed at the national level in most western democracies on the basis of a new politics programme (Poguntke, 1989). In Australia the only party ever to have attracted a large number of votes directly associated with the new politics (but gaining very little electoral representation) has been the Nuclear Disarmament Party (NDP). In 1984, it attracted 7 per cent of first preferences in elections for the Senate, a greater proportion of votes than the West German Greens attracted in the 1983 election to the West German Parliament. Following the demise of the NDP, the Australian Democrats are the only other minor party which wields political power (in the Senate) and places stronger emphasis on the new politics than the other established parties.

THE POST-MATERIALIST THESIS

As has already been suggested, it is perhaps misleading to label diverse issues and organisations the new politics. First, they are not strictly speaking 'new'. Apart from previous concern with the specific issues, arguments about fulfilling basic material needs before developing a concern with higher spiritual needs can be found in the work of Aristotle and have also been a standard argument of revisionist socialism from Bernstein (1899) onwards. Secondly, the implication of pursuing one policy may conflict with another. To take one example, support for Aboriginal rights may conflict with the goal of preventing uranium mining. Thirdly, the emphasis on individual freedom may conflict with the collective effort required to tackle either environmental damage or problems arising from social inequalities. Furthermore, it may mask the plurality of meanings attached to the 'defence of liberty'—for many, the defence of liberty is part of a protest against the bureaucratisation of social life, for others, it is a green light for the politics of greed, for freedom to speculate on the stock exchange. The libertarian element in the new politics may, for many individuals, conflict with socially responsible goals. As Flanagan (1987: 1316) has pointed out, libertarian values may involve more than an emphasis on participation and self-expression. They may entail a lifestyle that is highly materialistic, a lifestyle in which 'materialism may become an end in itself—a terminal value—because of the status, self-esteem, sense of achievement, self-indulgence and other gratifications that it provides'. Fourthly, there is concern that the main indicators for the emergence and salience of the new politics suffer from certain major flaws. For example, the oft-cited distinction between material and postmaterial values does not represent a simple division in society along a single dimension of conflict.

Inglehart (1971), using data from several European nations, has postulated the emergence of a new cleavage in society based on the attachment to material and postmaterial values. Respondents were presented with a card listing four goals for their country over the next ten years and were then asked to rank them in order of priority. The items focused on:

1 the maintenance of order in the nation;
2 giving people more say in government decisions;
3 fighting rising prices;
4 protecting freedom of speech.

Respondents who chose the first and third items were classified as materialists, those who ranked the second and fourth were postmaterialists and the remainder were assigned to a mixed group. This battery of items was later extended to twelve.

There have been many valid criticisms both of the methods used to measure postmaterialism and of the claims made by Inglehart on the basis of this scale (Jagodzinski, 1983; Boltgen and Jagodzinski, 1985; Offe, 1985; Papadakis, 1988). There is a tendency for Inglehart to argue for the almost inevitable triumph of postmaterialists over materialists. This deterministic approach to social analysis has been justifiably criticised for failing to analyse the complexity of social processes and institutions.

Nonetheless, the scale does provide us with an indicator of the propensity of some individuals to lay greater emphasis on participation and individual freedom than on traditional concerns with the economy and law and order. It has also provided a basis for comparing the relationship between values and political, economic and social indicators in a number of advanced industrialised democracies. The scale has been used repeatedly since the early 1970s, thus allowing researchers to test hypotheses relating to the significance of aspects of the new politics over a prolonged period of time. This is not to accept the claims about the long-term prospects for social change and the explanations for these changes offered by Inglehart.

As in many similar exercises, the scale oversimplifies the complexity of individual preferences and values. It does, however, have a basis in theories about human behaviour, especially in ideas about scarcity and socialisation. The notion of scarcity is derived from Maslow (1954) who postulated a hierarchy of human needs. Basic needs for survival, material needs, are located at the lower end of this hierarchy. Once these are fulfilled greater emphasis is placed on intellectual, social and aesthetic concerns. Hence, societies that experience a high degree of affluence are likely to be a more fertile breeding ground for postmaterial values than those in which there are high levels of deprivation. Economic recessions are, therefore, likely to lead to a decline in postmaterial values.

However, this decline may be less sharp if we consider the second hypothesis which argues that the socialisation (in other words, the process in which an individual acquires values) of human beings prior to adulthood is likely to have a long-lasting effect irrespective of change in economic and political conditions. One should therefore expect that people socialised under different conditions (be they of affluence or of economic decline or deprivation) will, in later life, relate to their socioeconomic environment in distinct ways. This proposition is not as controversial as it may sound. There is a large body of research on the socialisation of individuals identifying with a particular party from youth through to old age (see Inglehart, 1971: 992). For instance, people who grew up during the Great Depression are more likely to have a materialist orientation in later life than those who grew up during the post-war economic recovery and experienced unprecedented levels of affluence, even if the socioeconomic and political conditions change (Inglehart, 1981).

This provides us with a clue about the time-bound quality of the Inglehart thesis. It has been particularly successful in capturing shifts in values during the political, social and economic transition between the pre- and post-war world. However, the absence of similar data prior to the 1970s makes it difficult for us to test some of the claims about inter-generational changes in values.

The data in table 12.1 allow us to compare trends in material and post-material values in Europe, the United States and Australia. The data for Australia is less complete than for other countries. However, the trends are generally consistent with those in other countries. Inglehart had postulated a decline in materialists and an increase in postmaterialists (over several generations). The data lend some support to his hypothesis for this limited period of time which includes economic recessions (Inglehart, 1981).

This attempt to map out values that have been closely associated with support for new politics parties draws attention to processes of social and ideological change that may have contributed to the transformation of the party system.

These changes are by no means unidirectional. The greater the challenge from new social and political movements, the greater the need for established organisations to mobilise new resources and to alter radically their own structures. The discussion of values underlying the new politics and the apparent stability of preferences for postmaterialism provides important clues about its future prospects. However, there are problems attached to the claims by Inglehart to extrapolate long-term trends from survey data on values.

THE ADVENT OF THE NEW POLITICS

Arguments about changes in values have often been linked to the finding that traditional affiliations to political parties have been substantially altered over the past few decades. The class cleavages which formed the basis for the revolutionary interpretation of social change advanced by Marx and Lenin have been either considerably weakened or altered beyond recognition. Ever since the turn of the century, social democratic and communist parties have had to grapple with the problems of the rigidity of modern organisations, the necessity, in order to gain political power, of widening the social bases of support from the working class to other groups in society and the potential conflict between values pertaining to the fulfilment of needs on an everyday basis and those which imply a concern with the realisation of socialist principles in the future.

Any attempt to construct a new politics will be faced with similar problems (Papadakis, 1988). The new politics, though it suggests a partial explanation for the transformation of the party system, has not emerged as a strong alternative. Concern with postmaterialist issues is

Table 12.1 The trend in material/postmaterial values in Europe, the United States, and Australia (per cent)

Country	1970	1973	1976	1979	1982	1984
Great Britain						
Material	36	32	36	25	25	24
Mixed	56	60	56	61	63	59
Postmaterial	8	8	8	14	11	17
	100	100	100	100	100	100
* PDI	28	24	28	15	11	7
West Germany						
Material	46	42	42	37	32	23
Mixed	44	50	47	52	54	58
Postmaterial	11	8	11	11	13	20
	100	100	100	100	100	100
* PDI	35	34	31	26	19	3
France						
Material	38	35	41	36	34	36
Mixed	51	53	47	49	55	51
Postmaterial	11	12	12	15	11	12
	100	100	100	100	100	100
* PDI	27	23	29	21	23	24

The trend in material/postmaterial values in the United States (per cent)

	1972	1976	1980	1984
Material	35	31	34	21
Mixed	55	59	56	63
Postmaterial	10	10	10	16
	100	100	100	100
* PDI	25	21	24	5

The trend in material/postmaterial values in Australia (per cent)

	1976	1988
Material	24	27
Mixed	62	61
Postmaterial	15	13
* PDI	9	14

Note: * PDI (Percentage Difference Index) is the difference between the per cent with material values and the per cent with postmaterial values.
Sources: Kemp, 1978; Papadakis, 1990b; Dalton, 1988: 84–5

unlikely to lead to the formation of a new party system divided along the lines of materialism and postmaterialism (Dalton, 1988). Established parties can also make appeals to the new politics issues. It is also more difficult to institutionalise these concerns over specific issues than concerns attached to the development of specific social groups (or classes).

The old politics, as conceptualised by Inglehart, and for that matter by Aristotle, implied a concern with the fulfilment of material needs and with the conflict between clearly identifiable social groups over the resources to satisfy these needs. There is greater scope for the new politics once many of these needs have been satisfied and many of these conflicts have become either less sharp or been transformed into different types of conflict between groups organised on a different basis from those that dominated the old politics. This can best be illustrated by reference to the programmes of established political parties in western democracies (including Australia) which, in different ways, attempt to link new politics issues to old ideologies, to create a new synthesis between concern for the environment, for the quality of life and a belief in economic growth, the development of the free market, state interventionism, faith in scientific and technological progress and so on.

Most modern political parties in advanced industrial societies were formed before or around the turn of the century. The rationale for their existence was drawn partly from the major social conflicts of the time, particularly between groups in the sphere of production, religious conflicts and regional differences. These central cleavages, although they have become weaker in most countries, have persisted throughout this century. They have also undergone a transformation, especially in the years following World War II.

This is hardly surprising given the high levels of affluence enjoyed by most of the population, the increase in social mobility, the growth of the public sector, of the welfare state and of public employment, the decline of manufacturing industry and the rise of the service sector, the decline of agriculture and the exodus from the country to the city and the dramatic rise in access to higher education. Although it has been argued that the growth of the welfare state and the public sector has been less striking here than in other countries and that the economic development of Australia differs in many other significant respects from that of other countries (see Aitkin, 1983; Castles, 1985, 1988), in broad terms, the experience of affluence, government spending and changes in communications and transport is similar to that of other western countries. I am not suggesting a simple connection between economic changes and political ideas. Nonetheless, these changes may have prepared the ground for rapid communication of ideas associated with the new politics from one country to another.

CLASS POLITICS AND ISSUE VOTING

This section briefly examines another aspect of the changing basis for party politics. The most frequently cited indicator for this change is the decline in 'class voting'. Again Australia is seen as both similar and different.

There are strong similarities between western democracies to the extent that they have experienced a steady decline in 'class voting' since the turn of the century. There is one obvious explanation. As the non-manual groups decline in numbers, the major parties, in order to ensure their survival, need to broaden their appeal to other groups. Although there are problems with justifying the use of occupational status as a proxy for class, changes in the association between occupational status and vote do provide some indication of the fluidity of the major cleavages of the party system. This chapter has already suggested that the change in the occupational structure is connected with the nature and pace of economic developments. The decline in class voting applies to countries with different party systems, different degrees of polarisation between left and right and different patterns of electoral success and decline of the major parties (see Inglehart, 1987: 1229; for Australia, see Alford, 1963 and 1967; Kemp, 1978; Aitkin, 1982; Bean, 1988; Jones & McAllister, 1989). The main differences are in the relationship between the decline in class voting and the point in time at which this occurred. Statistical analyses of the structural bases of the Australian party system have pointed to the moderate decline in class voting from the 1940s until the mid-1960s, followed by an influx of non-manual voters into the ALP from 1967 onwards, after Whitlam had become party leader (Jones & McAllister, 1989: 15) and the stabilisation of this trend in the 1980s (Bean & Kelley, 1988).

Any attempt to argue for the salience and durability of the new politics also implies a challenge to the prevalent image of stability in the Australian party system. The commonly-used measures for stability include the capacity of the major parties (Labor and the Liberals in Coalition with the Country or National Party) to attract consistently about 90 per cent of the vote over the past four decades (Aitkin, 1985) and the apparent absence of volatility or vote-switching, hence the remarkable stability in individual voting patterns and the strength of 'party identification' (in other words the consistent and widespread loyalty of individuals to particular parties) (see Bean & Kelley, 1988). In this respect, Australia appears to differ significantly from other countries where there has been a striking increase in vote-switching and a decrease in party identification (Crewe & Denver, 1985; Dalton, Flanagan & Beck, 1984).

Some of these assumptions are open to dispute. Just as postmaterialism may mean different things in different countries, party identification is open to diverse interpretations. It is, in certain respects, unrealistic to compare the 'loyalty' of Australian voters to their parties with the volatility of voters in the United Kingdom and the United States since voting in the latter is voluntary whereas in the former it is compulsory. People are therefore more likely to think in terms of 'loyalty' to a particular party. A similar point is implied by Aitkin (1985). Furthermore, it has been suggested that Australian voters are far less likely to switch votes between elections. Yet the evidence is contradictory or, at least, incomplete. McAllister and Mughan (1987) have demonstrated that vote-switching has become much more common and is 'both a cause and a consequence' of the electoral victory of the Labor Party in 1972.

Turning to the capability of the major parties to attract most of the vote, one could raise several objections to this as a measure of 'stability'. As in most other advanced industrial countries, voting is much more heavily influenced than in the past by the mobilisation of the population around conflicts over issues or sets of issues. This development apparently has an inverse relationship with the decline of class voting (Dalton, 1988: 195). In other words, as class voting has declined, issues have emerged as stronger predictors of voting behaviour. Of course, these issues are themselves often proxies or 'intervening variables' for new group conflicts. Graetz and McAllister (1988) have argued for the salience of issue voting in deciding Australian elections.

TRENDS TOWARDS THE NEW POLITICS

The influence of the new politics has manifested itself in several ways. First, it has come to play a central role in the political agenda of all major political organisations. Although this may appear to be a recipe for consensus rather than conflict, the divisions both within and between major parties over environmental protection and other new politics issues have also become a source of instability. Secondly, new politics issues have not only disrupted the power of established organisations in setting policy agendas, they have spawned both new political organisations and come to play an increasingly prominent role in established ones. The Australian Democrats, for example, have increasingly taken on the role of a new politics party. Again, this should not be taken to imply that those who are not classed as postmaterialists will not vote for parties like the Democrats or that postmaterialists will not vote for the established parties. Thirdly, although the dominance of the established parties has not been successfully challenged by a new politics party, there are strong parallels between Australia and other countries with respect to the spread and the correlates of postmaterial values. Treated with caution, support for postmaterial values provides a further indicator of the significance of the new politics.

Similarities and differences across nations are compared in a brief discussion of the links between social location and political affiliation. Dalton (1988: 155) has plotted the links between this crude measure and party support across several countries and illustrates the broad similarities between nations, particularly the support by non-manual workers, those with educational qualifications and those in high status occupations for left-leaning parties. Graetz and McAllister (1988: 285) have carried out a similar exercise for Australia, mapping out the increase in support for the Australian Labor Party among non-manual workers and among the better educated between 1967 and 1984. For example, support for the Labor Party (as opposed to support for other parties) among those with tertiary education rose from 30 per cent in 1967 to 56 per cent in 1984, and among those with non-manual occupations, from 26 per cent to 49 per cent over the same period. These and other changes are consistent with the argument about the fluidity of the social and ideological bases of party systems. Above all, the drift towards left-leaning parties by non-manual workers and the better educated appears to tie in with support by these groups for postmaterialism.

Table 12.2 shows the association between support for parties that developed (in part) on the basis of a class cleavage and of the appeal they now hold for the middle classes. Class voting is far weaker among adherents of the new politics. This tends to support the argument about the relative autonomy of this group from traditional influences on political action. The lowest portion of the table highlights the differences in class voting between materialists and postmaterialists. (The Alford index is the Labor or Social Democratic party percentage of the manual vote minus the Labor or Social Democratic party percentage of the non-manual vote.) The biggest differences in votes for the Labor Party between manual and non-manual groups arises among materialists—a gap of 23 per cent. This gap is reversed if we turn to those with postmaterial values. The pattern is strikingly similar to that of the 1970 West German election. Even though this trend did not remain as strong in subsequent elections, there was a consistent association, in subsequent elections, between class voting and postmaterialism. These data provide us with further clues to the changing ideological and social bases of support for established political parties. Australia, whilst retaining its distinct institutional structures, is undergoing changes which correspond to trends in other countries.

Poguntke (1989) has found that voters for new politics parties tend to be postmaterialists, young, highly educated and new middle class. Although Australia does not have easily identifiable new politics par-

Table 12.2 Class voting by value priorities

West Germany

1970

	Total	Old Politics	Mixed	New Politics
Working-class	65	62	68	69
Middle-class	53	43	53	78
Alford Index	12	19	15	− 9
(N)	(1066)	(429)	(471)	(112)

1973

	Total	Old Politics	Mixed	New Politics
Working-class	65	59	68	79
Middle-class	49	33	55	67
Alford Index	16	26	13	12
(N)	(981)	(388)	(500)	(91)

1976

	Total	Old Politics	Mixed	New Politics
Working-class	58	56	58	85
Middle-class	45	26	47	72
Alford Index	13	30	11	13
(N)	(473)	(187)	(229)	(57)

Entries in the table are the percentage preferring the German Social Democratic Party of the two-party voting intention.

Australia

1988

	Total	Old Politics	Mixed	New Politics
Working-class	51	60	49	35
Middle-class	39	37	39	41
Alford Index	12	23	10	− 6
(N)	(592)	(170)	(343)	(65)

Entries in the table are the percentage preferring the Labor Party.

Sources: Hildebrandt and Dalton, 1978: 89–90; Papadakis 1990b

ties, recent data have shown that the new politics is likely to be supported by similar groups in this country to those in other countries.

Inglehart has argued that different generations would be socialised into different value orientations. There has been considerable dispute over whether these data reflect life cycle or generational changes. Statistical tests on panels of respondents from the United States, The Netherlands and West Germany over a period of eleven years, 1974–85, appear to support the argument of stability in postmaterialist values after primary socialisation (De Graaf, Hagenaars & Luikjx, 1989). Younger cohorts are far less 'materialistic' than the older ones. Young

Australians score low on materialism, although it should be borne in mind that the data for Australia were collected at a later point in time and may therefore exaggerate this effect (Papadakis, 1990b). Once again, there is a similarity in trends across these different countries. It is more than likely that the data show both life-cycle and generational effects (Jagodzinski, 1983).

Inglehart has also argued that expanding educational opportunities attached to post-war economic growth and levels of affluence would contribute to the growth of postmaterialism. In Australia, there is a strong association between high levels of education and postmaterialism (Papadakis, 1990b). With respect to the relationship between values and occupational categories, the results for Australia are again broadly consistent with those from the nine countries that belonged to the European Community between 1976 and 1979. Those in higher prestige occupations are consistently more likely to be postmaterialist than those in lower ones (Inglehart, 1981: 893; Papadakis, 1990b).

Those either with greatest access to or who actually form part of existing elites tend to be more postmaterialist than the general population. Although no data have been collected on the attitudes of political elites in Australia, evidence on the value orientations of candidates for the European Parliament points to the plausibility of these claims (Inglehart, 1981: 894). This has important implications for the likely success of the new politics, for its capacity to mobilise the most influential groups in society.

In many countries the association between value priorities and party support has at times been greater than the association between 'class voting' and party support. The gap between materialists and postmaterialists voting for a left-leaning party has been particularly striking in countries like West Germany (table 12.3). In Australia the gap for the Labor Party in 1978 was 25 percentage points, although this effect was no longer evident in 1988. The heaviest concentration of postmaterialists, however, could be found among supporters of the Australian Democrats who have emerged as the closest approximation to a new politics party.

CONCLUSION

There is, for all countries, insufficient evidence of long-term trends (Dalton, 1988). Moreover, in Australia the evidence suggests that the divisions over the new politics are generally articulated through rather than in outright opposition to established organisations. For this to persist, these organisations will have to be flexible enough to change and/or broaden their programmes and their social bases. In some countries, it may require changes in leadership style and in the internal organisation

Table 12.3 Value priorities and party support (per cent)

	Postmaterial	Mixed	Material
United States, 1984			
Democrat	66	53	50
Republican	34	47	50
	100	100	100
Great Britain, 1983			
Labour	52	30	26
Liberal/SDP	25	19	17
Conservative	23	52	56
	100	100	100
West Germany, 1983			
Green	23	5	2
SPD	54	48	37
FDP	6	6	5
CDU/CSU	14	41	56
	100	100	100
France, 1981			
PCF	14	13	8
PS	40	38	41
Other left	15	8	7
Ecologists	21	13	8
UDF	5	16	21
Gaullists	5	13	15
	100	100	100
Australia, 1978			
Labor	57	42	32
Liberal–National Country	27	40	58
Australian Democrats	7	4	3
Other	2	3	—
No party	7	11	8
	100	100	100
Australia, 1988			
Labor	47	46	48
Liberal–National	39	47	47
Australian Democrats	8	5	5
Other	6	2	1
	100	100	100

Sources: Dalton 1988: 171; Papadakis, 1990b; Kemp, 1978

of the party (for instance, the introduction, as in the West German Social Democratic Party, of minimum quotas for women candidates and officials).

It should be stressed that this chapter is neither postulating a straightforward relationship between values and political behaviour, nor making a claim for the long-term salience of the new politics as defined by Inglehart. Similarly, the various measures of class voting are not the most accurate measure of support by different groups in society for a particular party.

The claim is that the new politics has contributed to the transformation of the party system in western democracies. The impact in Australia has been as striking as anywhere else. It has affected the party system in terms of ideology, programmes or agenda-setting and social bases. Despite an electoral system that is heavily biased against minor parties, it made a strong impression in the 1990 Federal elections and ensured the re-election of the fourth Hawke ministry.

This chapter has focused on the significance of postmaterialist values in a comparative context. It has shown that Australia does not deviate significantly from other countries. It has also drawn attention to evidence of how issues like environmental policy have become much more important than in the past on the political agenda. However, the timing of changes in policy, the institutional forms and the specificity of programmes for change will obviously vary from country to country. There are important differences between nations and these are likely to persist for a long time to come. A similar argument can be applied to differences between nations on how to address issues (like defence and economic growth) commonly associated with the old politics.

A detailed examination of the new politics would consider institutional and historical factors. It would draw attention to the variety of characteristics of the new politics in different nations and show how it has been associated with the formation of new political parties and influenced existing parties. Although the underlying trends may be the same, developments in different countries will tend to be regarded either as models for stability or for change. The types of issues articulated by the new politics will also vary between countries. Concern about the environment can vary from a preoccupation with the protection of rainforests in Australia to preventing the construction of nuclear reactors in Western Europe.

Each nation offers different opportunities for the expression of the new politics. This applies to electoral systems and to organisational modes which might include corporatist incorporation of new political issues. There are of course some problems which have brought about moves for greater international coordination. These include environmental issues like the greenhouse effect and the depletion of the ozone layer. Social changes are also being linked with innovative proposals for greater integration between political institutions and for coordination of economic, social and environmental policies.

ACKNOWLEDGEMENT

I am grateful to Frank Castles, Barry Hindess and Robert Jackson for helpful comments on aspects of this chapter.

REFERENCES

Aitkin, Don (1982, 2nd edn) *Stability and Change in Australian Politics* Canberra: Australian National University Press
—————— (1985) 'Australia' in *Electoral Change in Western Democracies* edited by I. Crewe and D. Denver, London: Croom Helm
—————— (1983) 'Big government: the Australian experience', *Australian Quarterly*, 55, 2, pp. 168–83
Alford, Robert (1963) *Party and Society* Chicago: Rand McNally
—————— (1967) 'Class Voting in the Anglo-American Democracies' in S.M. Lipset and S. Rokkan eds *Party Systems and Voter Alignments* New York: Free Press
Bean, C. (1988) 'Class and Party in the Anglo-American Democracies: The Case of New Zealand in Perspective' *British Journal of Political Science* 18, pp. 303–21
Bean, C. and Kelley, J. (1988) 'Partisan Stability and Short-Term Change in the 1987 Federal Election: Evidence from the NSSS Panel Survey', *Politics*, 23, pp. 80–94
Bernstein, E. (1899) *Die Voraussetzungen des Sozialismus und die Aufgaben der Sozialdemokratie*, Stuttgart: J.H.W. Dietz (translated by E.C. Harvey, 1961, *Evolutionary Socialism: a criticism and affirmations* New York: Schocken Books)
Boltgen, F. and Jagodzinski, W. (1985) 'In an environment of insecurity. Postmaterialism in the European Community, 1970 to 1980', *Comparative Political Studies*, 17, 4, pp. 453–84
Castles, F.G. (1985) *The Working Class and Welfare* Sydney: Allen & Unwin
—————— (1988) *Australian Public Policy and Economic Vulnerability* Sydney: Allen & Unwin
Commonwealth of Australia (1989) *Our Country, Our Future, Statement on the Environment* Australian Government Publishing Service, July
Crewe, I. and Denver, D. eds (1985) *Electoral Change in Western Democracies* London: Croom Helm
Dalton, R. (1988) *Citizen Politics in Western Democracies. Public Opinion and Political Parties in the United States, Great Britain, West Germany and France* Chatham NJ: Chatham House
Dalton, R., Beck, P. and Flanagan, S. eds (1984) *Electoral Change in Advanced Industrial Democracies* Princeton: Princeton University Press
De Graaf, N., Hagenaars, J. and Luijkx, R. (1989) 'Intragenerational stability of postmaterialism in Germany, the Netherlands and the United States' *European Sociological Review*, 5, 2, pp. 183–97
Flanagan, S. (1987) 'Value Change in Industrial Societies', *American Political Science Review*, 81, 4, pp. 1303–19

Graetz, B. and McAllister, I (1988) *Dimensions of Australian Society* Sydney: Macmillan

Hildebrandt, K. and Dalton, R. (1978) 'The New Politics: Political Change or Sunshine Politics' in M. Kaase and K. von Beyme eds *German Political Studies* Beverly Hills: Sage

Inglehart, R. (1971) 'The Silent Revolution in Europe: Intergenerational Change in Post-Industrial Societies', *American Political Science Review* 65, pp. 991–1017

——— (1977) *The Silent Revolution* Princeton: Princeton University Press

——— (1981) 'The Silent Revolution in Europe', *American Political Science Review* 75, 3, pp. 880–900

——— (1987) 'Value Change in Industrial Societies', *American Political Science Review*, 81, 4, pp. 1289–1303

Jagodzinski, W. (1983) 'Materialism in Japan Reconsidered: Toward a Synthesis of Generational and Life-Cycle Explanations' *American Political Science Review* 77, 4, pp. 887–94

Jones, F. and McAllister, I. (1989) 'The Changing Structural Base of Australian Politics since 1946', *Politics* 24, 1, pp. 7–17

Kemp, David (1978) *Society and Electoral Behaviour in Australia* St. Lucia: University of Queensland Press

McAllister, I. and Mughan, A. (1987) 'Party Commitment, Vote Switching and Liberal Decline in Australia', *Politics* 22, 1, pp. 75–83

Maslow, A.H. (1954) *Motivation and Personality* New York: Harper

Miller, W. and Levitin, T. (1976) *Leadership and Change* Boston: Winthrop

Offe, C. (1985) 'New Social Movements: Challenging the Boundaries of Institutional Politics', *Social Research*, 52, 4, pp. 817–68

Papadakis, Elim (1984) *The Green Movement in West Germany* London: Croom Helm

——— (1988) 'Social Movements, Self-limiting Radicalism and the Green Party in West Germany', *Sociology*, 22, 3, pp. 433–54

——— (1989) 'Green Issues and Other Parties. *Themenklau* or New Flexibility?' in *Policy Making in the West German Green Party*, edited by E. Kolinsky, Berg Publishers, pp. 61–85

——— (1990a) 'Environmental Policy' in *Consensus and Restructuring: Hawke and Australian Public Policy*, edited by C. Jennett and R. Stewart, Macmillan, 1990, pp. 339–55

——— (1990b) *A Survey of Attitudes to State and Private Welfare in Australia* Canberra, Political Science Program, Research School of Social Sciences, Australian National University

Poguntke, T. (1989) 'The "New Politics Dimension" in European Green Parties' in F. Müller-Rommel ed *New Politics in Western Europe. The Rise and Success of Green Parties and Alternative Lists* Boulder: Westview Press

——— (1987) 'The organisation of a participatory party—the German Greens', *European Journal of Political Research*, 15, pp. 605–33

13 Why has the women's movement had more influence on government in Australia than elsewhere?

MARIAN SAWER

In 1902 Australia became the first country in the world where women had both the right to vote and to stand for the national parliament. Despite this early success, the political influence of women remained minimal until the 1970s. Since the 1970s the Australian women's movement has regained an international reputation for its success in imprinting its demands upon government—particularly in terms of sophisticated bureaucratic machinery government for monitoring and auditing the effects of government policies and programs on women. The network of women's policy units found at Commonwealth, State and Territory levels of government has been a signal achievement of the Australian women's movement.

Australia has also been ahead of most of the English-speaking world in the creation of a wide range of government-funded services run by women, for women, usually in accordance with collectivist principles, however diluted by the demands of government accountability. There is no equivalent in the USA or the UK, Canada or New Zealand, for example, of the women's information and referral services funded by governments and run by women in all Australian capital cities and a number of regional centres. These services, provide a bridge to government for women, particularly those isolated at home and provide important feedback on the impact of government policy changes on women in the community:

> . . . the aim is to provide a range of information and advice to women in a way that is caring, empowering and comprehensive—and in an environment, a workplace, where power is shared and the operations of the organisation reflect the democratic principles of information transfer at work (Treloar, 1987: 10).

By 1989 some 203 women's refuges, largely run in accordance with feminist collectivist principles, were being funded by government, as well as rape-crisis centres, incest centres, domestic violence crisis services, women's health centres and the women's information services referred to above. Even services operating in conjunction with the police, such as the twenty-four hour ACT Domestic Violence Crisis Service, have remained collectivist in form (despite the formal concession of a 'coordinator') and have in their constitutions aims such as the following:

- to change the inherent power difference between women and men which creates and perpetuates domestic violence;
- to work towards the empowerment of all women and children . . . (Constitution, ACT Domestic Violence Crisis Service, cited by Heather McGregor and Andrew Hopkins, 1991).

Women's services have provided an important input to government policy and legislation. Community education campaigns funded by federal and State governments, for example on rape or child sexual assault have been notable for their feminist perspectives. Public endorsement has been given to the view that the answer to the abuse of male power lies in the empowerment of women (see, for example, the National Domestic Violence Education Program launched in 1988). The latest domestic violence legislation (which varies from State to State) includes the provision of 'ouster orders' so that perpetrators can be removed from the home and kept in custody for up to four hours while the victim applies for a restraining order from a magistrate.

Feminist analysis of intra-family transfers has been important in the direction of social security payments to primary carers in low income families (for example, family allowance and family allowance supplement). Feminist analysis of the 'invisible welfare system' has also been important in achieving improved support services for primary carers of the aged and the disabled, for example, under the federal Home and Community Care Program. Childcare has become a major electoral issue as demand continues to outstrip supply of government-funded community-run childcare centres. In the 1984 election the promise of another 20 000 places was the largest spending commitment made by a federal Labor government committed to public sector restraint, and another 30 000 places were committed in 1988. Prompted by the Opposition's offer of substantial tax rebates for childcare fees, in 1990 the Labor government again made a childcare commitment the centre of its spending proposals. An additional 50 000 places were promised, as well as fee-relief and other subsidies for employer-provided and commercial centres.

The taxation system has retained the individual as the unit of account, thus avoiding the disincentive for secondary earners contained in overseas taxation systems such as that in the USA. In 1987, women employed full time in the paid workforce earned 82 per cent as

much as full-time male employees (ordinary time earnings) meaning
that the wages gap was far less than in comparable countries such as
Canada, where full-time women workers earned 66 per cent of male
earnings in the same year.

On the other hand, the social policy outcomes achieved by women in
Australia, still lag well behind the achievements of two generations
of social democratic government in Sweden. Australia has still not
achieved paid maternity leave outside some areas of the public sector,
let alone the generous paid parental and family leave available in
Sweden. Nor has Australia achieved the level of female political participation and participation on government appointed bodies to be found
generally in Scandinavia (by May 1990 women constituted 12 per cent
of elected MPs in Australia's federal parliament compared with 38 per
cent in Sweden's Riksdag).

Where the Australian women's movement has been outstandingly
successful has been in the creation of specialised bureaucratic machinery, and this will be the main subject of this chapter. The fact that the
women's movement in Australia has operated through government to
such a large degree has given rise to neologisms such as 'femocrat' and
'femocracy'. A number of books have appeared recently, exploring the
sometimes uneasy relationship between feminism and the state in Australia (Franzway et al., 1989; Sawer, 1990; Watson, 1990; Yeatman,
1990 and Eisenstein, 1991). Feminists within government often lament
that there are not enough feminists left outside to maintain the pressure
for continued progress from within.

The reasons for the relative success of the Australian women's movement in effecting change in government policies and structures over the
past two decades may be summarised as follows:

1   the Australian political tradition whereby radical social movements
    have automatically looked to government to satisfy their demands;
2   the window of opportunity provided by the election of reformist
    governments at national and State levels at a time when the political
    energy of the contemporary Australian women's movement was at
    its height;
3   the lack of effective opposition—anti-feminist organisations did not
    win the credibility with mainstream political organisations that they
    achieved most notably in the USA;
4   the existence of a centralised wage-fixing system.

INFLUENCING GOVERNMENT

From the 1970s there was a steady influx of women into Australian
parliaments rising to 12.6 per cent of MPs by December 1990. The
majority of these (61 out of 108) were Labor MPs, assisted by the par-

ty's national affirmative action policy adopted in 1981. In 1972 a reform wing developed out of the women's liberation movement, focusing on getting women's demands onto the political agenda and getting more women into political positions. The new body, known as the Women's Electoral Lobby (WEL) was a non-party organisation, with members from all political parties. It provided a political training ground for many women who moved into important political or government positions. A survey of State and federal women MPs in 1985 found that 28 per cent had been, or were still, WEL members. In 1990 three out of the four women Cabinet Ministers in Western Australia were former WEL activists, including the State Premier, and two out of three in South Australia. WEL also provided an organised lobby group for anti-discrimination measures, equal employment opportunity (EEO), women's policy machinery and the government provision of childcare and women's services. It was the Australian Labor Party and Labor governments which were to prove most receptive to the demand for specialised machinery to ensure government addressed women's needs.

The development of Australia's national machinery began under the reformist Whitlam government, which appointed the first women's adviser to the Prime Minister in 1973. The question of how to introduce feminist machinery of government was the subject of much discussion by WEL members and the first femocrats who were brought into the Whitlam government during the years 1973–75. One problem was how to develop bureaucratic machinery appropriate to the structural philosophy of the feminist movement. The movement had developed non-hierarchical collectives intended to empower women; the bureaucracy was characterised by hierarchies of power and status. Another problem was how to combine the need for concentration of resources so as to achieve some clout in the bureaucracy, with the need to prevent marginalisation in a separate department or agency. The answer was a centre-periphery model, with the hub in the major policy coordinating department and spokes in functional departments and agencies.

Australian feminists decided to avoid the model of a separate ministry of women's affairs with responsibility for program implementation.[1] Instead the fate of women's policy mechanisms was tied closely to the role (and ambitions) of Prime Minister's and Premier's departments. The approach adopted, which focused on policy development and coordination, released energy for the development of mechanisms for auditing the impact on women of the whole gamut of government activity. While feminist in aim, this machinery was forced to become internally hierarchical, like the surrounding bureaucracy, and unlike the government-funded women's services referred to above. So feminists in the hierarchy became advocates for their sisters in the service collectives—a relationship not without tensions.

By the beginning of the 1990s Australian women had achieved specialised government machinery not only at the federal level, but in every State and Territory. This machinery was in most cases established by Labor governments, the exceptions being Victoria and the Northern Territory. Queensland, the last State to acknowledge that specialised machinery was necessary, elected a Labor government committed to women's policy units in December 1989.

The major strength of Australian women's policy machinery has been the recognition that no government activity can be assumed to be gender neutral in its effects. Because men and women have different roles in the family and the labour market, government policy is likely to affect them differently. For example, in the area of public transport a decision to save costs by concentrating on peak hour commuter routes will have a particularly adverse effect on women. Women are more dependent on public transport than are men, and are the major users of suburban services needed to get to the shops, to the baby health centre or to visit family members. Similarly, a decision to introduce timed local telephone calls will have a major impact on women, who use the telephone to maintain family and other social networks and to tide family members through life crises (part of women's role in maintaining the invisible welfare state).

Recognition that outcomes are different for men and women has been entrenched in mechanisms for monitoring and auditing government policy for gender impact. These mechanisms are now regarded as exemplary within the British Commonwealth and the United Nations (UN) bodies concerned with the status of women, as well as within the OECD. Australia was the first country to introduce the kind of comprehensive disaggregated analysis (gender breakdowns) presented in the annual Women's Budget Statement.

In other words, Australia has tried to build into its government machinery means of monitoring and evaluating the outcomes for women of all government activity, and not simply of programs specifically intended to advance the status of women. The latter constitute only a relatively small part of total government activity affecting women.

KEY ELEMENTS OF AUSTRALIAN WOMEN'S POLICY MACHINERY

The key elements of Australian machinery for advancing the status of women (for more detailed information see Sawer, 1990) include the following:

• Location of the central women's policy coordination unit within the main policy coordination agency of government (Prime Minister's Department, Premier's Department at State level or Chief Minister's Department in the two Territories). In addition to advising and coordination functions these central units have responsibility for monitoring Cabinet and budgetary material for impact on women and for producing annual women's budget documents.

- Existence of departmental women's units intended to ensure that the department or agency's policies and programs have a positive impact on women. Women's units which focus on impact of government on women in the community are structurally and functionally distinct from equal employment opportunity units which coordinate programs to improve opportunities for women and designated groups in public sector employment.

- Monitoring at the political level of impact of government policy on women by status of women committees within the Parliamentary Labor Parties. The Labor Party is currently (December 1990) in government in five out of six States and at the Commonwealth level.

- Advisory or consultative bodies which provide a link between government and non-government women's organisations and are usually serviced by the central women's policy unit. In addition to the peak advisory bodies which advise the Prime Minister or Premier and Ministers Assisting on the Status of Women, there are often portfolio-specific advisory bodies such as the Women's Employment, Education and Training Advisory Group which advises the Commonwealth Minister for Employment, Education and Training.

- Intergovernment mechanisms include quarterly meetings of Commonwealth/State and Territory women's advisors (heads of central women's policy units). The meetings are also attended by the head of the New Zealand Ministry of Women's Affairs. Other intergovernment mechanisms include working parties and taskforces which report to the relevant annual meetings of portfolio ministers, for example, the Women's Housing Issues Working Party reporting to the Commonwealth/State Housing Ministers' Conference and the Commonwealth/State Task Force on NESB Women's Issues reporting to the Conference of Ministers for Immigration and Ethnic Affairs.

- Women's information services run by women, for women, are funded by Commonwealth, State and Territory governments. In addition to providing information, support and sometimes advocacy, these services conduct phone-ins on, for example, the impact of social security changes on sole parents and feed this information back into the policy process.

- Reporting mechanisms, for example, the annual public reports required on progress of the National Agenda for Women, the Australian Women's Employment Strategy and the National Policy for the Education of Girls in Australian Schools.

- Development of performance indicators relating to government outputs (such as the performance indicators developed by agencies as part of the women's budget process and the performance indicators contained within the Australian Women's Employment Strategy), and relating to more general social outcomes (such as the gender equality indicators included in the National Agenda for Women and used to track changes in the status of women relative to men over time).

In 1990 the Hawke government included in its fourth term election proposals the creation of an additional element of intergovernmental women's policy machinery—a twice-yearly Ministerial Forum bringing together Commonwealth and State Ministers responsible for the status of women.

Australia has also played a major role in strengthening the international instruments and mechanisms for the advancement of women, which in turn have provided the basis for domestic initiatives. For example, the UN Convention on the Elimination of All Forms of Discrimination Against Women (CEDAW) underpins the constitutional authority of the Commonwealth Sex Discrimination Act. An Australian, Justice Elizabeth Evatt, now chairs the CEDAW Committee, which oversights the implementation of CEDAW through a reporting process and interprets its articles for the benefit of the 104 countries which have ratified. Australia's first CEDAW implementation report was regarded as a model of its kind, and Australia is currently convening, together with New Zealand, a regional seminar aimed at countries which have not yet ratified the convention. By contrast, the USA has yet to ratify CEDAW, while the UK has ratified but with a remarkable eight pages of reservations.

Australia has also been an active member of the UN Commission on the Status of Women, and has played an important role in the development of the various international plans of action for the advancement of women adopted by the UN General Assembly. The most recent of these, the Nairobi Forward Looking Strategies (1985) has in turn given rise to Australia's own National Agenda for Women (1988), which performs a useful function in pushing planning beyond the time frame provided by Australia's short-term electoral cycle.

WOMEN'S POLICY MACHINERY COMPARED

The concept of the need for specialised national machinery for the advancement for women first received widespread acceptance during the UN Decade for Women. The UN Branch for the Advancement of Women (BAW) began regular surveys on the subject of national machinery during the decade. Of 126 countries which provided information on the origins of their national machinery, eighty-seven gave dates between 1975 and 1984 (BAW, 1987a: 21).

An early pioneer in the field of national machinery was Canada, which hosted a UN seminar on 'National Machinery to Accelerate the Integration of Women in Development and to Eliminate Discrimination on the Ground of Sex' in 1974. Canada had allocated portfolio responsibility for the status of women in 1971 and Status of Women Canada, the central coordinating agency, was created in 1976. In the same year 'integrative mechanisms' were adopted within each federal department to achieve early intervention in policy development and to monitor for differential impact. Canadian and Australian machinery had many points of similarity; the machinery in the two countries was developed in parallel, but independently. Canada, supported by Australia, has played an important role in the integration of plans of action for women into both UN machinery and into the activities of the British Commonwealth. Canada was chosen to host the 1990 meeting of British Commonwealth Ministers Responsible for Women's Affairs, intended to monitor progress in implementing the Commonwealth's Plan of Action for women.

However, by the late 1980s, the Canadian political environment had become more unfavourable than that in Australia to the further progress of feminist interventions in government. The free trade agreement with the USA was viewed as likely to undermine feminist gains. In February 1990 the Canadian government announced that as part of its deficit-reducing strategy, it was converting its funding of women's centres from an operational to a project basis. A nationwide campaign of demonstrations and occupations of Secretary of State offices followed, during which women's organisations pointed out that the government was now spending more money on security than it had saved through the cuts to operational funding. In May 1990 the government at least partially reversed the cutbacks, restoring funding for women's centres (but not feminist research organisations) for one year and for a second year on a cost-sharing basis with the provinces.

As of 1985, 137 countries claimed to have national machinery for the advancement of women, or structures performing functions usually attributed to such machinery (BAW, 1987a: 18). Of these, ten had a Ministry of Women's Affairs, and eleven had a Ministry substantially concerned with women (for example Women and Community Development). A further fifty-five countries had women's desks, bureaux, or divisions within a Ministry or major government unit with other purposes. Of these, twenty-two were located within the office of the Prime Minister and twenty-nine within the social welfare area (BAW, 1987a: 20).

Other types of machinery included advisory commissions (twenty-two countries), a subset of which focused on investigatory or legislative aspects of the advancement of women. A large number of countries (thirty-six) designated non-government organisations, whether party political or otherwise, as performing national machinery functions of advancing the status of women. During the period 1968–1985 there has been a general shift in the pattern of national machinery from a predominance of non-government organisations and advisory commissions in 1968 towards the establishment of government units (rising from 13 per cent of the total in 1968 to 54 per cent in 1985).

Of countries most often regarded as comparable to Australia, some were notable for their lack of the kind of central agency and integrative machinery found in Australia and Canada. For example, the UK was able to list as its 'national machinery' only the Equal Opportunities Commission and the Advisory Committee on Women's Employment (BAW, 1987b: 118–119). The USA did not respond at all to the UN survey, and like the UK has no central agency or integrative machinery. Sweden lists the Equality Affairs Division of the Ministry of Labour, as its 'national machinery'. Bodies associated with the Equality Affairs Division include advisory, research and complaints bodies associated with the Swedish Equal Opportunities Act.

In 1989 the (renamed) UN Division for the Advancement of Women reported on the general picture as follows:

> During the United Nations Decade and afterwards over two-thirds of the countries have established national focal points for the advancement of women. Since the Nairobi Conference these national machinery have continued to receive international attention and the importance of their role of presenting women's concerns within the government has been underlined at many expert groups and seminars, both regional and interregional, as well as by the Commission on the Status of Women. There have been efforts to support networking among national machinery.
>
> Most, however, suffer from lack of staff and resources. Many are located away from the main sources of decision-making. Yet, if 'mainstreaming' of women's concerns is not to mean their disappearance in practical terms, the national machinery has an essential role of advocate, monitor and advisor in national decision-making. As the expert group on equality in political participation and decision-making recommended: 'National machinery should be strengthened by enabling it to monitor the incorporation of women's concerns in all government ministries, including their budgets, and be provided with adequate resources to carry out their tasks ' (DAW, 1989: 6–7).

POLITICAL TRADITION AND THE NATURE OF THE WOMEN'S MOVEMENT

In Australia there has been a long tradition of radical movements looking to government to meet their demands and a long tradition of administrative innovation to encompass the new areas of activity demanded by radical agendas. Chartism was a long-standing influence on Australia's political history, giving rise to pioneering democratic innovations such as manhood suffrage, the secret ballot and the payment of MPs in the nineteenth century. Echoes of chartism are to be found in the Australian Women's Charter movement during the Second World War, the 'six demands' of women's liberation on which Women's Electoral Lobby campaigned in 1972 and the Working Women's Charter pushed by women unionists later in the 1970s. The development of innovatory bureaucratic machinery to translate the demands of the women's movement into the sphere of government has analogues in the development of conciliation and arbitration machinery early in the century in response to the demands of the labour movement and in the more recent development of complex administrative responses to the demands of the environmental movement.

There are many similarities between the political traditions of Australia and her close neighbour, New Zealand (see Castles, 1985). The development of New Zealand's women's policy machinery, in particular the Ministry of Women's Affairs formally established in 1985, has occurred in close consultation with Australia. New Zealand's women's policy machinery was a brave attempt to develop and model feminist political structures in government: 'We have worked hard to develop decision-making structures which are based on feminist and bicultural principles and which involve team work and collective decision making' (O'Regan, 1988: 2). This also included a much more overt commitment to lesbian rights than would have been considered politically wise in Australia, such as consultation days with lesbian women (Washington, 1988: 13).

The attempt of the Ministry of Women's Affairs to model feminist structures and processes of decision-making has since 1988 largely fallen victim to the New Zealand Labor government's headlong dash into corporatism, although the Ministry has increased in actual size (to thirty-five positions). Most of the original staff members, who had been recruited from the women's movement, left the Ministry when the original collectivism and solidarity was replaced by hierarchical management structures and more individualist performance norms. As of May 1990, bipartisan support for the Ministry was still lacking and there was some suggestion that if the National Party came to government they would turn it into a Ministry of Family Affairs.

The USA's women's movement, in keeping with more individualistic political traditions, has focused on lobbying from outside and on litigation, rather than on entrenching women's policy machinery within government. This tendency has been reinforced by the obstacles to legislative reform posed by the separation of powers between executive and legislature in the American political system and the capacity for mutual frustration (Summers, 1990: 18). The USA, despite the creation of a Women's Bureau in the federal Department of Labor as early as 1920, has no governmental machinery comparable to the women's policy machinery found at federal and State levels in Australia and no counter-part to the networks of government-funded women's services or to the award conditions which have been achieved for women through the Australian Council of Trade Unions (ACTU). In the USA the women's health movement, for example, focused on the creation of self-help groups rather than on public sector funding as in Australia. The tradition of individualistic 'equal rights' feminism in the USA has meant that feminist organisations have tended not to campaign on issues such as maternity leave. The National Organisation for Women (NOW) feared, like its predecessors, that recognition of the special needs of women workers (rather than their equal rights) would give rise to discrimination against them. As noted, the USA has not ratified CEDAW and has provided no information to the UN on national machinery for the advancement of women. Were it to do so, it would have little to report beside the Equal Employment Opportunities Commission and the similar beleaguered Office of Federal Contract Compliance Programs.

Scandinavia has, like Australia, a political tradition of using the state to achieve social goals. However there has been relatively little development of distinctively feminist political or bureaucratic structures, something attributed by commentators to cooption or pre-emption by the prevailing social-democratic tradition (see, for example, Haavio-Mannila et al., 1985; Gelb, 1987).

In the UK, ideological tendencies within the contemporary women's movement have tended to inhibit more pragmatic reformist activity. These tendencies have been described as 'ideological purism and localised structure' (Gelb, 1987: 285). Many feminist writers came from sociology departments where Marxism was a dominant influence in the 1970s. Ideological purism characterised both socialist feminist and radical feminist groups and led to uncompromising views of the state as the instrument of capitalism or patriarchy:

> It is often suggested that, partly as a result of this leftism . . . British feminism has had no 'mainstream' voice, and has therefore been easily marginalised. Certainly, there was little interest in the early years in the advancement of women in existing political structures . . . (Wilson, 1986: 98).

> Attempts to work within state arenas were viewed with suspicion and likely to be regarded as co-option . . . This standpoint was dominant during the seventies in Britain with lasting implications for feminists and activists. As a result of adopting such a position less energy was put into trying to enter the bastions of power, in particular the Labour Party, and the civil service (Watson, 1989: 4).

In one comparative survey of European politics Britain has been described as 'perhaps the country in which institutions and structures have altered least to accommodate women's demands' (Lovenduski,

1986: 256). As we have seen, the UK was unable in 1985 to cite any central government machinery for monitoring or auditing government policies for gender impact.

By comparison, as we have seen, the Australian women's movement manifested a relatively pragmatic attitude towards the state, in line with Australian political traditions, and perhaps benefited from that lack of a feminist theory of the state which was of concern to some feminist academics (see Franzway, Court and Connell, 1989). As with the labour movement at the beginning of the century, the program tended to be 'ten bob a day and a bit of state intervention'. The outcomes, however, more than matched those in countries where the women's movement had spent longer debating the relationship between capitalism and patriarchy or between feminism and the state.

The Australian women's movement in the 1980s has also been characterised by alliances between newer feminist organisations such as Women's Electoral Lobby and more 'traditional' women's organisations such as Business and Professional Women, Young Women's Christian Association (YWCA), Nursing Mothers' Association and a host of others, which have joined together on issues such as support for anti-discrimination legislation, the extension of women's policy machinery, women's services and women's grant programs, and on tax reform. Such alliances between 'traditional' women's groups and newer feminist groups have not been possible in the UK due to perceptions of the latter as 'lesbian and anti-male'—a perception reinforced by sensationalist media coverage (Gelb, 1987: 275). On the other hand there are no Australian feminist organisations with a mass base comparable to that of the USA National Organisation for Women, which grew to a membership of about 250 000 during the Reagan period.

POLITICAL OPPORTUNITY

In addition to the ideological predispositions of the British women's movement in the 1970s, there was also a lack of political opportunities for feminist influence on government. Neither the Wilson nor the Callaghan Labour governments were susceptible to feminist reform, much less the Thatcher government elected in 1979. Ironically it was only after the election of the Thatcher government that a political opportunity presented itself in the form of the Greater London Council (GLC) under its leader, Ken Livingstone. The GLC Women's Committee, established in 1982, set up feminist structures and funded innovative projects (by 1984 its budget was almost £7 000 000). A number of other London boroughs followed suit. This window of opportunity was largely closed with the abolition of the GLC in 1986 and the crackdown on local government by the Thatcher government.

In the USA, feminism has become in the 1980s identified with the Democratic Party. By 1980, women had won the right to half the delegate positions at the Democratic national convention, and in the same year women became more than half the Democratic constituency (the 'gender gap' of 8 per cent more women than men favouring the Democrats had opened up). By 1984 the Democrats 'adopted the feminist perspective on all public issues directly affecting women' (Freeman, 1987: 231). Unfortunately, in terms of presidential elections (as contrasted with Congressional elections), feminists were now associated with the losing side.

Despite attempts by the National Women's Political Caucus (NWPC) to influence the national conventions of both Democrats and Republicans in the 1970s, the political environment within the Republican Party was becoming increasingly hostile. The Republican Women's Task Force organised by the NWPC was identified with the declining liberal wing of the Republican party. 'The political culture of the Republican party gives greater weight to personal connections, and the personal connections of Republican feminists have not been to the winners of intraparty political struggles' (Freeman, 1987: 215). An anti-abortion plank was added to the Republican platform in 1976.

The Reagan victories in the presidential contests of 1980 and 1984 meant that USA feminists were forced to mobilise to defend what were viewed as fundamental rights such as the right to choose (abortion). However, this mobilisation of women to defend the right to choose (more women marching than at the height of the Vietnam War) has had the effect of mobilising many young women, who had tended to take the achievements of feminism for granted. It has also had significant political effects in countering the work of pro-life groups in persuading politicians that a pro-abortion stance was a political liability. In the gubernatorial elections of November 1989 'pro-choice' Democrats won governorships is several states and there was a resurgence of a 'pro-choice' wing among the Republicans.

Australia had the advantage in that not only did the height of the political energies of the feminist movement coincide with the election of reforming governments, but the federal system has meant that those levels of government in which feminist gains have been greatest have been able to maintain the momentum and eventually pull along those in which the political environment was temporarily less favourable. Some States in which the creation of feminist machinery came late, such as Western Australia, were able to draw on the accumulated experience of other administrations to make rapid strides. The Northern Territory, with a continuous history of conservative government, was nonetheless able to draw on experience shared through Commonwealth/State women's affairs mechanisms, and not only develop its own machinery but also, by 1989, pass the most advanced domestic violence legislation in the country.

LACK OF EFFECTIVE OPPOSITION

In the USA the early successes of the women's movement gave rise to a well-organised and well-funded backlash, both from the Moral Majority and from anti-feminist organisations such as the Eagle Forum, founded by Stop-ERA (Equal Rights Amendment) campaigner Phyllis Schlafly. Women's anti-feminist organisations have a special role in lending credence to anti-feminist positions. By 1980 Schlafly had become the arbiter (through Reagan adviser Ed Meese) of Republican policy on women and feminists no longer had access to the Republican party leadership or administration (Freeman, 1987: 239). By 1984 Republican feminists had been read out of effective participation in the party (Freeman, 1987: 240). Republican leaders preferred the 'other', (anti-feminist) women's movement led by Schlafly.

In the UK the women's movement has not had the kind of influence on government likely to give rise to organised anti-feminism. Local successes like the Women's Committee of the Greater London Council certainly gave rise to a hostile backlash in the popular press, but feminist interventions were generally treated as simply exemplifying the excesses of the 'loony left'. In 1987 the Cleveland child sexual abuse cases diagnosed by the Australian doctor Marietta Higgs gave rise to a backlash in defence of the family against interfering professionals rather than against feminist influences. The 'feral women' camping at Greenham Common in the 1980s in the attempt to stop the introduction of Cruise missiles did give rise to Lady Olga Maitland's attempt to mobilise a counter campaign. This was at first called 'Women for Defence' but was changed to 'Families for Defence' because 'unlike Greenham we're not a feminist campaign and the men are coming on board and playing a role' (Campbell, 1987: 135). The campaign did not attract wide support, however, as few Conservative women were attracted to the idea of direct action at Greenham, Molesworth or Trafalgar Square.

In Australia an anti-feminist group similar to the Eagle Forum emerged in 1979 to oppose the influence of the women's movement on government. The Australian group was called Women Who Want to be Women (WWWW, now Endeavour Forum) headed by the indefatigable Babette Francis. Much of the initial energy of the group, which had close links to the Catholic National Civic Council and access to church networks, was devoted to parliamentary petitions seeking the abolition of the National Women's Advisory Council and to disruptive activities relating to the UN Decade for Women. The influence of WWWW peaked in 1980–82, when its anti-feminist message coincided with the small government views then being expressed by some members of the Coalition government on the need to 'strengthen the family' as an alternative to expensive welfare provision. WWWW participated in pre-Budget consultations and was able to ensure that anti-feminist groups received government funding to attend the mid-Decade UN conference in Copenhagen. However the extremist views of WWWW were not palatable to most Australian conservative politicians. While feminist strands within the Liberal Party have been weakened with the move to the right of the party in the 1980s, they are still sufficiently strong, particularly in South Australia to provide a basis for bipartisan support for women's policy machinery. Women's advisory bodies have been a useful means to garner such bipartisan support.

After the election of a federal Labor government in 1983 groups such as WWWW which were opposed to the UN Convention on the Elimination of all Forms of Discrimination Against Women (CEDAW) were excluded from advisory bodies or grants programs designed to promote the status of women. Mrs Jackie Butler, Queensland Coordinator of WWWW, was the lead signatory of a propaganda sheet, circulated through church networks which gave rise to a flood of petitions, letters and telegrams to federal parliament, claiming that ratification would lead to the Bible becoming a banned book, the state taking control of children from infancy and Australia being placed under the control of foreign powers. Despite becoming politically marginalised at the federal level, WWWW continued to receive a sympathetic hearing from the Bjelke-Petersen National Party government of Queensland. With the fall of Bjelke-Petersen, the subsequent revelations of the corruption of his government and the election of a reformist Labor government in Queensland in 1989 the WWWW lost its last bastion of governmental influence.

WWWW borrowed many of its tactics from the USA. For example, while Schlafly's campaign against ERA included presenting State legislators with home-baked bread 'from the breadmakers to the breadwinners', Francis presented a cake during 1982 pre-Budget consultations to federal Cabinet 'To the Men in the House from the Women in the Home'. However, these tactics did not have the same resonance in a country where the power of religious fundamentalism was much weaker. WWWW proved a disruptive presence at the federal level for a time, and may have had an influence in delaying federal anti-discrimination legislation and preventing government adoption of a plan of action for the second half of the UN Decade for Women. In Queensland it waged a campaign against the setting up of a women's studies program at Griffith University. In Victoria it harassed the Women's Information and Referral Exchange with a successful legal action against its exclusion from the management collective, and its ACT convenor was elected to the ACT House of Assembly in 1982. It did not succeed in undoing the gradual entrenchment of women's policy mechanisms at federal and State levels. The fact that it tied its political fortunes to the fundamentalist Bjelke-Petersen wing of the National Party contributed to its demise as a political force. Its influence has been summarised as follows:

With the exception of the issue of sex education in Queensland, where the New Right succeeded not merely in eliminating humanist programmes but also in getting a Christian-based substitute recommended to government, the most that has been achieved . . . is delay of reform and some access to policy processes (Webley, 1983: 19).

The 'pro-life' movement has also copied techniques from the USA, such as harassing women arriving at abortion clinics and targeting MPs believed to be soft on abortion for electoral 'punishment'. Pro-life legislative initiatives have included the unsuccessful attempt in 1989 to introduce a private members' bill into federal parliament aimed at ending Medicare funding for abortions. (Medicare is Australia's universal health insurance.) There is no immediately likelihood that such moves will be successful, but, on the other hand, the pro-life movement has made parliamentarians sufficiently nervous to balk at further liberalisation of existing State abortion law. In most Australian States abortion is technically illegal, although generally available due to liberal judicial interpretations. Abortion was decriminalised in South Australia, the Northern Territory and the Australian Capital Territory before the formation of 'Right to Life' organisations. The situation was thus similar to that in the UK, where the Abortion Act of 1967 was passed before the appearance of organised opposition. Subsequently, British feminists have had to expend considerable energy in defending the Act from repeated attempts to amend it.

EXISTENCE OF A CENTRALISED WAGE-FIXING SYSTEM

The existence of a centralised wage-fixing system in Australia made possible a significant narrowing of the gender-gap in wages once the concept of equal pay finally displaced the concept of the family wage in the early 1970s. The centralised system compensates for the relative industrial weakness of the feminised sectors of the labour market.

The 'comparable worth' or 'pay equity' principle—allowing the comparison of dissimilar male and female work on the basis of a points system evaluating skills, effort and responsibility—has been rejected in Australia as incompatible with historic wage-fixing principles. Nonetheless Australia has achieved a greater narrowing of the wages gap than countries such as the USA and Canada where this principle has received acceptance but must be implemented at the enterprise level. The gender-gap in Australian wages does, however, remain higher than that in Sweden, where wage bargaining is centralised and both blue-collar and white-collar unions have pursued policies of wage solidarity benefiting low-paid workers.

In a survey of seven OECD countries, based on information supplied by Australia, Canada, Japan, New Zealand, Portugal, Great Britain and the United States, the gender gap in full-time earnings was smallest in

Table 13.1 Ratio of women's to men's earnings, 1984

Australia	81.2
Canada	65.5
Japan	55.3
New Zealand	79.4
Portugal	73.1
UK	73.0
US	69.9

Source: Women's Bureau, 1987: 67. Data received varied by basis of measurement (hourly, weekly, monthly etc) and inclusion of overtime and cannot be treated as strictly comparable. The Australian data excludes overtime.

Australia, followed by New Zealand. The greatest gap was in Japan. The centralised wage-fixing systems of Australia and New Zealand enabled relatively rapid progress in implementing equal pay decisions, once the concept of the 'family wage' had been abandoned.

From the late 1970s the peak union body, the Australian Council of Trade Unions (ACTU) has become increasingly committed to feminist issues such as pay equity and the achievement of award conditions which accommodate the family responsibilities of workers. It has run important test cases which have led to the Australia-wide achievement of maternity leave (1979), leave for adopting parents (1985) and parental leave for mothers and fathers (1989–90). While its comparable worth test case ran into the sand in 1986, the ACTU successfully negotiated with the Labor government for the establishment of a Pay Equity Bureau within the Department of Industrial Relations in 1990. The ACTU has attempted to compensate for the increasing emphasis on productivity principles in wage-setting (difficult for women to establish in the service sector, and virtually impossible in the human services) by an emphasis on improving wage outcomes for low-paid workers and the extension of award coverage to groups such as outworkers and family daycare workers. The ACTU has also provided crucial support for equal employment opportunity legislation and programs covering public and private sectors.

The support provided by the ACTU for feminist initiatives in the industrial arena and for equal opportunity and women's policy machinery within government reflects a number of changes within the union movement. The largest unions affiliated to the ACTU are now the teachers' and public service unions—both with coverage of feminised areas of the workforce and with strong feminists among their leadership. Women's policy units within government and working women's resource centres funded by government have worked closely with the ACTU and relevant unions on issues such as improving industrial protection for migrant women workers in the clothing industry and improving awareness of maternity leave and anti-discrimination provisions relating to the workforce.

CONCLUSION

Hester Eisenstein has compared the women's movement to a great river in flood, which as it runs down to the sea moves most easily through pre-existing channels, carved into the landscape by previous floods (Eisenstein, 1991). In the Australian case, the pre-existing channels included those carved out by previous waves of radicalism, such as those stemming from the labour movement and from small farmers. This was a tradition of regarding the state as an organ of 'syndical satisfaction' and of developing new forms of state action, such as the conciliation and arbitration system and the multiplicity of quangos dealing with primary industry, to encompass movement concerns.

While the women's movement has had greater influence on government in Australia than elsewhere, particularly in the realm of national machinery, the gains are vulnerable to a range of factors. The influence of new right agendas and of economic rationalism have brought to prominence those trained in insensitivity to gender-specific distributional outcomes and hostile to the forms of social investment needed by women. 'Femocrats' are often engaged in achieving 'least worst' outcomes rather than optimal ones. A recent example has been in the area of higher education funding—when the push towards the 'user pays' principle became irresistible, there was a feminist 'save' which substituted a tax on graduate earnings above a certain level for the proposed 'up front' fees which would have excluded many women.

The attempt to carry feminist organisational values into government, including an emphasis on process and empowerment (entailing a referring back of issues to the wider group), has been put at risk by the rise of managerialism. Instead of collective work, group solidarity and empowerment, there has been an increasing stress on the individual manager, competing for performance pay, managing for results, and deriding those who are 'client-driven'. (As already noted, the Ministry of Women's Affairs in New Zealand, intended to model feminist principles of collective decision-making and consultation, has exemplified the impact of top-down managerialist approaches on feminist organisational principles.) While all attempts to work through government involve compromise and speaking the language of the day, the present language is particularly unsympathetic to feminist values.

The energies of the Australian women's movement have been dispersed into a range of issues, in particular, environment issues, and the political pressure needed to consolidate feminist gains in government is not always available. Women who might have jumped up and down about the exclusion of women from tripartite economic advisory bodies, may be away mobilising resistance to large capital projects, such as the Very Fast Train, which threaten rural communities and natural habitat. Nonetheless, despite the present unsympathetic environment, the 1990 federal election saw the major political parties competing to provide an unprecedented level of expenditure on childcare, as well as greatly increased expenditure on breast cancer screening. Bipartisan support was promised for existing women's policy machinery and Labor offered to expand that machinery in various areas, including a twice-yearly ministerial forum, a pay equity bureau and a work and family unit to assist with implementation of ILO Convention 156.

ILO Convention 156 (Equal Opportunity and Equal Treatment for Men and Women Workers with Family Responsibilities) mandates the accommodation of work and family responsibilities in such a way that fathers are able to play a more equal role raising their children. Ratification of the Convention will put Australia among countries such as The Netherlands, Norway, Finland, Sweden and France, and ahead of Canada, let alone the USA or UK.

In summary, the Australian women's movement, by working through government, has succeeded in mitigating the retreat from the welfare state characteristic of the English-speaking democracies and continued, with some exceptions, to expand the range of services meeting the specific needs of women. A major achievement has been the institutionalisation within government of the feminist insight that all policy has differential impact on men and women.

ENDNOTE

[1] In New Zealand, the Ministry of Women's Affairs was established in 1985 with a remit as a policy rather than a service delivery body—making it similar in objectives to Australian women's policy coordination units although having a ministerial structure.

REFERENCES

BAW (1987a) 'The Development of National Machinery for the Advancement of Women and Their Characteristics in 1985' Background Paper for Seminar on National Machinery for the Advancement of Women, Vienna, 28 September–2 October
——— (1987b) 'Draft Directory of National Machineries' Background Paper for Seminar on National Machinery for the Advancement of Women, Vienna, 28 September–2 October
Campbell, Beatrix (1987) *Iron Ladies: Why do Women Vote Tory?* London: Virago
Castles, Francis G. (1985) *The Working Class and Welfare: Reflections on the Political Development of the Welfare State in Australia and New Zealand, 1890–1980* Wellington: Allen & Unwin/Port Nicholson Press

Dahlerup, Drude (1986) *The New Women's Movement: Feminism and Political power in Europe and the USA* London: Sage

DAW (1989) 'Information on the Preliminary Results of the Review and Appraisal of the Implementation of the Nairobi Forward-Looking Strategies', Vienna, October

Eisenstein, Hester (1991) *Gender Shock: Practising Feminism on Two Continents* Sydney: Allen & Unwin

Findlay, Sue and Randall, Melanie (1988) *Feminist Perspectives on the Canadian State, RFR/DRF* 17, 3

Franzway, Suzanne, Court, Dianne and Connell, R.W. (1989) *Staking a Claim: Feminism, Bureaucracy and the State* Sydney: Allen & Unwin

Freeman, Jo (1987) 'Whom You Know versus Whom you Represent' in Mary Fainsod Katzenstein and Carol McClurg Mueller *The Women's Movements of the United States and Western Europe* Philadelphia: Temple Press

Gelb, Joyce (1987) *Feminism and Politics: A Comparative Perspective* Berkeley: University of California Press

——— (1987) 'Social Movement "Success": A Comparative Analysis of Feminism in the United States and the United Kingdom' in Mary Fainsod, Katzenstein and Carol McClurg Mueller *The Women's Movements of the United States and Western Europe* Philadelphia: Temple Press

Haavio-Mannila, Elina et al. (1985) *Unfinished Democracy: Women in Nordic Politics* Oxford: Pergamon Press

Lovenduski, Joni (1986) *Women and European Politics: Contemporary Feminism and Public Policy* Brighton: Wheatsheaf

McGregor, Heather and Hopkins, Andrew (1991) *Working for change* Sydney: Allen & Unwin

O'Regan, Mary (1988) 'Mary O'Regan, Secretary of Women's Affairs 1985–1988' in *Newsletter/Panui* 9 (June), Ministry of Women's Affairs, Wellington

Sawer, Marian (1990) *Sisters in Suits: Women and Public Policy in Australia* Sydney: Allen & Unwin

Summers, Anne (1990) 'Sisters Out of Step' *Independent Monthly* July, pp.17–19

Treloar, Carol (1987) Speech to Women's Information Services National Conference, Alice Springs, 5–7 May

Washington, Sally (1988) 'Great Expectations: The Ministry of Women's Affairs and Public Policy' *Race, Gender, Class,* 7, (July) pp. 7–15

Watson, Sophie (1989) 'Unpacking "the State": Reflections on Australian, British and Scandinavian Feminist Interventions' Draft Working Paper presented to the Working Group on Feminist Politics' Oslo, December

——— (1990) *Playing the State: Australian Feminist Interventions* Sydney: Allen & Unwin; London: Verso

Webley, Irene (1983) 'The New Right and Women Who Want to be Women in Australian Politics in the 1980s', *Hecate* 9 (July), pp. 7–16

Wilson, Elizabeth (1986) *Hidden Agendas: Theory, Politics and Experience in the Women's Movement* London: Tavistock

Women's Bureau (1987) *Pay Equity: A Survey of 7 OECD Countries* Canberra: Australian Government Publishing Service

Yeatman, Anna (1990) *Bureaucrats, Technocrats and Femocrats: Essays on the Contemporary Australian State* Sydney: Allen & Unwin

Index